THE HORSE
CRUCIFIED AND RISEN

by

ALEXANDER
NEVZOROV

The Horse Crucified and Risen

Published by Nevzorov Haute École

www.hauteecole.ru/en

Second edition.

ISBN: 978-5-904788-21-6

Cover Photo Lydia Nevzorova

Photos provided by Lydia Nevzorova, Sophia Spartantseva, Natalya Bykova, Maria Sotnikova, Georgi Gavrilenko, Svetlana Gorovaja

CONTENTS

ACKNOWLEDGEMENTS

*I would like to thank Roy Cochrun, Varvara Lyubovnaya
for their work on translation,*

*Kris McCormack, Stormy May,
Cloe Lacroix, Donna Condrey-Miller,
Marie Duizidou and Victoria Reesor
for their assistance with editing the final translation,*

*Sofia Spartantseva, Natalia Bykova, Svetlana Gorovaya
and Maria Sotnikova for their incredible disclosing photos
of equestrian sport.*

PROLOGUE

am positive that for those who have made equestrianism, harness racing, flat racing, driving and the like their profession or their hobby it is not worth reading or even opening this book.

Sportsmen, jockeys, riders and their ilk will neither find nor learn anything good about themselves in it.

If anything, just the opposite.

At any rate, such an audience, with the spite, thick-headedness and phenomenal aggressiveness it displays in defending its right to abuse and torment horses, is not wanted among the readership.

I would prefer to be left alone with those few who either already understand or are honestly trying to understand the essence of man's relationship with the horse.

By any stretch of the imagination, it is very difficult to find a subject more steeped in deception than the relationship of man and horse.

Even in the most inferior of religions either the lie is smaller or it is skillfully infused in some proper psychological dogma and directed after all at the person, that is, at the being for whom the right always remains to send the liar to that well-known place in hell.

But, to be perfectly honest, I have very little interest in people.

This book is not about them, but about the relationship of man and horse.

It is about the horse's cardinal secrets: his phenomenal nobility, intellect, ability to love and to be friends, and about his primary misfortune — his association with man.

I, perhaps, more competently than anyone, can speak about these traits, having trained without any coercion, without any crudeness, without straps, iron and crops a sufficient number of horses.

When I fasten my eyes for the first time on a horse I intend to train in the most complicated of elements and figures for the Haute École,[a] train in a spirit of friendship yet with the horse recognizing my right of seniority, I, as a rule and as is the custom of the school to which I belong, silently say to myself: "Shunka-wakan kile nagi-ki uachi elo," which translated from the Lakota[b] means, "I need the soul of this horse." Just the soul, and if I win it — everything will turn out alright.

Then this horse — without any bridle, without any coercion — will be obedient and favorably disposed. He will do incredible things: lie down when I knit my brows, sit and remain seated, do the Spanish walk,[c] the piaffe[d] or the capriole.[e]

At the same time, the right to train this being is based by no means on the fact that I am a human, but on the fact that he is a horse.

Not one horse recognizes seniority according to this extremely farfetched principle.

Fortunately, we — both horses and beings from the hominoid superfamily, hominidae family, homo sapiens species, that is, people, — are of the same animal kingdom, giving us a surprising kinship, a common origin and almost identical physiological and metabolic features. We are, astonishingly, related!

Only, in us — we being from the order of primates — the physiological and metabolic features of a low biological origin (according to Darwin's brilliant treatise) are more evident.

The horse has them, too, but his beauty, you will agree, overshadows them.

In a subsequent chapter, I will speak in detail about all this and about the fact that the greatest stupidity of all is the attempt to create one's own relationship with the horse from the position of thinking oneself a more advanced being.

But first, the lies, the stupidity and the myths.

One may look practically at any era and find everywhere a staggering number of lies relating both to the relationship of man and horse and to the training of the horse.

Abysmal lies, told with great glee.

Intoxicating lies.

From sickly sweet tales and delusional thoughts about a horse's stupidity to the instructions of the sadist James Fillis[1]* — "to burn a horse."

Without inconvenience, one may look nearer home — it is so simple these days — at any kind of sporting competitions, such as the Olympics.

Without fail, you will see there a horse whose whole chest and front legs are inundated with foam (frothy saliva), pouring from his mouth, a mouth packed with "iron," special apparatus for inflicting great pain on the horse. This is a traditional and typical scene, obligatory for competitions in the sport of "dressage."[f]

It is like a nightmare. The physiological cause of this drooling is tragic.

But no one is punished for it.

Just the opposite! There, at the competitions, this is considered an excellent sign, is welcomed by the judges and is a source of the sportsmen's special pride. When the frothy drool is not flowing or flowing only a little, the judges purse their lips and the sportsmen are embarrassed.

The flowing drool is supposedly evidence that the horse "is working its mouth well."

Or "chewing the 'iron' well." That very same "iron" which has no other purpose but the infliction of pain in the mouth.

We will examine the schizoid sporting verbiage further on, in the chapter about equine "iron," but now let us look at the situation strictly physiologically.

Try to press your tongue firmly against your lower palate and keep it in such a position for about five minutes.

Even if you are not a horse in dressage, but just a reader of these lines, you will drool without fail right onto the pages of this book.

And if you also stuff some kind of sizable piece of iron into your mouth (and even better, two, as is common in equestrian sport), "iron" that will be pressing on your tongue, pounding on your teeth and gums and painfully gouging into your upper palate, and at the same time you instinctively attempt to get away from it by trying somehow to move your tongue and cheeks, then the drool will pour forth as foam and completely cover both the text and the pictures.

Further reading of this valuable volume will become impossible. And almost unnecessary. You will understand everything instantly.

---

* Here and below the numerals mark the Notes reference.

Of course, for a horse in such a situation there are a multitude of grave physiological consequences. First is the critical drying up of his throat from the impossibility of swallowing his saliva. There is the crushing of the parotid gland and similar problems.

But it is considered good in equestrian sport for the drool to stream from the horse's mouth. And the sportsmen are awfully pleased about it.

Frothy foam flowing from any living being would seem to be a most striking example of some sort of physiological problem (to put it mildly) — a sign of discomfort, pain, distress, even of anguish, of something very wrong... But no, in equestrian sport it is welcomed!

Broad-bottomed ladies in old undertaker hats — the Olympic riders — proudly pose for calendars on horses inundated with drool.

If something similar to what happens with their horse were to happen with their cat, or their grandmother, they would call a doctor immediately. They would be especially apprehensive, and they certainly would shed a few tears.

But here they are happy. These "ladies" (of both sexes), being predominately small-minded people, are convinced that everything is fine regarding the horse's bridle, that the horse has been inundated with frothy saliva because he has happily and willingly chomped at the iron instrument of torture they stuck into his mouth and then tightly fastened there.

Such a "lady" will, without fail, even argue passionately — in the name of the speechless horse — about her horse's love for this torturous instrument, the bit.

Though it is enough to open any handbook on equine dentistry and have the eyes fall immediately upon an article about terrible injuries to the lips, gums, teeth, palate and similar sensitive parts of the mouth that are caused by bits, or simply to know that sporting horses without fail break their first premolars (the so-called "grinders"), that is, the teeth in closest contact with the "iron," impacting the secondary premolars, that is the stronger teeth that don't splinter as quickly as the first.

And this is only the simplest and most basic example of a horse's constant trauma.

Is it even possible to talk to such people about the desire or ability to understand the horse?

And this is only the simplest and most elementary example not only of man's cruelty and stupidity and the awful lies about everything connected with the horse and riding, but also of the absolute unwillingness and inability of man to understand the horse.

In these endless lies, in which many have already permanently entangled themselves, you can no longer make out just which is greater — stupidity or innate malice.

There are lies here, there and everywhere.

Take the rodeo, for example. 99.9 percent of mankind is convinced that boys in hats sit down on wild and violent horses that are trying to throw them at any cost. The whole spectacle of a rodeo draws on the cowboy hero and symbolism; a ritual has been developed and there is strict choreography of the boys in hats.

And it all is a deception.

All the horses used in a rodeo demonstrating violent hysterics to the public, bucking, "rearing," "sun-fishing" from side to side and moving about the arena in wild jumps are normal, delicate horses that have been exhausted and submissive for a long time.

They simply tie a strap tight around their genitals, causing awful pain, before letting them out of the box into the arena.

The task is simple — cause the horse severe pain (and in such a sensitive location yet) to make him mad, frantic and furious and then pose on him, pretending to be an animal trainer.

There are few who know that the convulsive flailing of the hind legs, the prancing and bucking and jumps to the side are caused not at all by a desire to throw the rider, but only by despair and a desire to be rid of the pain.

If one takes any serious boy in a hat, steals his fringed chaps [g] and jeans from him, ties his testicles with thick rope and begins to jerk on that rope, the boy in the hat will be leaping, yelling and waving his legs too.

Unfortunately, such entertainment is not practiced.

There is no way I can say that all of this is my personal discovery.

It is not a discovery at all. Everything that I say in this case has been known for a very long time. And it can be understood by anyone who tries to meditate on it.

Very far from any equine horrors, a founder of the great spiritual and philosophical system called Taoism, Zhuangzi, [2] having looked closely at the relationship of man and horse as early as the 4th century before our era, in the epoch of suppressed ancient Sinicism, wrote that the bridle tortures a horse.

Being a first Taoist, that is, a perceiver of the phenomenally strong and subtle connections among the living beings which populate the world, Zhuangzi empathized with the horse and tried to guess his main secret: how can one be with a horse, be one with a horse and on a horse, not against his will, but with his consent.

He understood first that there is such a secret and that such a thing was possible in principle. He did not, however, manage to find the secret.

But Zhuangzi had another occupation — he was a philosopher and a great rogue, he was very busy — establishing one of the most fulfilling spiritual traditions of the world — and he didn't have the time and capability to search for a solution to the secret of the true relationship between man and horse.

Yet, the ancient sage became intoxicated by the horse's beauty, by his physical nobility — and he damned the "master horsemen" of his time, who were guilty of the torment and death of horses. That, very likely, is everything. But in his "Outer Chapters" he had already articulated the problem, for which, properly, we bow low to him.

Zhuangzi died, glancing a final time at his ancient Chinese sky.

A black lacquered lid with a ruby-red dragon was placed on his coffin, which the sobbing ancient Chinese fortunate enough to have heard Zhuangzi while he lived stuffed into a narrow, dusty grave.

And the "master horsemen" with their iron pieces and thousands of virtuoso methods to torture the horse have survived into our time, and still they injure and humiliate horses.

And lie.

To themselves. To you. To us. To everyone.

* * *

Consider jumping competitions.

Jumping is when people in specially tailored red or blue coats and velvet riding hats, looking as if they are occupied with something extremely important, whip their horses, already perspiring from pain and terror, to force them to jump across assorted painted poles.

It looks very serious and intense.

The bell rings (usually it is a pilfered ship's bell), the judges excitedly sit back on their haunches, the loudspeaker screams, the crowd of spectators roars and the painted poles are lifted rather high, and there is the hope that one of the participants will break his neck or at least break his back.

The men in tight fitting breeches and velvet helmets — just as wide-bottomed as the ladies in the dressage arena — having driven the horse out of its mind with the pain jumping all the painted poles, force their way toward the television cameras, in whose field of view they assume an especially daring air.

They willingly give interviews, where they are certain to lean on their own certain contact with the horse, and even blab the obligatory something about the horse's love for jumping the painted poles.

And now, imagine that by some magic the bridles have been removed from all the horses.

That instrument which cruelly controls the horse by great pain in the mouth, is no longer functioning. The horses are free.

They all scatter instantly. And it becomes clear that there is no real contact at all and there never was, that the horses were restrained and constrained only by pain.

The men in tight-fitting breeches, the squealing ladies in hunt ties, with pin, letting drop the whips and velvet helmets, all run like hell, scattering from the horses who have gone mad with the joy of their sudden freedom.

All of them...

The moronic amusement called equestrianism ceases to exist as soon as the painful component of control is removed.

Without pain to control the horse, there are no competitions, no victories, no interviews, no myth. There is no sport.

A rustling of the competition program, recycled and softened for a certain understandable use, is heard from the crooked wooden toilet behind the empty bleachers.

The sport has ended.

* * *

Of course, during 30 centuries of history there were a million reasons preventing man from understanding the horse and establishing with it natural and tender relationships, during which a horse's obedience, readiness to be a friend and to serve would have remained the same, but it would exclude completely the stupid, painful action which always provokes war and mutual hatred.

It has been very thoroughly botched through anthropocentric religion.

A simple example.

The autumn of 1535. Europe.

Six bishops and devout knights, 43 coats of arms in all, beneath a sky pierced by the ringing of bells, in a great procession with singing and crosses, were leading a horse possessed by the devil to a fire that had been prepared for it.

Annabelle, judging by everything, a devilishly talented horse from a travelling circus, had been caught in direct communication with the devil. Confirmation of the communication was, in the opinion of the tribunal of bishops, the horse's supernatural abilities.

History has held back what she was good at and at what she wasn't.

I suppose it was a commonplace diversity of subjects, the ability to sit down, to count and so forth, expressing itself in circus jargon, "stunts," which today can be taught to any horse in a week.

Generally they burnt anything that they could not explain.

The method, of course, is impressive, but not too effective. They burnt cats, dogs, heretics, wrongly shaped crosses, learned men who went too far, fellow Christians who folded their hands in a different way and chickens who blasphemously were able to peck at grain scattered in the shape of a cross.

And it also happened to horses.

So the case with Annabelle was by far not the only one. Having perused the chronicles, it is possible to name, through the most approximately of counts, no fewer than 100 similar cases. And this was only the horses.

I didn't count dogs and learned men.

The church stood fast.

The presence of intellect in any being, besides man, thoroughly demolished the dogma and the existence of the faith itself. It brought the most offensive discord. Not to the intellect, but to a certain acceptable world order.

It, of course, is excused partly by the custom for sacrifice that spreads through any dogma, paraphernalia and centuries of any priestly societies. (Christian

priests are no exception.) A fire lit by Christians with something alive in it that dies in the fire is the expression of a normal, archaic pagan desire to sacrifice the enemy to god.

The obsequious desire to tickle the nostrils of the authorities with the smell of the burning flesh of its enemies is acceptable.

A nasty little desire, of course, but explicable. I don't recommend taking seriously all the same the church's lies that the church was only isolating and recording with its tribunal a certain anomaly, and really the stupid civil authorities were burning the "abnormal" living creatures (learned men, astrologers, witches, dogs and heretics.)

But let's return to our story.

Before ascending to the fire, the circus horse Annabelle was subjected to all the horrors of the rite of exorcism, that is the expulsion of the devil.

They shoved burning coals into her ears, cut crosses with a knife on her flanks and hindquarters, and they even wanted to disembowel her in order to ascertain if the devil was hidden in her belly, but they didn't. They decided that if they ripped her open, she would die on the spot and the pious public would be deprived of an enormous edifying diversion.

To the wild howling of the crowd, the singing and the bells, to the muttered Latin of hundreds of pale lips and the clank of "armor iron," they pushed the horse into a gigantic square of over-dry brush, tied it with chains to the wall, heaped up hundreds more bundles of brush, and lit it afire.

The worn and tormented half dead horse resisted desperately and neighed so awfully that several of the knights decided to stab it to death in order to put it out of its misery.

The bishops were opposed and set the guards against the kind-hearted ones — and a human slaughter began around the gigantic heap of burning brush in which they mutilated and slaughtered people in the heat of the moment, ten from each opposing side, it appears. But the fire turned out to be weak.

The horse, judging by the description of the pious chronicler, didn't burn up immediately, as had been thought by the priests, but — having been burnt alive — agonized the rest of the whole day in the cooling coals.

The reason here is not only medieval Christian schizophrenia. It is absolutely understandable and is not being discussed.

Had the church acknowledged the presence of intellect and a soul in the horse, it would have destroyed itself instantly by this acknowledgement. I will not cite the canonical and dogmatic foundations of this assertion, they are widely understood. Christ, as you remember, never sat on a horse.

He took an ass at the local livery for his triumphant entry into Jerusalem.

It matters little to me overall what the church has given mankind.

But that at least ten centuries were wasted entirely through its fault is completely accurate. A colossal amount of time, fully suitable for researching a horse's soul, for serious attempts to understand what is the essence of the relationship of horse and man, was frittered away.

It is stupid, by the way, to blame Christianity alone.

Both the Muslim world and Judaism were also useless in this sense.

Little-by-little, very weakly and sluggishly, something glimmered in Taoism, in Zen-Buddhism, while absolutely, incidentally, in light of our subject, not influencing these doctrines the nations had adopted. Chinese brutality toward the horse was in no way distinguishable from Italian brutality.

Though, as I already have said, inspiring names and thought were flaring up slightly in the old Zen manuscripts and Taoist chronicles.

In the 12th century, the flames of the Jurchen ripped open the huge belly of the celestial kingdom, rolling over all of China's northern and northeastern provinces.

The story of a Taoist hermit, Yue Fei, applies to this very same time.

The Jurchen slaughtered a whole monastery, burnt everything and killed so many people that, craving something different, as a dessert for their Jurchen show, they blinded two living old things: an elderly monk and a very old horse, on which the monks took scrolls into the city. (Taoist scholars made money on the side with calligraphy.)

For the Jurchens, probably, this seemed a brave and splendid novelty, fundamentally new ground in the business of burning mountain monasteries.

Having cut out the eyes of both of them, they sent the two blind beings to wander throughout the region.

Yue Fei did not know how to ride, having never been on a horse and he just plodded alongside the blinded horse, warming his freezing palms on his neck.

When the blind horse lay down in the snow, the monk settled down between his legs and, having warmed up, fell asleep.

Goodness knows what he then understood and how, this old Taoist man. But he understood something.

On the tenth day a goddess with a silver face blocked the meandering path of the blind horse and the blind monk — the merciful Kwan-Yin.

The gods had sent her, having given her with the eyes of the Taoist monk which had been washed and healed in heaven and bade her to return them to Yue Fei.

But Kwan-Yin, a well-known mischief-maker, decided to have a little fun and proposed that Yue Fei make a choice.

She said: "I am able to return the ability of one of you to see the world. Chose whom it will be."

Yue Fei didn't think even for a second and replied to the goddess with the silver face: "The one who understands it correctly must see the world. Return the eyes to the old horse."

And Kwan-Yin acted as the monk had decided. She gave to the horse the eyes of the Taoist, eyes that had been washed and healed in heaven, and which were filled with great wisdom and great kindness.

This poignant story has had no influence on the course of the history of the horse in the world. It is likely those who love to rummage around in dusty Taoist legends have shed a few tears over it several times over the intervening eight centuries, but nothing more than that.

Relationships with such a striking being as the horse show just how stupid, ruthless and cruel man can be.

Or, conversely, how noble, kind and inspiring.

Unfortunately, one must devote a lot of attention in this book to the first, wicked version, inasmuch as it is the generally more common and accepted one.

After all, the conflict of man and horse is already many thousands of years old.

There is no special sense required to imagine the conflict's human participants.

They are all the same, the stupid Mongol who laughed at the freshly cut horse and the fat-bottomed girl in the old undertaker's hat who stuffed the horse's mouth with "iron," and the hoarse, idiot coachman — the inventor of the Russian troika.

You can't list them all, by the way, there are far too many of them — and what unites them all is their inability to understand or even give a thought to what they are doing with the horse.

There are many of them and they are devilishly similar.

If you lined them all up, how vividly awful would be this crowd who yells and whoops, who shakes the whips, the crossbeams of obstacles, the collars, capes, hitches, polo mallets, and who clank spurs...

And also the red-nosed, emaciated and hoarse jockeys, personally sending horses to kingdom come in torment by tearing their lungs to shreds (the statistics!).

Here are the old cavalrymen of all eras, who dug holes into the ribs of their tired horses with their spurs and abandoned them on the march to die in ditches.

Here are the red-jacketed competitors and the girls from the dressage arena, pumping up their biceps like Hercules by jerking on equine muzzles.

Here are the polo players, the harness racers, and the "troika drivers," who, to please a drunken coachman's aesthetics, turn at the gallop until they break the horses' vertebrae by drawing their necks to the side and drive them along the icy posts of the Russian roads until they die.

Here are the rejoneadors and picadors[h] embroidered in gold, who always place the horse in danger of the bull's horns first of all and leave the arena, tangled in bull and horse entrails.

And here are the weather-beaten faces of the unsanitary girls from the urban stables, spiteful 15-year-old fools who squeeze from the dirty, ill, emaciated horses the last drops of life in the town squares.

Their name is Legion.

And everything is for show.

And they all are noisy and aggressive, and each has an abundance of tall tales about the love of man for the horse and of the horse for man, and an abundance of delusional notions about what a horse is and what has to be done with "it."

And against them, against all this gigantic, excitedly cackling, swaggering crowd, we will be able to gather and place only a few silent figures from all of time...

Here is the Taoist elder who died two and a half thousand years ago in China who looked into a horse's eye with infinite agony.

Here is a pair of long-haired 17th century Frenchmen in collars and jackboots, the fathers of the Haute École.

Along with them, their long grey tresses draping over their woven woolen robes are elders of the Great Plains, Indian medicine men from the Shunka-Wakan Yuga Wichasha tribe… and even a few of our own contemporaries… That's all.

No… not quite all.

With them, behind them are all the horses of the world.

Of all the eras and continents.

The living and the dead.

And, I have forgotten one of the main personalities of "our" small equine side — the Dean of the Cathedral of St. Patrick in Dublin.

An intriguer and brilliant writer, who didn't know how to ride and never was a master of horse training, Mr. Jonathan Swift.

As you recall, Lemuel Gulliver ends up in the country of the Houyhnhnms, that is to say, horses, on one of his voyages.

The Houyhnhnms were perfect. Noble, honest and wise.

Not being a master of the "Haute École," not working daily with horses, Swift nonetheless absolutely understood the horse's nature and its main traits.

The Houyhnhnms have the Yahoos enslaved. These Yahoos are lying, aggressive and lustful creatures. It is very easy to recognize man in them.

For the Yahoos hate the Houyhnhnms and live with the thought of taking vengeance on them.

Generally, it was and is considered that the brilliant Swift defamed mankind with this book.

The idiocy and primitiveness of human nature, as Swift well discerned, was most apparent in mankind's relations with the horse.

And the image of the Houyhnhnms is a classical literary device, a great way to once again belittle mankind which was not dear to his heart. But here, it is not merely a device. Here it is sincere, unbearable pain, the origin of which is in love for the horse, in the perception of a horse.

He looks fine, this sarcastic, sharp-tongued, English intriguer, standing with the tribal chiefs and medicine men, and the lion-maned fathers of the Haute École in their quilted collars.

I can easily imagine Swift as the elder Dean of St. Patrick's Cathedral.

It is daybreak. His wig is jauntily atilt.

On his old cheeks are blue and ruby blots, shadows cast by the stained glass window. He is muttering, nibbling from his fingers some wax clinging to them, and the freshly extinguished candles trace flourishes of smoke in the colored, dawn gloom of the library.

"These idiots, (I mean the reading public), have exhausted themselves! They terribly want to prove that what has been written in Gulliver's travels, the Lilliputians, giants and Houyhnhnms are all a lie and fantasy. They look for proof. They look for the sting of the giant wasp, they look for the miniature sheep. They look and they do not find" ...

Somewhere in Swift's letters it is recognized that he suffered a great deal from the fact that he did not have a worthy companion. Of course. I myself hadn't been born, yet. For some reason we missed each other by about two hundred years. But our meeting is easy to imagine.

His old English, hook-nosed and lop-eared physiognomy is illuminated by a great and triumphant mischief.

"There is one proof that everything is true. There is, yes. It is here, in the conservatory. Let's go!"

On the way from the library to the conservatory he continues to clown about, making outrageous remarks and showing off his verbal skills.

In the conservatory, in shackles, sits his main proof. A living Yahoo from the island of the Houyhnhnms.

The Yahoo has especially favorite toys: A red redingote, a jockey cap and a whip.

Usually he is occupied by defecating, spreading around the feces, scratching, stuffing himself with a really rotten calf's head, dozing, howling or reading newspapers.

But always he waits for when they will remember him and bring him toys.

He accepts them with awe and is so overcome by the tawdry "treasure" that he doesn't get into the sleeves of the redingote right away.

It is a symbolic, significant, astonishing spectacle. The Yahoo, this creature, is always agitated by the prospect of playing with his toys, by the emotions aroused by his game.

He puts on the redingote, fastens the jockey cap, snatches the whip and begins to imitate a rider, beating an imaginary horse with all his strength, while pulling it mercilessly by the mouth.

Oh, he knows well what his toys symbolize.

He goes mad, imagining beneath him that stirring embodiment of beauty, kindness and nobility, which in Swift's great book is called a Houyhnhnm, is in his complete control, paralyzed by the pain in the mouth.

He thrashes and thrashes some more, pulls fiercely and thrashes again...

Though he has likely witnessed this spectacle more than once, Swift's jaws are clenched in anger so great that somehow even his sagging, old English cheeks are sucked in. "See? Tell me, has the idiot yet been born who said that Yahoo is a proud name?"

I nodded.

He knew the answer already, but he soured nonetheless:

"The poor Houyhnhnms"...

* * *

They're all like this. The sweet tales about the relations of man and horse are just tales. And it is no accident that Swift's Yahoo is presented to us in a red redingote and jockey's cap.

It is in equestrianism that man's desire and ability to torture the horse has become concentrated.

Though, more about this a bit later. In the corresponding chapter.

First I want to explain to you the iron in all its forms, and impart its history.

---

[a] Haute École (French "High School") — speaking f.iguratively, the designation of the highest skill in working with a horse. The standard is different for each era, of course. In the 17th century it was simply the performance of very complex elements or movements on horses in full collection which was achieved by painful action, using the spurs and bridle. Somehow or other, it was the height of perfection for that era, better than the masters of the Haute École, for at

that time no one in the world was working with horses. In the 20th and 21st centuries, the fulfillment of all elements devised in the 17th century is considered the crowning achievement of working with a horse, but no longer using any means to coerce the horse. Moreover, teaching horses all the most complex figures and gaits should occur at the horse's full discretion. Neither bridles nor spurs nor halters of any type are allowed during training. Any punishments are categorically forbidden. In the 21st century, Haute École still designates the highest degree of complexity and skill.

[b] Lakota — a language of the North American Sioux Indians.

[c] Spanish Walk — a Haute École element consisting of a very rhythmic and gentle movement of the horse forward with an extreme accentuated lifting of the forelegs.

[d] Piaffe — a trot, or passage, practically in place.

[e] Capriole — the literal translation is "goat jump." A Haute École element, when the horse forging into a courbette sharply leaps up into the air, practically straightening his hind legs.

[f] Dressage — a sporting discipline that includes several basic movements or elements developed as the horse's response to the rider's harsh painful action.

[g] Chaps — a cowboy's leather leggings which are worn over jeans.

[h] Rejoneadors, Picadors — mounted participants of a dastardly amusement which ends in the public murder of cattle.

"IRON"

Chapter One

T he history of equine "iron," that is, of snaffles, curb bits, and spurs, cannot be examined and understood except in the context of the very dramatic history of the relationship between man and horse.

A history of the iron in and of itself would not be very well understood and would, most likely, be terribly boring.

In any event, it is not important whether the chomping abrasions on Scythian snaffles were being induced or what the curvature of the psalium of Greek or Persian curb bits was, but, rather, the fact of how this iron worked and that it transformed the relationship of horse and man into an eternal problem.

The iron of every era is fantastically informative. Iron in general, is very truthful, very direct and straightforward. The masters of bas-relief, painters, and men of letters can lie artistically as much as they like and however they like about the relationship of man and horse and they can create a certain romantic illusion, but by looking closely at the iron of one era or another, the truth becomes clear.

It becomes clear what kind of relationship it really was, what man wanted, what the horse did not want, what riding was like and how great or worthless was the rider's skill.

Using the truest imagery, I want it to be as clear for you as it is for me when I go over the innumerable snaffles, curb bits, and spurs of all eras, from the times of the Lurs to the Napoleonic days.

In each piece of iron — and the cruelty of the designs is staggering— is a breathtaking quantity of information about riding styles, about the characteristics of the horses, about the ambitions and customs of the era, about the peculiarities of war, and about human stupidity and the horse's pain.

That is why I wrote this chapter and, in particular, why I am starting the book with it, because iron in particular always was, is and will be the most fundamental and determining factor in the strange and very dramatic relationship between horse and man.

Generally, it all was very much the same everywhere.

Whether in ancient Scythia, Assyria, or the Kingdom of the Lurs; whether in Rome, Egypt, or in the ancient caverns of the Celtic smiths; or beneath the piercingly white full-spectrum bright-as-daylight lamps in the workshops of modern England and Germany — over a period of almost 3,000 years the same exact activity has been and still is taking place, namely, the manufacture of metal contraptions, pieces of metal with differing forms which give man the illusion of authority over the very free, very strong and very defenseless horse.

From the moment man first understood that it is only with pain that he can force a horse to bear him on her back, he has contrived and concocted unbelievable contraptions, first trying to lessen the pain he causes with the movement of his hand while holding the reins, then driving that pain to the limit.

The iron in the horse's mouth has become, for man, some kind of indispensable attribute of the relationship, a magical key for control of the horse.

For all that, I will not be starting from the very beginning.

One may boldly scroll through any of the archaic times.

Let's take a certain high point, the moment when control of the horse was converted into a very complex art achieved by very few, but which enraptured — and continues to enrapture — the whole world.

France, the 17th century.

Here by this time the great riding school named Haute École, that is "high school," had been created and had gained its fundamental features which maximized exploitation of the horse's capabilities.

Haute École has at least eight canonized founding fathers.

They are Frederico Grisone, Pignatelli, Salomon de la Broue, Piniatelecci, Cesare Fiaschi, Antoine de Pluvinel, Francois Robichon de la Gueriniere and Chevalier de Nestier. These are the only legitimate, canonized fathers.

And I am not talking about any historical small potatoes [3] that hint at their paternity in the memoirs of that time. There are about 30 men, and all of them, as they say, had their hands in it, but they were not canonized.

Both the canonized and minor fathers of Haute École were masters of very complex dressage. They were rough, tough horsemen with dismal biographies and physiognomies, confirmed libertines, ready for a fight.

What is interesting, save for the heavily and noisily boozing Cesare Fiaschi and the quietly imbibing Piniatelecci, all of them were men who were teetotalers.

The charm, swagger and reputation of these wizards opened doors and hiked many skirts for them.

These maestro horsemen, who sold their talent at all of Europe's royal courts, were more valued than the most famous poets. Every literate person was able to dash off some verse in those days.

But hardly anyone was able to teach a horse the courbette[a] — a majestic and formidable jump on the hind legs when the horse rises up into a pesade[b] that, because it is so high, the effect of the jump increases a meter more! — except these men that smelled of horses. These were the cocky and coarse maestros who calmly gave blood princes a box on the ear and thrashed marshals and ministers on the hand and back with a whip for any error at a lesson.

Their commodity and their talent was in incredible demand.

One just has to imagine to what extent the knowledge of riding was valued in those days and how the knowledge to teach a horse at least a little was worshipped.

Everyone rode then, but they rode hideously and toward the end of the 15th century they were beginning to understand that.

The Gothic era bequeathed to Europe a nasty riding seat in which the rider openly interfered with the horse's movement. This resulted in a tendency to terribly beat the horse, to use very bulky iron in the horse's mouth, and spurs with necks which reached as much 35 centimeters. But chiefly — the gothic seat contributed nothing to the understanding of the horse's balance beneath the rider, even the horse could not find it.

Here, and further on in the text, I am examining only a certain upper class of horse in the equestrian world hierarchy created by man — namely, saddle horses.

Those horses, whom it would be possible to combine under the general category of "non-saddled" — draft horses, farm horses, carriage pullers, city dwellers — over the centuries had the same fate at the hands of all peoples. The fate and life of the workhorse of the Gothic era in no way differed from the fate and life of the ancient Egyptian horse or the horse of a Russian peasant. The fashion, trends, birth and death of the various schools in no way ever influenced the monstrous life of these horses, a life replete with beatings and other indignities.

The fundamental tasks of a saddle horse in Gothic times were the following:

- delivery of a load, in the form of a rider, roughly to where he needed to go;
- to trample and bite someone along the way wherever possible;
- not to die in a year's time from decaying and inflamed wounds and abrasions which were caused by armor and the very complex and always poorly fitting accoutrements.

The marching, fighting, tournament and parade horse of the middle ages simply carried the rider along a certain specified trajectory and it wasn't important what the trajectory was — from Paris to Liège or from the flag at one end of a tournament barrier to the flag at the other end.

The control of a horse was uncommonly crude and feeble.

It was no accident the knights' tournaments always were performed across a barrier, a plank wall nearly 120 centimeters high.

If not for this wall, any Raymond of Toulouse and Lionheart attempting to joust with one another would have amused the public with their repeated unsuccessful attempts to actually meet within the confines of the tournament field on their horses — which were nearly uncontrollable or able to be controlled only very crudely.

Training of a tournament horse was primitive; they taught the horse by any means to gallop as swiftly as possible in all this idiotic iron along a wall, which also served as a reference point. Nothing else was required of the horse.

There is also a separate history regarding "swiftly," by the way.

The pages and squires, or the "tournament guards," in order to raise the knight's horse into a gallop, thrashed her from behind for all she was worth, which was not prohibited by the rules of the tournaments.

The horse galloped along the wall and at a defined point met the other steed, which was moving in exactly the same way along the other side of the barrier. The knights began manipulating their lances at this point.

This was all there was to the equestrian part of a classical tournament.

Status Armarium, the tournament rules, stipulated a mandatory bend at the dividing barrier's end, about which there is this extremely eloquent quotation: "They did it in order to prevent the accelerating knight from running into the barrier or the spectators' stands."

In these words are summed up for you all the characteristics of a real knight's riding.

And this wasn't entirely attributable to the stupidity of the Bohemonds of Taranto, the Rolands or the Cids. It was simply that the subtlety of controlling a horse was totally unknown. And it wasn't the horses' doing.

I must surmise that the French king, Henry II was able to select any steed he desired, but nevertheless it was he, who, at a tournament, incidentally, and only because of his inability to control his horse, was simply stabbed in the head by the lance of his respectful opponent who absolutely had not intended to hit the king, but — just the opposite — had intended to lose the engagement.

Henry, by the way, died right there on the tournament field.

The cinematic versions of tournaments without barriers or battles in a clear, open field are pure fantasy, and they are possible only because of countless rehearsals and the abilities of the stunt horses, which are taught first to converge on each other and shoot on past at a precisely specified distance.

Such stunts were too much for real knights' horses.

But times changed. The tournament ideal of riding "faded" along with the knights' standards.

It would have taken a long time for it to die due to "natural causes," but the Renaissance burst forth, which drove the first serious nail into the coffin of Gothic riding almost immediately, because it brought to god's earth classical ideals and the "picturesque ease," "elegance" and "power" of the "classical seat" — (that description being a myth if ever there was one).

The Renaissance, as you recall, rapidly became ingrained in life.

Translated into modern terms, it was an ordinary cultural revolution.

Gothic culture, including its style of riding, was destroyed in approximately 80 years.

And then we see the appearance of the Haute École masters, who finished off the old beliefs about riding and presented to the world examples of an unimaginable perfection and a fundamentally new way of riding, so-called "school riding".

And when it was understood that school riding is an art, magic and religion simultaneously, there was no end of those wishing to kiss the hems of the tunics of the gods of this religion, which is how the fathers of Haute École were presented to the public.

The blood princes, the grocers, the suppliers of lacy linens to the bordellos who had grown rich, the powdered provincial nobles, officers of all stripes, men of letters, kings, retired inquisitors, successful artisans, actors and grandees — they all rushed to learn and grasp school riding.

It was the height of swagger to nonchalantly drop a phrase like, "yesterday Monsieur Pluvinel complimented my seat at the old Versailles manège..."

Having said such a thing, a man was able to count fully on the grandiose success of his persona in any enlightened society, regardless of the actual quality of his persona.

All the masters of Haute École, both Neapolitan and French, began with absolutely nothing; with only one shirt and that without any lace, with only one shabby Louis d'or sewn into the collar lining which smelled of manure; with begging, sour wine, fights and very cheap prostitutes.

But by their zenith or, at the worst, the twilight of their lives, almost every one of them had attained the right to be rude to kings and have a queue of counts, viscounts and dukes line up at their doors.

All the Haute École maestros resembled spiders in a jar — they divided Europe, struggling for the right to hold sway over any kind of royal court.

All the Haute École men were unable to endure each other and squabbled unceasingly while ascertaining who was whose pupil, who invented the pesade and who the capriole.

It is well-known that both Salomon de la Broue and Pluvinel were actual pupils of Pignatelli, but both disassociated themsleves in every possible way from the teacher at any opportunity.

We hear nothing about friendship among the maestros, but we do know for certain that when the time came and one of them was dying, no thoughts arose in any of the others to pitch in for a wreath or to go to the funeral.

They were neither a "department" nor a clan, nor even a group of like-minded people, they competed rather sternly for the right to hold sway over the European royal courts.

The maestros bickered terribly while dividing Europe.

It is true, someone got Versailles and someone the dismal manège of a mean Danish king at Fredericksborg Castle.

Antoine de la Baume de Pluvinel was the master of his talent best of all.

Endowed with one and only one gift, to train a horse in the Haute École tradition in a way he alone had devised, he became the Duke of Anjou's equerry, a chamberlain, France's ambassador to Holland, a member of the Council of State, the Duke of Vandom's tutor, a fashionable writer, and a holder of a very respectable status and all the imaginable regalia of that time.

Except for the Marquise de Marialva and William Cavendish, the Duke of Newcastle (wealthy and enlightened enthusiasts counted among the non-canonical "fathers"), the titles and "genealogies" of other equine maestros of the 16th and 17th centuries, were, I suspect, mostly counterfeited or purchased, but this didn't bother anyone. Maestros were able, after a few lessons, to obtain a new or additional title at any European court.

Moreover, what is really surprising, the majority of them had remarkable literary talents (a strange natural addition to their ability to work with a horse).

Salomon de la Broue made a brilliant display with a most celebrated book which brought together all the instructions outlining his method. Cesare Fiaschi, Grisone and the Duke of Newcastle all wrote numerous interesting books in which riding methods and operations were intertwined with a very original philosophy of understanding the horse's place in the world of people.

The work of Frederico Grisone, with an account of his view of the horse and her training, was honored with the blessings of the pontiff. (I am not joking,

the book received the Vatican's full approval and the official blessing of Pope Julius III. Grisone's work was republished eight times!)

Antoine de Pluvinel, in particular, wrote a best seller for his time, modestly calling it "A Manual for the King."

Francois Robichon de la Gueriniere created another absolute "hit" of the century, the "School of Horsemanship."

Besides a very competently laid out "equine" practical section, both these books were written brilliantly and have been republished and are still read today.

True, Gueriniere in his work very spitefully comments on the principle work of Haute École. Pluvinel's composition, from which, per se, everything started, was the first and most successful attempt to classify the school's attributes.

Now to the most unpleasant thing. All these "teachers," practically without exception, made use of extremely cruel, awful iron and without fail contributed to this problem something brand new, their very own, original designs.

To this very day, we classify rare bits according to the names of the Haute École maestros.

We say: Here's the curb bit mouthpiece devised by the master Grisone, and this is what Piniatelecci's cannon looks like.

There are cannons invented by Fiaschi, Gueriniere and Pluvinel (see table III *).

The methods for training horses relied mainly on force and were often simply loathsome.

The aspiration to collect a horse at any cost, that is to have her lift and bend her neck in such a way that the poll becomes the upper point, and the hind legs are brought far under the body, providing simultaneously strength, gracefulness and maneuverability, has led to the use of idiotic methods.

Cavendish (a famous wealthy English enthusiast), for example, lashed hedgehogs to horses' tails, in an attempt to push the horses legs further beneath the body.

Fiaschi hooked the horse's hindquarters, attached reins to the hooks which the rider held in his hand and, in response to any attempt by the horse to thrust out her rear, the rider tugged at these hooks, causing the horse terrible pain in her hindquarters.

---

* Text tables are marked with Arabic numerals, appendix tables — with Roman numerals.

The invention and usage of a sharp-toothed serreta (the creator is unknown, but possibly that very same Fiaschi) added a constant pain on the horse's muzzle to the pain caused by the iron (see page 168).

There are more than enough disgraceful and outrageous pages in the history of Haute École. But, in addition to cruelty and stupidity, there was also the determination to push ahead, all-in-all toward the light, to achieving the perfect balance of the horse, to her athletic development, and on the part of some of the "fathers," to maintaining the gentleness and trust of the horse.

Balance is the only thing that allows a horse to be used as a mount without her rapid breakdown. Artificial balance, that is, balance achieved through iron in the mouth, only postpones the time until the total breakdown, and delays somewhat the most terrible diseases of the spine, legs, neck, the muscles and ligaments, arthritis and arthrosis.

But for those days, it wasn't enough.

While criticizing the savage methods of the founding fathers of the Haute École, one must always remember what exactly they had to break through after at least 25 centuries of absolute incomprehension of even primitive functions of a ridden horse.

They, of course, were great riders for their time. Great riders are born very, very rarely, more rarely than great violinists or great writers.

How and why history concentrated them in such numbers in the tight space of two centuries is a mystery.

But, Haute École was born as a result of this concentration.

So, the mustached maestros smelling of horse prowled the European courts, gave lessons, wrote books, amassed wealth, hiked the skirts of duchesses, trained their husbands "school" horses that cost unreasonable sums, while not understanding themselves, incidentally, that they were creating the main, basic worldwide school which would, for centuries to come, be the absolute standard of skill for handling a horse. Right up to the end of the 20th century, when several people at different ends of the world refuted the basic thesis of classical riding and work with the horse in general, the thesis that the horse can work only while having iron in her mouth, a certain instrument which had a painful influence on her.

That is what happened in the 16th and 17th centuries, to put it mildly.

The Haute École maestros brought to the traditional nobility's cavalry primitive discipline and school figures, that is, certain exercises they had devised for the horse to perform in the hands of or under the saddle of a master.

And look what they started!

As early as the middle of the 17th century, there were at least 107 such figures.

But the fact is, almost nothing had been discovered.

The natural movements of the horse that she demonstrated in a close engagement or in games with another horse or when a stallion mated with a mare were the actual basis of the figures.

All the elements of Haute École, the capriole, the courbette, the pesade, the terre à terre, [c] the Spanish walk, the douze [d] and the piaffe are the unrestricted, natural movements of a healthy and wild horse.

Man only desires that the horse demonstrate them at the right time, in the right place, without the need of natural external stimuli like a mare in season or a stallion approaching strange mares.

Generally this statement is irrefutable. I will gladly send those who do not know horses well or who have been sold a bill of goods by the reasoning of stupid grooms about the artificiality of Haute École movements, to one, though not perfect, book devoted to horse behavior, by George H. Waring: "Horse Behavior".

In the chapter "Motor Patterns," is cited a whole list of all of a horse's movements in tabular form.

Of course, in the table you will find the ballotade, [e] the capriole, the courbette, the croupade, the levade and the mezair.

There is a description of the movements where a horse stands more or less vertically on her hind legs, now loosely lumped under the term "pesade," and also of the Spanish or school walk where the horse performs a high lift of the front legs combined with forward movement.

There also are phase-by-phase pictures of a horse's movement during her demonstration of the capriole, croupade, courbette and so forth.

By the way, all the Haute École figures have a purely manège and parade origin and purpose.

Contrary to popular opinion, they never were intended for war nor for equestrian combat nor duels.

Suffice it to say that while the war horse was dressed in armor, she was able to move only a little, her natural balance was destroyed, and the complex movements based on perfect equilibrium and balance, like the terre à terre or the capriole, were simply unrealistic.

As soon as firearms began to dominate wars, the Haute École figures became even more useless: whether you pirouette in front of an enemy or not, they will knock the brains out of both you and the horse at the same time from a safe distance.

The so-called "school" horse, that is, a balanced horse that has Haute École training and has been taught the Spanish walk, the Spanish trot, the passage, [f] piaffe, pirouette, terre à terre, mezair, [g] douze, sentavo, [h] pesade, courbette, ballotade, croupade, [i] capriole, saraband, a reverse pirouette on three legs, couchez, centado, [j] levade, [k] lansade, [l] balance [m] and other figures and elements is an absolute work of art that demands many years of effort, special veterinary services, feeding and care, which are unrealistic under the conditions of any war of that time and which, at the time, cost fabulous amounts of money.

Such a horse was fully comparable in price with a picture from the brush of Velasquez or Van Dyke.

And, as you may imagine, no one ever sewed army tents from the canvasses of these men.

There is one invincible argument in favor of the uselessness of the "school" elements and figures in the theatre of military action: practically all require a special area of land, a manège. Their execution is impossible on the hills, in the swamp, in the sticky sands and in slush, that is, on the terrain of a real war. A horse in nature, living free, can, in a moment of fighting or courtship, perform those movements which served as the basis of the Haute École elements. Of course she does this on almost any terrain, but she does so without a load on her back, that is, without a rider who destroys her natural balance, and with an unrestricted head and neck. In addition, as I have been able to observe, stallions select the place for a fight very carefully and perform more successfully if the ground beneath their feet is more solid and flat. Mares are not as squeamish about the footing, but they also are not so sweeping and exuberant in angry or aggressive movements.

And the main thing: There is no need for a horse to execute a capriole or a terre à terre in war; what is needed is the ability to stay alive after a week's march in the mud, a week's hunger, with open wounds on her body, with mange, with scratches eating away at her legs, and with an idiot cavalryman on her back along with his 50 kilograms of pistols, carbines, bullets, extra horseshoes, pots, long underwear, tankards, blankets, broadswords, tobacco, sandwiches (figuratively speaking) and other stores, all the bag and baggage necessary in a campaign.

Of course, even in ancient times, both in the times of the knights and the time of firearms, in the Arab, Scythian, Persian, Indian, Greek, European, Chinese and similar armies, there were horses that were trained, for example, to buck and bite or rear up at the right moment.

Rearing up, speaking literally, is the "pesade," and it served not as a fighting method, but only as an opportunity to shield oneself with the horse's chest and neck from arrows or bullets.

But, I repeat, all these movements of fighting horses had nothing in common with the Haute École figures that are based on a horse's perfect balance, her many years of athletic training and the rider's perfect seat.

And there was another significant factor: cavalrymen, as a rule, didn't know how to ride, in the lofty Haute École sense of this word.

They only held onto the horse; they never created a cohesive whole with her and neither their saddles, nor their seat, nor their training, nor their main duties required this. This statement sounds extremely paradoxical, but I am able to prove it easily.

Let's take Murat's splendid Napoleonic cavalry.

Let's take the Hussar, as the utmost embodiment of military riders.

It was already the 19ᵗʰ century, by which time the cavalry should have been able to be taught anything.

Let's open the Russian translation of a "sainted" Hussar writer, the famous de Brack book, "Light Cavalry Out-posts." In the chapter "Cavalrymen's Wounds and Injuries," what do we encounter first? — "injuries to the 'danglers.'" Such injuries, the book tells us, "are encountered extremely frequently among cavalrymen, almost always occurring as a result of the 'danglers' repeatedly pounding the saddle."

What the hell are these "danglers"?

Further on in the text, the mysterious term is decoded: a "suspensorium" is recommended for any cavalryman as mandatory personal equipment... roughly speaking, a thick quilted, soft diaper.

I quote further: "This is a reliable method for protecting delicate organs from battering during a horse's intense movements"...

The fact that they got such injuries shows to what extent they did not know how to ride, and this is highlighted by the fact that the army handbook, attempting to prevent this commonplace injury, stipulates bringing along special regulation Pampers!

And these were Napoleon's Hussars, the flower of European Cavalry!..

I can affirm that such an injury is evidence not simply of a rider's bad seat, but of the complete lack of a seat as such, and the tragic inability to ride a horse.

The most delicate part of a man's anatomy mentioned by de Brack, and called "danglers" by him, can suffer only in the event that a rider at every step, or throughout every stride, strikes — or speaking more figuratively — when he frankly beats the saddle with that part of his body. The assertion that the cavalrymen were very bad, if not to say the worst, riders seems paradoxical only at first glance, and then only under the condition that one forgets that the real figure of the cavalryman was replaced in the public consciousness by his depiction in popular film.

The much injured "danglers" of the Napoleonic Hussars are all in all a very telling illustration, but besides de Brack, who unintentionally bore witness to the want of even elementary riding skills among the elite cavalry units, there is a whole series of historically indisputable, most influential authorities who speak with all candor about the fact that "cavalryman" and "the art of riding" are mutually exclusive terms.

Count Drummond de Melfort, who published his "Essay on the Light Cavalry" in 1748, was absolutely convinced about this.

He speaks with all sincerity about the impossibility of the cavalrymen's attempts to teach any "refinements of the riding art."

"All refinements of the art are redundant for cavalry."

It is curious at that, but Melfort also includes under "refinements of the art" such primitive things as "stronger support on one stirrup than on the other."

This essay became the basis for all training codes and ordinances, such as the book of Monsieur de la Porterie, "Military Instructions for the Cavalry and Dragoons, Published by Monsieur de la Porterie, as Leader of a Camp of Dragoons," or the "Royal Ordinance" published in 1755.

General de Bohan, who published "Principles of Sitting on a Horse and the Training of Military Horses" in 1781, categorically protested in it against any refinements of training in the training both of cavalrymen and cavalry horses.

Frederick of Prussia hated any academic techniques even more passionately.

But a good rider, even in the simplest and most narrow meaning of the word, can only be one who has not just studied these academic techniques, but also had the ability to practice them over about 10 years.

However, let's return to the story of Haute École and to the iron. There exists an entirely scientific point of view regarding the horse's surprising talents, discovered by the Haute École founding fathers. They put forth that the horse's ability to perform the most complex figures beneath a rider, are only the consequence of using a new form of iron, more refined and cruel than those developed by the equestrian nations, like the Scythians or the Sarmatians, or the primitive iron of the Middle Ages, both early and Gothic.

Let's try to examine this assertion.

As you already understand, there exists a great illusion which consists of the point that man controls the horse in sports, in front of the cart and in the cavalry.

That is not true.

Pain controls the horse.

They stop the horse with pain, they direct her with pain and they turn her with pain. As a matter of fact, the whole history of riding is a history of equine pain.

And it all began very simply, with a small ring. Many thousands of years ago, wishing to control the horse, man used a ring, which was driven into the skin and cartilage horse's nostrils, breaking the nasal septum.

Who was the first to think of this stupidity?

Sumerian images (2500 B.C.) have been preserved in which this ring in the horse's nose is clearly visible.

This is evidence only that the Sumerians knew how and loved to draw, and not that they were the first or second to do this, and not that other peoples did not practice this method.

One way or the other, whoever it was, it gave rise to something bad.

Thanks to the Sumerian picture, it is easy to imagine the technology for installing the ring.

A bronze ring was driven into the nostrils, into the nasal septum, breaking through it, and then it was clamped.

One or two cords were tied to it, and the rider was able crudely and roughly control the horse while sitting on her or while standing in a cart or chariot attached to it.

The method was absolutely impractical.

First, there was great difficulty in the installation of such a ring.

There were no tranquilizers, and the ability to lay down a horse quickly, accurately and without any gadgets was still unknown, so the horse had to be thrown down by ten people and her legs bound. The procedure itself of hammering the ring was sickening (owing to the clamping of the ring or the connecting of it, if the ring was wooden) and rather difficult.

Antibiotics, of course, were unknown, the bronze and wooden rings were responsible for the most acute inflammation initially, and then necrosis and the break down of the very thin nasal septum.

Then man began to seek out in the horse a somewhat simpler, albeit just as vulnerable, tender and sensitive place from which he could gain control.

He found this place — it turned out to be the mouth.

And that is when the so-called "equine iron" was invented.

In the 2,500 years that passed from the time of the creation of the Sumerian picture "with the rings," humans have invented an astonishingly long list of devices for use in the horse's mouth.

The principle always remained about the same, but the degree of cruelty varied.

There were, for example, the Scythian snaffle bits with the so-called "barbed psalium" (see Table II, **6**), which, at a pull of the rein on the required side, deeply pricked the horse's lips, facilitating for the Scythian rider a turn of the horse's head in the necessary direction and, accordingly, the rest of the equine body as well .

The fashion of the "barbed psalium" stayed in vogue for all of the 4th century B.C.

It is noteworthy that the sharpening of the twin barbs on all four shanks of the psalium was so thorough that even now, after having lain 2,400 years in a Scythian chief's burial place, it can cause a finger to bleed at the lightest touch.

Snaffle mouthpieces, meaning, the parts that are directly inside the horse's mouth, are not the only abomination with which horses were burdened. There were also the rings that cut the gums, and spines and teeth, and a special screw to increase the painful effect.

The Haute École maestros of the 16th and 17th centuries continued this tradition of mankind; they jeered, they devised brutal curb bits and they did it devotedly, or so it appears at first glance.

Grisone's regulation iron (see table III, **3**) was provided both with a sharp spade for piercing the upper palate and additional chains for restraining the tongue and long (31 centimeters) arms, the so-called shanks or branches, which were connected to each other for strength by two more chains that are called chainette.

I won't even talk about the crudeness and strength of the main curb chain, the gourmette, which put pressure on the trigeminus nerve and jaw bones from below.

Pignatelecci's regulation iron is a bit more modest, without any special frills in the mouth, but just as murderously hard on the palate and the trigeminus nerve (see table III, **1**).

All Haute École curb bits, no matter what the design of the cannons, are based on the same principle and have an average shank length of 30–32 centimeters and a weight of approximately 550-600 grams. Owing to its length, the very powerful shank lever sets the curb bit mechanism into action with the slightest movement of the reins: the curb chain digs into the jaw bone, compressing the trigeminus nerve, and the port, a bend in the middle of the mouthpiece to form a raised "arc," digs into the palate. The chainette holds the shanks tightly together; once slid apart, they would allow the bit to lie flat on the tongue; held together, the bit digs constantly into the horse's palate. Everything combined assures the maximum painful impact on the horse's mouth.

Jokers such as Grisone, Pignatelecci and Fiaschi even invented special devices which were secured to the bit to maximize the painful impact.

They were the rosaire or the chapellete, steel beads which caused a sharply pressing action almost on the very root of the tongue, the trebuchet, which resembled a small catapult, or the coquille, shaped like a shell, which scraped the palate.

A rarer example of a device intended to increase the severity of the curb bit mouthpiece, the designer of which is not known, is called the chardon (all the elements of curb bit are presented in table 1). It is a little mechanism which is set into action by the rider, who with a light pull of the rein exposes the special barbs so that they are brought into contact with the horse's mouth.

By the way, even without the chardon and the trebuchet, the iron of that era is monstrous in its force of impact.

Thus the combination of iron's maximum cruelty, spurs, the correct seat, and devices like the pillars (invented by Pluvinel, these were fixed posts in a manège, between which a horse was tied making it possible to do to her what you liked from all sides), led also to discovery of the horse's staggering abilities and then the devising of figures and elements which became fundamental both for original Haute École and for competitive dressage, as well as for circus riding.

Although this is absolutely the accepted point of view, I can assure you that it is total nonsense.

First, very pure iron existed as far back as Persia and Greece, in the Scythian and Cimmerian worlds and with the Sarmatian cavalry and the Huns (see table I, II).

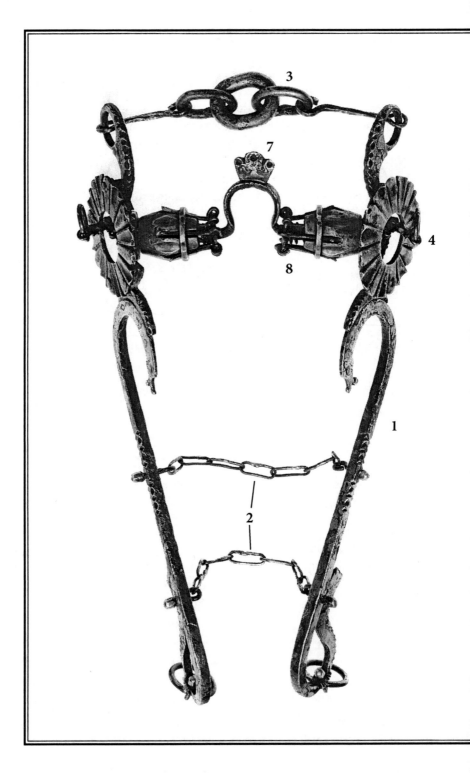

Table 1

1 — branche; 2 — chainette; 3 — gourmette; 4 — boufette; 5 — rosaire;
6 — trebuchet; 7 — coquille; 8 — chardon.

The Greek curb bits of Athenian and Spartan types are devices that, thanks to thorns, are no less cruel than the Haute École curb bits (see table I, **4**).

And even a bit more cruel, a mask of bronze bands was put onto the horse along with such a curb bit and the fine hooks on the psalium played the role of fastening it as a unit to the mask.

And why? No particular reason. There was no special effect obtained. There were no courbettes and caprioles, no special dressage ability and no balance. Riding had not become an art, although the Greek world, too, had its own ideals of lofty dressage and reasonable horse training — as described by Xenophon. (By the way, the ancient world still was unaware of the stirrup.)

As shown by excavations of a Congaeti burial pit, ancient Iberia, approximately the 4th century B.C., also was not especially timid in the selection of painful methods of influencing the horse (see table I, **2**).

Complex bits related to multi-jointed snaffles with psalium that have been excavated are typical for that era and also are designed to inflict acute and extraordinary pain in the region of the soft palate, as well as exert a constant strong painful impact on the gums and teeth. I would attribute them not to the Congaeti or Akhalgori cultures, but, rather, would classify them as typical equine accessories of Northern Parthia that ended up in the Congaeti burial mound as a war trophy.

And again, there's nothing special obtained, only an uncivilized, primitive ride with a complete lack of ability even to balance the horse beneath the rider.

One may look at Europe's Middle Ages.

Take, again, the 14th and 15th century military curb bit that was standard for those times.

With a shank up to 50 centimeters long, the mouthpiece was provided with hooks for tearing up the palate and with spiked cylinders for the gums and to make a deep impact on the lissa, the cartilage of the tongue (see table IV, **2**).

And all for nothing... nothing except an extremely ordinary, tame ride at a trot and sometimes at a canter. It was all romanticized and poeticized, and later even motion pictures had a hand in promoting the fantasy.

The main practice was the so-called "ramming motion", a heavy, unbalanced trot which was the primary gait of any medieval attack.

The Arabian East, professing without exception the principle that "one must treat a horse in the barn as a friend and brother, but when you ride on it, as the most evil of enemies," also devised iron of an extreme nature.

Eyewitnesses described it as "terrible and agonizing horse equipment, which is so disastrous for horses that it can sometimes break their jaws and even crack their bones inside."

True, this "terrible and agonizing iron" of the 13th century would eventually be in common usage in Europe where it was called "Arabian," "Turkish," or simply "hunting" iron.

The eyewitnesses themselves described the style of Arabian riding.

Using their own, Arabian type of iron, these peoples rarely stopped a horse without filling its throat with blood or without it being in a tormented, terrible and miserable condition.

All of their horses are reined in powerfully by the sudden and powerful impulse of the Arabian curb bit, from which the whole croup sometimes is broken."

In the same work, "About Asiatic and African Horses" there also is evidence of Arabian spurs: "Likewise, even the spurs of these riders, which look larger than nails, are used by them with great inhumanity; and in Barbary one can see at a stable horses in such pitiful condition that their blood streams from their snouts and sides."

The Arabian spurs from my collection confirm the validity of this work which was published as "long ago" as 1824 (see table V, **4**).

Despite the ferocity of these gadgets, the Arabian, and even any oriental rider, always was very primitive.

The end of the 18th century did not bring anything new to the art of riding; actually, it would become considerably more primitive and crude.

The artificial balancing of a horse through iron in her mouth and the displaced croup discovered by the founding fathers of Haute École would become the standard everywhere, except the cavalry.

But!

Complex elements which required a rider's virtuosity were virtually disappearing.

The fact of the matter is that in France, the French revolutionaries who had put the great manèges out of business and shot the students and masters, finished off Haute École, a completely aristocratic attribute, with special enthusiasm, using the butts of rifles.

(The revolutionaries used de la Gueriniere's famous manège for meetings of their schizoid tribunals.)

And de Nestier himself, by the way, "went missing" in the revolutionary years.

True, it wasn't only in the revolution.

By the middle of the 18th century, two deadly enemies to Haute École tradition had appeared.

The "High School's" first enemy was the cavalry, with its desire to see the horse only as fodder for one or two battles and as a means of transport.

The second enemy was the Anglomania which infected Haute École's homeland with a love for things primitive and the excitement of races.

Two non-canonized masters of the School deserve special respect and a posthumous good word: D'Abzac and de la Bigne. These two struggled desperately, both in the manèges and in living rooms, with the English influence that was so disastrous for the School. England, with its races, with a veneration for abominable riding and with its primitivism and coarseness as regards man and horse, turned out to be the grave digger of the art of riding.

D'Abzac forbade everything English in the manège, including the English style of boots and the English hunting whips that were coming into fashion then.

De la Bigne refused to take even the most profitable and titled pupils only because they were English. These two, unfortunately, were in the minority.

"English style," the style of red-nosed squires who recklessly rode after the fox, was killing school riding with its search for contact with the horse, its complexity and inspiration.

England was victorious because she was able to offer the world more primitive, democratic riding standards which by the 19th century had already completely forced out Haute École.

Conflict between the pro-cavalry academies and the classical schools began to appear as early as the 18ᵗʰ century.

The Saumur school, founded in 1763, was the main ideologue of military horsemanship, having united the Luneville, Angers and Saint Germain schools under a banner of hostility to the "academicians."

Resisting them was only the Versailles school which had maintained authentic classical traditions, that is, those which professed a fine, masterly and sparing practice for the horse in comparison with the primitive cavalry.

It didn't resist for long, and then its foundations, too, were shaken by the influence of the cavalry generals and society's enthusiasm for English races; soon Versailles's traditions were totally, physically, eradicated.

Into the basket beneath the guillotine of the French revolution, along with pomaded and empty heads slid, in the best traditions of the gallant age, unfortunately, also the severed head of Haute École.

The art of riding, per se, was returning to the level of the 15ᵗʰ century.

Only now, man-made collection using iron was taking the place of spurs of a hellish length — thus becoming a new variety of torture for the horse.

Pluvinel never would have allowed himself to hold a horse in an artificial collection for more than several minutes at a time.

He understood the kind of tension that occurred in the entire cervical area of a horse's spine and in her whole muscle system. Being, roughly speaking, the inventor of this collection, he always remembered that a free horse collects itself only for several moments.

"Clowns" like F. Baucher, the Golden Duke or J. Fillis spent hours collecting a horse and taught this to their adherents.

The severity of the iron — curb bit — of this time was the last straw. Take for example this generally rustic curb bit of the "Jineta" type, weighing 850 grams, with a boffette of carved bronze and a shank 20 centimeters long. Here it is easy to notice that the four-link curb chain, which is traditional for Haute École curb bits, has been replaced by a steel pear-shaped ring, which clasps the horse's lower jaw, not so much to be able to affect the trigeminus nerve, as simply to break the jaw with a light pull of the rein (see table IV, **12**).

This type of iron was so widespread that it even has been cited in a number of typical works, in "L'Encyclopedie" by Diderot and d'Alembert in the volume "Art du Cheval", in the chapter "Eperonier". This mouthpiece of a curb bit is, per se, the European version of the common Arabian iron discussed above.

The 18th century itself returned to the ancient tradition of installing sprocket teeth on the bit, which, ramming the palate vault, sharply impacted the minor palatine nerve and the maxillary nerve branch (see table IV, **8**).

Moreover, the mouthpiece had become solid again, it was no longer jointed. Because of the solid-mouthpiece design, the severity of equine iron, was growing extensively, and its "destructive force" was growing as well.

But even where the quantity of pins, rings, cylinders and the length of shanks were not shocking to the eye of the beholder, the severity and cruelty of the iron was unchanged. One may take the simplest Scythian snaffle bits of the 6th to the 4th centuries B.C.

They look perfectly harmless (see table II, **4**, **5**). But the problem is that in principle harmless, painless iron does not exist. Any iron shoved into a horse's mouth has one purpose, to cause pain.

A horse's iron, roughly speaking, is divided into two categories — "trigeminal" action (when the branches of the trigeminus nerve, which pass along the bones of the horse's lower jaw, are chosen as the main point of pain-infliction) and "dental" effect, where the very tender toothless areas — the bars, the teeth (first and second premolar teeth), tongue, palate and gum are subjected to a direct painful influence — that is, direct pain which acts upon the minor palatine nerve, the branches of the maxillary nerve, the sublingual nerve, the alveolar nerves and the facial nerve. [n]

Trigeminal action iron is based more on intimidation. The horse, being a phenomenally intelligent creature, always will remember what kind of "mine" was put into her mouth by man. Such iron causes not a steady, cruel pain, but inflicts only one-time, short "injections" of this pain into the horse's brain and consciousness.

The Scythians, Cimmerians, Sarmats, Huns, Alans, Antes, Sogdians — almost all of the ancient world — used dental effect iron.

It fully assured control at swift gaits, stopping, backing up as well as submission to primitive turns on one hind leg — the kind which are practiced today in circuses, where they are called "spins" — but nothing more than that.

Dental effect iron assumes constant usage of the rein, what now is called by the amusing phrase "contact with the mouth" — that is, these bits constantly remind the horse of her place and her servitude by inflicting continuous pain and discomfort.

It is difficult to say which type, the trigeminal or the dental, is more cruel.

I believe that they are approximately equal in cruelty.

Any trigeminal iron provides a direct painful impact on the minor palatine nerve, the branches of the maxillary nerve, the sublingual, the lingual and the branches of the trigeminus nerve (see table 2).

This is a dry anatomical fact. There's no way around it.

Any dental iron provides a direct painful impact to the minor palatine nerve, the branches of the maxillary nerve, the sublingual and lingual nerves and the alveolar and infraorbital nerves.

Modern equestrianism has put these two types of iron — the trigeminal and the dental — in the horse's mouth at the same time.

The curb bit with a mouthpiece resembling Pingnatelecci's iron, except that it is even more severe, is shoved into the horse's mouth. Moreover, the mouthpieces are in no way designed differently than the Mongolian or Scythian.

As we might expect, nothing startling happens.

Moreover, competitive or sporting dressage, timidly hinting that it is one of the "High School's" heirs, proves to be completely unable to reproduce the really complex and spectacular elements like the terre à terre, the capriole or the sentavo.

Only the most primitive elements, such as the passage and pirouette remain.

And this is despite the fact that the horse's undisguised agony, which continues for hours — a combination of the effects of the different irons, the blows, the forced collection, mutilation of the neck and spine, the use of electrical shock and striking of the legs — has become the absolute norm.

In this respect Haute École's fathers must be given their due, for they did not commit the sin of striking the legs, that is, rhythmic beating with sticks on the horse's legs in order to attain a higher lift of the legs in the passage, the piaffe and the "balance."

However, today's dressage "queens," be they Russian, German, or from anywhere else in the world, generally do not operate without striking the horse's legs.

Moreover, while in the classical schools (the Royal Andalusian, the Spanish school in Vienna) patterned in the image of the Haute École, exercises with the horse continue not more than half an hour, sporting dressage torments the horse for hours on end, with sessions lasting two or three hours each.

And still the result is nil.

This means that the severity of the iron gives no help toward revealing the horse's startling capabilities.

And spurs don't make the point either.

Spurs in combination with iron in the mouth, by the by, were used as early as the time of the Huns.

I have a very rare example of Hun spurs, these are more cruel in their effects than the Haute École or Mexican type. (see tables 3, 1; IV, 3).

It is of course a bit difficult to compare with the Gothic European spur which is a completely pathological and outrageous variant.

Besides this is a direct action spur! (see table 3, 2).

The peculiarity of the medieval seat (legs firmly forward with firm support in the stirrup) in no way warranted such a length and sharpness of spurs, nor the capability of cutting into the horse's belly in any extreme situation, even against the rider's wishes. (The horse can fall down, the rider's leg can "slide" back and sideways upon colliding with another rider or a man on foot and the horse, finally, can jump over something, inevitably dislodging the rider's legs.)

This example of the spur is pathological in it's brutality, but it was common in 13th–15th centuries. They loved to use it in combination with the "sweet" military curb-bit (the one with hooks on the mouthpiece). Such shameless lethality of the spur, and in particular that such a variant was widely adopted for combat, once more demonstrates that the medieval horse was, roughly speaking, "a horse for one battle," a valuable creature, but nonetheless less valuable than the one-time opportunity to win or run away.

The Haute École spur (see table 3, 6; V, 10) employs a completely different principle and, in comparison with the Gothic spur, the spur of the Huns, and the Mexican and German spurs, it is, in general, an example of delicacy and gentleness.

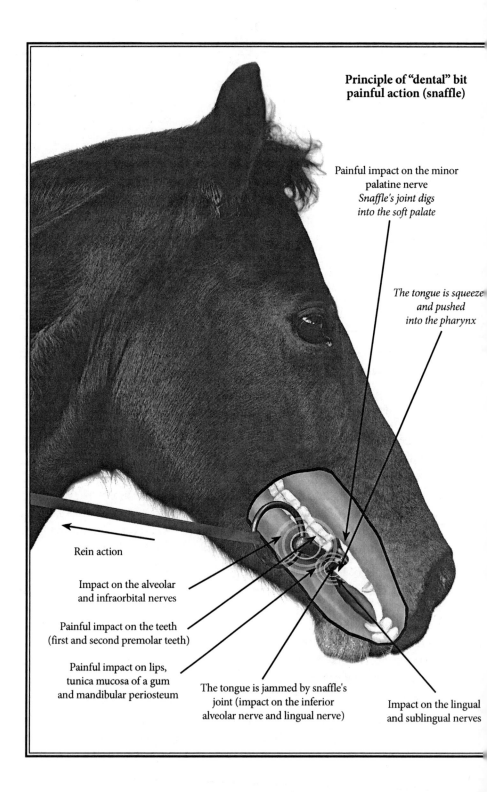

Principle of "dental" bit painful action (snaffle)

Painful impact on the minor palatine nerve
Snaffle's joint digs into the soft palate

The tongue is squeeze and pushed into the pharynx

Rein action

Impact on the alveolar and infraorbital nerves

Painful impact on the teeth (first and second premolar teeth)

Painful impact on lips, tunica mucosa of a gum and mandibular periosteum

The tongue is jammed by snaffle's joint (impact on the inferior alveolar nerve and lingual nerve)

Impact on the lingual and sublingual nerves

Table 2

Principle of "trigeminal" bit action (curb bit or pelham bit)

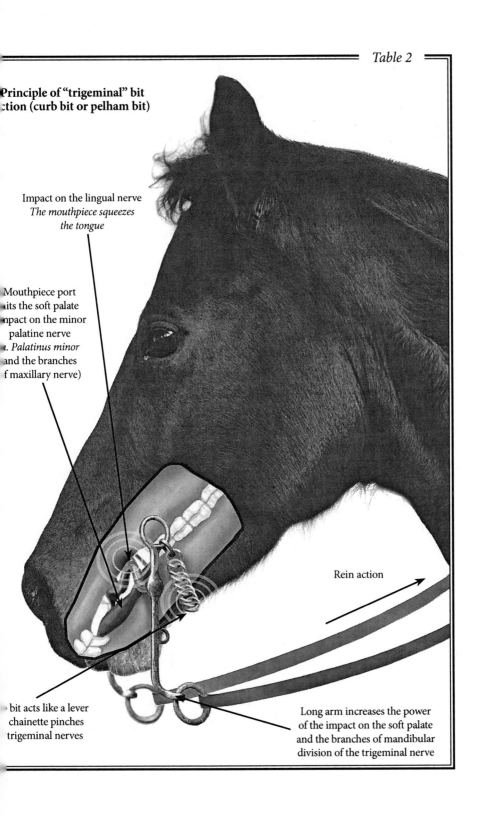

Impact on the lingual nerve
The mouthpiece squeezes the tongue

Mouthpiece port hits the soft palate Impact on the minor palatine nerve (n. *Palatinus minor* and the branches of maxillary nerve)

Rein action

bit acts like a lever chainette pinches trigeminal nerves

Long arm increases the power of the impact on the soft palate and the branches of mandibular division of the trigeminal nerve

This leads us to believe that these glorious adventurers of the 16th and 17th centuries who smelled ripe with horse sweat, guarded a secret that did not lie in the iron nor in cruelty.

At the end of the 20th century, it was demonstrated in the most convincing form by several people in various countries almost simultaneously that the horse can beautifully perform the most complex Haute École elements and the most breathtaking figures without any iron at all and without any devices that control her head or cause any kind of pain.

Moreover, several people in the world already know how to train horses using only kindness and understanding and obtaining from the horse the purest and most correct collection, without using any iron pieces or straps at all.

In these cases, I am speaking about "pure" versions, not about situations when the horse has been trained using iron, and then "stripped" and shown bridleless only for purposes of a demonstration or other performance.

I am speaking of the versions in which the horse really has been trained and taught without any painful coercion of the iron type, and without halters, when all training has been built from the start by appealing to her astonishing mind and readiness to be friends with man.

The North American Indians from a special caste of "horse whisperers" practiced similar methods in the 18th and 19th centuries in very rare instances.

This was done at a time of training rare, "custom-made" fighting horses, each of which was pure gold. For example, the Commanche gave up 100 to 200 regular horses for one combat horse, that is one trained by the whisperers.

By the way, the usual, widespread practice of the North American Indians in regard to other horses was a rope loop around the lower jaw of the horse, which was called a "wikan."

This rope has little to distinguish it from iron in its effect.

* * *

J.R.R. Tolkien who, judging by his biography, was absolutely not a horseman, and who lived in the everyday reality of one of the most cruel countries with regard to horses, that is England, also probably either pondered this subject or felt something.

Table 3

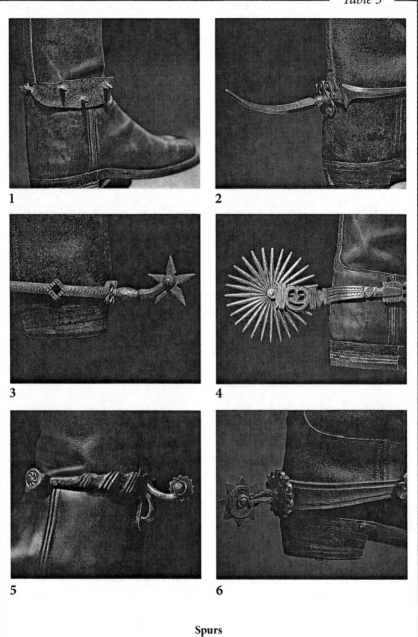

Spurs

1 — Hun (3^d-4th centuries); 2 — Gothic (Europe, 14th century); 3 — Europe (15th-16th centuries); 4 — Mexico (19th century); 5 — Austria (18th century); 6 — France (18th century, Haute École)

At least, the central character of his brilliant trilogy, "Lord of the Rings," Gandalf, constructs his own relationship with a horse without any iron and without any bridle, which is emphasized by Tolkien.

Swift, in the enchanting epilogue of Gulliver's journey to the country of the Houyhnhnms writes: "The very first spare cash I used for the purchase of two stallions, which I keep in a beautiful stable... The horses understand me sufficiently well; I talk with them at least four hours every day. They don't know what a bridle is..."

* * *

The ancient world also knew riding without a bridle.

True, in a somewhat anecdotal version.

The Parthians and Numidians were first, in this sense, to be recorded in the world's chronicles, but both they and others used collars raised very high, practically beneath the jowl.

And since they rode very small and, as a rule, worn out horses, they were able to "choke" the horse when necessary so that she began once more to obey.

If one is to believe Plutarch, Julius Caesar practiced riding without a bridle, but one must remember that this very same Plutarch explained Alexander the Great's conception by the fact that lightning had struck his sleeping mother between her legs.

Montaigne cites relatively credible evidence on this subject in his "Essays." Quintus Fabius Maximum Rullianus (3rd century B.C.) in a battle with the Samnites, despairing of breaking through the Samnite defense with the Roman cavalry after their third or fourth attack had been repelled by the Samnites, commanded his riders to remove the bridles from their horses as he galloped along the lines of his cavalry.

The Roman cavalry complied, removed the bridles and routed the Samnites, breaking through their lines almost at once and scattering them to the devil.

The infantry immediately entered the breach in the Samnite defense and slaughtered them.

They were victorious over the Samnites, but the down-on his-luck victor Rullianus was gathering his cavalry for a long time thereafter.

And a second lover of bridleless attacks, Quintus Fulvius Flaccus, gave almost the very same orders.

It is known that he dispersed and killed an enormous army of Celtiberians.

The practice did not take root solely because the consequences of such victories were more severe than any defeats would have been.

Having trampled the Celtiberians into their native soil, the Roman horses, without bridles and sensing their freedom, shook off the Roman cataphracts or bolted in such a mad gallop that the rider had to decide how to carefully get off the maddened horse of his own accord rather than be borne further into the unknown.

For a long time thereafter the Romans were busy trying to round up their horses, chasing them through the fields of Celtiberia, and covering their cataphracts in bandages.

No one else made any more such attempts in Roman history, although Livy in his famous works also urged the military leaders: "*Id cum maiore vi equorum facietis si effrenatos in hostes equos immittitis*" (You will do your business with greater advantage of your horses' strength, if you send them unbridled upon the enemy. Livy — XL-40.)

At any rate, there is no further serious documented evidence of similar attacks either in Roman history or in the history that followed. [4]

A horse without a bridle, that is, without an instrument of pain to control her, would, for centuries, be synonymous with peril, with dangerous self-will.

The Russian language, for example, can serve as the best illustration of this.

There is a most vivid, very powerful Russian word which means an irrepressible, malicious outrage, a desire to violate the rules of decency, to be spitefully willful.

This word is "разнузданный, разнузданность" (unbridled, lack of restraint, dissoluteness), that translates, whether strictly or loosely, to "an absence of a bridle."

Not only in Russia is a horse without a bridle imagined as dangerous, uncontrollable and capable of nothing but violence.

There also is a word in English with such a meaning — "unbridled" — and it also is unrestrained, dangerous and undisciplined. And literally it is "without a bridle."

It would be a mistake to think that all the horrors of iron have remained in the past.

Today's iron is in no way distinguishable in design from the iron of past centuries.

That same monolithic mouthpiece of the curb bit is still crammed into the arch of the horse's palate, we still fasten that same chain that causes painful paralysis with its strong pressure on the trigeminus nerve.

Modern iron is divided into the iron of dental action and that of trigeminal action in exactly the same way as its historic counterparts.

And it is used in precisely the same way.

It has become a bit less intricate, the shanks have been shortened a bit, different metals have appeared, but its essence has not changed at all.

Only the design is different. The rosaire, chappellete, trebuchet and coquille have disappeared, because it has become clear that for the purpose of inflicting very strong pain and to have an effect on the main nerves of the head, a fixed bit, either with a curved port mouthpiece or a mouthpiece which is broken in two, is fully sufficient.

The colossal shank length disappeared on its own, because any ignoramus was able to break the jaw of too many horses too easily, which meant that the horse simply was murdered, since it became unable to eat and slowly, before everyone's eyes, died of starvation.

Plainly speaking, the rate of attrition was too high.

A principle was at work which generally governs the modern physical culture of primates, the "law of economy."

For efficient torture of the horse, the shank length of modern curb bits is fully sufficient.

The snaffle bit has not changed at all.

No one, it is understood, has undertaken any attempts to listen to the horse's soul or to become friends with the horse.

The best-known Russian horseman, the connoisseur Ivan Severyanovich from Leskov's "The Enchanted Wanderer," is a specimen of an obtuse jerk, completely lacking any ability to understand the horse.

All conflicts with the horse which are described in "The Enchanted Wanderer," can be resolved with gentleness and patience much more rapidly and effectively than by the idiotic breaking of a bowl on the horse's head, or by beatings, blinding and similar outrages.

Ivan Severyanovich is a representative example and not an isolated one, of the common national attitude toward the horse.

Moreover, Ivan Severyanovich's boorishness is romanticized and heroized; he is without question considered a nice, positive character, who is very popular.

There is a Russian proverb which is very expressive of this attitude: "Don't trust the horse. If you find a mare's skull, bridle it too!"

Almost no one believes that there is another way besides the loathsome and dead-end path of pain and torture of the horse. Almost no one believes in a path of kindness that is strikingly simple and effective.

Nonetheless, let's return to the fathers of Haute École.

As I already have said above, they were not like-minded persons and they did not create a coherent doctrine of equestrian training. Some of the School's "fathers" made use of the most barbaric methods.

Yet it is worth singling out the primary figures.

They are, undoubtedly, Pluvinel and de la Gueriniere.

They were the first in the history of mankind, after Xenophon, whom they read, studied and quoted, and after Zhuangzi (Chuang Tzu) about whom they had no knowledge, to speak of gentleness and friendliness as a fundamental key to a relationship with the horse.

This in and of itself was an absolutely shocking position in the eyes of all of their contemporaries.

The stupid human world had by that time accumulated notions about the horse, which was seen as a biological mechanism that is brought into action by pure cruelty and nothing more.

De Pluvinel banished from the "School" those pupils whom he caught being cruel to a horse. And by old age he had become quite intolerant in this regard.

Francoise Robichon de la Gueriniere already had written directly about gentleness as a fundamental method.

It was a tiny, timid step forward, and possibly, much more important than the contrivance of collection.

Not one of the "teachers" would have been able to take the giant step from fierce "school" curb bits to full "bridlelessness" and kindness, and to friendship with the horse, — it was unthinkable, it completely contradicted the then-held view of the horse's essence and her functions in the military and manège .

The whole concept was simply incredible and fantastic and there would be no guarantee it would be understood in their century.

It is stupid now to condemn the fathers of Haute École because they stayed with the iron, and with their spurs and pillars.

Yes, they stayed with it all. But they, and no one else, imparted a certain powerful drive, a movement in the direction of changing the relationship with the horse.

It is, by today's standards, a trifle, but then, everything begins from a trifle.

Years of work with the widest variety of horses taught the founding fathers of Haute École to listen to the horse, and set them to thinking about the fact that everything is not as simple as it seemed to their contemporaries.

They were the children of their time, they were cruel, and their guilt with respect to those specific horses that came into training with them is enormous. But they were talented and, glancing into the striking eyes of the horse, they grasped her pain, her weariness.

And having grasped it, they changed themselves. They knew how to draw conclusions. The horse's torment became their torment.

The Roman cataphract, the Gothic knight, the Scythian rider were completely indifferent to what the horse was experiencing. It fully sufficed for the fulfillment of their utilitarian military or transportation tasks that the horse was simply mobile. The quality of the movement played no role, the horse's mood did not matter at all; as long as the horse ran and did not fall, everything was alright.

The founding fathers of Haute École were the first who dealt, roughly speaking, with equine choreography.

They desired a very complex result, and were first to understand the dependence of this result on a relationship with the horse and her condition.

For years, line by line, working with the horse under saddle and on the ground, they patiently completed their "masterpieces" — the capriole, "balance" and piaffe, forever in contact with the horse's soul, pride and kindness.

They sincerely searched for training methods gentler than those that had been adopted everywhere.

Pluvinel in particular introduced into Haute École practice the "lunette", special glasses for the horse, which tightly closed her eyes and fully deprived it of the ability to see everything else that was happening at the manège .

He wanted the horse's utmost concentration and did not wish to punish her with a whip or iron. He tried to put the horse into a very calm and meditative state in which she would be able to concentrate fully on the trainer's voice and her own sensations. The "lunette" was not very effective and not even a very smart idea, but it says something about Pluvinel.

The founding fathers of Haute École desired from the horse the most complex movements of which she was capable, and they were the first to elicit highly organized, complex actions. They earnestly called the horse, and she earnestly responded.

And in this lay the reason for their striking discoveries and successes, not at all from iron and spurs.

Only because of this did some of Haute École's founding fathers courageously and rightfully make progress in the world history of the horse.

Their progress had nothing to do with the diverse listing of tortures of the horse.

It had nothing to do with that which they traditionally write and rewrite on all the continents. That is not the history of the horse; it is the history of human stupidity. I am referring to the authentic world history of the horse, which at some time will have a certain high point.

The high point will be when iron, — the symbol of man's fear of the horse, fear of her power and love of freedom, a symbol of man's continual defeat in 3,000 years of relationship with the horse — ceases to be necessary for anyone.

What trifles man has already hit upon indeed, like the structure of the atom.

The horse's soul and the ability to penetrate it are more complex undertakings.

But there is a hope.

Although there also is the temptation of the most primitive, most brutal way.

The way of Swift's Yahoo.

* * *

The apogee of cruelty, stupidity, inability and unwillingness to understand the horse has resulted in equestrian sports.

P.S. I deliberately have not mentioned stirrups in this short history of equine iron, since they were never a means of control and had little influence on the horse's feelings.

I have collected and classified everything I have at my disposal regarding spurs (see the Appendix 2).

---

[a] Courbette — the horse rises on her hind legs with haunches flexed and lowered, and takes a series of jumps with an obligatory landing on her hind legs. The forehand is raised higher and the cadence is more sustained than in the mezair.

[b] Pesade — the horse raises herself high on her hind legs.

[c] Terre à terre — a Haute École figure invented by Gueriniere which consists of a uniform and very rhythmic lift of the fore-body with an abrupt forward movement of the hind legs.

[d] Douze — a very old version of "balance" characterized by a high raising of the body during a shift of the weight from one leg to the other, a lesser amplitude of swaying and collection, which is absolutely absent in the usual balance.

[e] Ballotade — one of the "school" jumps. The horse, having jumped, tucks in the forelegs and relaxes the hind a bit in the hocks, but tenses them in the fetlocks and shows the soles of its rear hooves. Per de la Gueriniere: "In the ballotade, when the horse is at the apogee of its jump, she turns up the hind feet as though it intended to kick, without however doing so as she does in the capriole." She remains there for a short time and again comes down onto the hind and then onto the forelegs. I don't know one "school" horse right now in the world that could do the Ballotade. It is not the complexity of teaching this element, as it is very simple to teach, but it is effective only in engravings and photographs, and as a live demonstration it is too fast and does not make the necessary impression.

[f] Passage — a very rhythmic and slow trot with a high, accentuated lifting of the legs. There are a multitude of varieties of the passage. It is a very simple element, performed everywhere and there is no clear leader in its performance.

[g] Mezair — "a demi-courbette, the movements of which are less removed from the ground, more rapid, and characterized by greater forward motion than a true courbette, but at the same time higher and more measured than the terre a terre".

[h] Sentavo — an advance of the horse on her hind legs.

[i] Croupade — a conventional jump in place. It's height is low, not more than 50-70 centimeters. It is important that all four of the horses feet are in the air during this jump. According to de la Gueriniere "…when the horse has all four legs in the air she draws the hind legs and hooves under the belly without showing the bottoms of the feet." I teach the Croupade to all horses, since this movement, which the horse masters perfectly, allows her to transition to the more complex jumps, the ballotade and capriole.

[j] Centado — an exercise where the horse sits on her rump for several seconds.

[k] Levade — a semi-pesade with a pause (3–5 seconds) at the highest point.

[l] Lancade — a jump of the horse in which the horse lands on the forelegs. The element is easy to teach, but absolutely unspectacular.

[m] Balance — a rhythmic and extensive swaying of the horse, which throws the body weight from one foreleg to the other. The hind legs either stop during it or do a slight piaffe.

[n] I understand all the conventionality, plainness and some inconsistency of these terms, and some were not invented until I did so. But it is nevertheless necessary to classify and divide the horse's iron according to the principle of "the primary area of injury," as in actuality the two types of iron are extremely different.

EQUESTRIANISM

Chapter Two

England.

The 21st century.

Rossdale & Partners veterinary clinic, Newmarket.

The dreams of the young racing mare Theresia III, that ended up here, on the red and blue oilcloths of the operating table are enchanting and peaceful.

It is absolutely quiet here.

Absolutely sterile.

State of the art medical equipment, and the great hands of Richard Payne, star of veterinary surgery known throughout England.

The filly Theresia III is lying on her back.

Her stomach with its tiny, prim udder with two teats has collapsed deeply.

Her neck, the very long and almost straight neck of the costly English pure thoroughbred, is extended its full length, and blue corrugated hoses lead into the mouth, feeding the blood and lungs of the filly pure halothane, the gentlest anesthesia.

All her legs have been lifted and the washed hooves are in clear plastic bags.

Richard Payne, who is glancing at the monitors around the operating table, is digging into a foreleg carpus with an intricate, shiny instrument while happily mumbling something through his mask.

On the monitors is seen the arthroscopic operation and the broken joint in which the instrument rummages.

Besides Richard Payne, chunky English nurses are fussing around with the sleeping horse on the table.

One of them constantly lifts the filly's eyelids and shines a light into its eyes, while at the same time she taps on a keyboard with a gloved hand. (The stage of the pupil's dilation, most likely.)

Theresia III sleeps. The pain has left the joints broken by the races.

And the gaseous halothane anesthesia bears her, the sweet beautiful mare, away from the table, into a huge pasture covered with high grass, to her mother and to her sisters. It carries her into a space of freedom, into love and happiness, to the life for which she was really born.

And the life that people created for her is forgotten.

A life overwhelmed by pain in her broken legs and in her burning and bursting lungs, a life which passes in the darkness and the stench of the stall from which they suddenly pull her into the blinding glare, to the shouts, to the din and stench of thousands of Yahoos and they begin to break her mouth with iron and to beat her.

But now on the red and blue oilcloths of the table, this second life which people have conceived for her has disappeared somewhere.

Memories of it have melted away, as the pain has melted away. And then the filly Theresia begins her run!

And how she runs! How freely, how extensively and powerfully… The racecourse visitors in checkered caps who make their money on races would howl and scratch their ugly mugs in complete ecstasy!

She runs in her dream, but her hooves in the clear plastic bags run too, and gauze pads, hoses, oilcloths, nurses, bags and sensors fly all around the operating room.

There is static and a gray rippling line on the monitors.

In her reeling, droppers and clusters of vials crash to the floor, and the great Richard Payne himself rebounds and his blade, having traced a sparkling track in the sterile air of the operating room, sticks exactly into the center of the schedule board of operations.

The sleeping beauty gallops, while laying on her back, amidst the lively chaos in the operating room.

But several minutes will pass and it all will be restored.

They will pick up the droppers. They will adjust the monitors. They will give him another blade, and clear bags will once more be placed onto the calmed filly's hooves which are raised toward the sky.

Horse races have maimed the filly Theresia, as they have thousands of other horses. Her fate, her pain are typical for a horse after the first racing season.

Today Richard Payne, undoubtedly, will heal her, having performed a madly expensive and complex arthroscopic operation.

Of course, he will heal her only so that she can race again, destroying her joints and tearing her tendons and lungs.

But once the cost of the treatment exceeds the cost of the filly herself, Theresia's owner will buy herself another horse, and the filly Theresia will go nowhere.

She will go to slaughter, or be killed on the training grounds, or she will die slowly under the fat-bottomed girls who play with her life in their sport.

One way or another the filly Theresia III will be sent to a heavenly pasture, to her own equine god.

* * *

It is not totally by chance that I have begun this chapter about equestrianism with an episode that relates more to horse racing, although, if one is oriented toward the concepts generally accepted in the equestrian world, horse racing and other horse sports do not have any relationship to each other.

But I long ago consolidated for myself all human amusements, that are based on torture and a lack of understanding of the horse, into one whole. I believe that troikas, racing of all kinds, the horse corrida and the circus, eventing, dressage, "pleasure" riding on rented horses, and show jumping all are, per se, one and the same. For simplicity, we shall call them "equestrianism."

All of these disciplines have one main, unifying feature: they all are based on a complete lack of understanding of the horse, ignorance of it, "not hearing" it and they all conceive of the horse as a biological mechanism that is obligated to serve man for his entertainment, simply because… well, because it is obligated to do so.

There is a definite cruel logic in this.

In the animal world there is a leader from the order of primates, the suborder of the higher humanoid (Darwin's ingenious wording, by the way), and he, on the strength of his "highly evolved state" claims the right to eat what he wants and to amuse himself however he wants, without any consideration of the feelings of the one being eaten or the perceptions of the one he has chosen for his amusement.

In other words, an ape which has progressed to the mobile telephone, television serials and handheld stun guns, calmly violates the world and its inhabitants as he chooses, including the horse.

That's the way it is and it is stupid to argue with it.

I would say that this is a certain biological reality, not so much disagreeable as it is unflattering.

There is, true, one small problem — this biological reality does not entirely conform to those myths which the developed primate has proclaimed as the reality about himself, and which he and his kind have believed about themselves over a period of 35 centuries.

I have in mind all the trifling but sweet myths about a soul, about a conscience, about kindness, about a god and nobility, etc. — their full range is widely known.

The origin of almost all the world's religions is a direct consequence of mankind's universal inferiority complex and its aspiration to distance itself from the fussy, fidgety, hairy, stinky and very inconsequential ancestor, the ape known as *Pierolapithecus catalunicus* or *Paranthropus*.

This clear perception of the insignificance of its own origin has been humanity's special "quirk" in all centuries and eras. If Darwin had us being derived, for example, from the panther or something just as spectacular and heroic, I assure you there would be thousands of times more Darwinists.

But, here's the problem! We are really counted in the classification of living creatures as follows:

1) in the class of mammalia,

2) in the order of primata,

3) in the family of Hominidae,

4) in the sub-order of anthropoids,

5) in the family of Homonoids (humanoid primates).

And so forth… One simply wants to cry!

But! I draw your attention to point 3.

Clearly stated here is "the family of Hominidae."

Hominidae has been guaranteed to us by science.

But only "Hominidae."

That is, similar to that being, which, being ashamed of its nature, laid down myths about itself, believed in them and is trying to live and feel in accordance with them, despite its abominable biological origin.

A certain loophole, take note, has been abandoned.

A wee one.

But it exists.

And it is perfectly within our power, either to remain "Hominidae" or voluntarily take upon ourselves the whole load, the whole accumulation of a fascinating falsehood, absorb it, merge with it and transition to another category.

Those who have accomplished this merger between a descendant of monkeys and Paranthropus become composers, martyrs, philosophers, writers, saints, warriors, or artists.

But in his relationship to the horse, man always was, and still is, merely a monkey, a being from the order of primates.

Hominidae. (I have already spoken about the rare exception of the Zhuangzi or de Nestier type.)

And equestrianism, its philosophy, its practices, its customs and its procedures fully confirm this thesis.

By the way, Jonathan Swift had laid down all this brilliantly.

And it is no accident that we represent Swift's Yahoo here in the red riding coat and jockey cap, the traditional attire of the quintessential equestrian sportsman.

Cavalrymen, water carriers or miners, for example, were, of course in no way better, often even worse, but they lived according to the laws of their time, of their war, or of their hellish labor. For war, the conveyance of water on horses dying from joint pain and strain, and nightmarish labor in mines where a horse was lowered down approximately as shown in this document (see table 6, 4), where it first went blind and already having gone blind pulled a cart, and then took a long time to die, having been cast into the secluded corners of the mine and there spitting up black coal dust, is all disgusting, but it came about because of a certain earnest need. It was not for mere amusement.

But sportsmen and wannabe sportsmen are simply being entertained, amused.

You must be aware that all the "important proceedings" — the ritual installation of colored sticks at a definite height for show jumping, the clattering of the starting bell, the doping inspection, the points and penalties, the styles of the caps and iron, the idiotic Olympians, the dashing troikas, the steeplechases, the harness racing, the horse corrida — all of them are nothing more than entertainment, amusement.

Equestrianism is, as is well-known, is not at all a necessity; this phenomenon did not arise out of any kind of need for survival. Equestrianism is entirely optional. It does not have to be.

No one's fate, health or life is at stake.

An urgent dispatch, so to speak, is not being conveyed across the front line.

Those who earn money with this business simply devise a way to obtain payment for the amusement, no more than that.

Sportsmen, in proof of the seriousness of their diversions and with a goal of imparting certain tragic "gravitas" to their activities, very much love to discuss the dangers of equestrianism. But the hemorrhoids, calluses, injuries, sweat, broken noses, broken backs and concussed skulls of the sportsmen should not evoke anyone's sympathy. After all, no one forces sportsmen to amuse themselves in just this way.

The extensive "martyrology" of steeplechase [a] and show jumping and other amusements of equestrianism in which, thank goodness, the actual torturers of horses frequently break their own necks, are entirely the problem of the torturers themselves.

The injuries of a mere sportsman — the blood and even the death of an idler who decided to have some fun, who wanted an adrenalin rush, some "self-glorification" or a hundred rubles — should not be confused with the sacred blood of a gladiator, who was forced into the arena at spike-point.

So, let's call things by their true names.

Equestrianism is the amusement of people who lack the ability to feel the horse's pain and appreciate the horse's spirit and are convinced with all the passion of the hominidae primate that the creature who is, in their opinion, inferior is obliged to entertain them and to be subjugated by them simply because it is obliged.

As much as the horse does not want to participate in their amusements voluntarily, these people use instruments for the infliction of great pain in the horse's mouth, in the lower jaw, in the poll and the neck, and in the loins and the muzzle.

This pain is so severe (in any competition one can see a horse who is experiencing a painful clonic convulsion, and the sportsmen nearby giggle, convinced that the horse is simply tossing its head) that ordinary horses, horses that are not very strong in spirit, are quickly destroyed.

Sometimes, however, the standard means of inflicting pain are insufficient to assure the horse's obedience. "Resistance" to the standard means has nothing to do with the strength of the horse's spirit, but only on how badly the horse wants to escape, even for a moment, the terrible agony he is experiencing. When the horse "resists" standard means, then other means are used — electroshock, ordinary beatings, refined beatings, "multiple floggings," beating with sticks on the legs, compressed air weapons and frankly torturous means of continuous action: martingales, checks, overchecks, spiked serretas, side reins, chambons, de Gogues, standing martingales, driving reins for work in-hand and similar abominations.

This torturous arsenal allows, for example, fastening a horse's head tightly to its chest and immobilizing it that position (side reins) or, conversely, pulling the head high, fastening it to the horse's back and immobilizing it in that position (the check). And then they compel the horse to perform with its head tightly fastened.

These things are done in order to crush any resistance and in order to correct the horse's movements to the standard acceptable to the type of sport.

I have enumerated only two positions of eight or ten, but the others, too, have a purely painful purpose. The martingale, for example, is a strap construction which makes any normal sharp upwards movement of the head ultra-painful: one type of martingale fastens tightly to the girth at one end and at the other, to the rein, that is to the iron in the mouth. A jerk with the head upwards is a sharp blow to the nerves of the gums and teeth in response. And it is like that for hours.

By the way, all this filth is an indispensable, most commonplace appurtenance of equestrianism and an assortment is found at any stable where there are sporting horses. True, the stun guns, and in general the electrical pieces are attributes only of expensive, "advanced" stables where they are engaged in so-called dressage or show jumping.

One needs to imagine too the incredible, spectacular mediocrity of the sportsmen, be they sulky drivers, troika drivers, jockeys, or the riders competing in dressage, show jumping, or eventing.

They, as a rule, are convinced that the lengthy list of torturous means are all normal, everyday objects which one needs to use to train the horse or improve its movement.

Yet, if there is a talent for riding, not one of these "tools" is at all necessary — either from the standard assortment or from the extreme.

And it is terribly offensive and unacceptable to the sportsmen and the wannabes to acknowledge this fact.

Why do you think the Russian world of "horsemen" trembles so from the sound of my name alone?

Yes, of course, for them I am a loathsome, insulting spectacle. They see how a man calmly sits on a wild, lively four-year-old stallion without any bridle or similar stupidity, and this stallion, who has remained absolutely free, unconditionally obeys and performs whatever "haute école" figures it is permissible for horses of this age to do.

Of course, it is unbearable for these "horsemen" to look at this.

One wants to kill such a man immediately.

I understand them.

The very fact of my existence leads inexorably to the following conclusion: the presence of any painful device — be it simple dental or trigeminal action iron, the martingale, side reins or an overcheck — is evidence of the "horseman's" complete inability to understand the horse and to be understood by her.

Accordingly, and according to sensible and simple logic, if you do not have the capabilities to explain to the horse what it is you want from her without any bridles and iron pieces, you should not be near a horse, and you, unfortunately, are not gifted in this business, so you need to occupy yourself in some other way.

I understand that so-called "horsemen," sportsmen and jockeys, want to be involved with horses very much.

And they are involved with them.

But, what if you have no ear for music at all, but want very much to give a solo vocal concert at La Scala?

What will happen? Nix.

No one ever will allow you onto La Scala's stage, because you don't have an ear and you cannot sing.

But if you don't have "equestrian" talent you are nonetheless able to become Russia's champion in dressage, for example.

Or Germany's champion in show jumping.

It's easy!

For there is that assortment of painful devices that ostensibly can replace talent.

In equestrianism, success is guaranteed if the humanoid primate has firm confidence in his right to inflict pain on a creature he believes is a lesser one; if he is willing to resort to absolute cruelty and does not mind that the path to his goal is over the dead bodies of horses. In that case, the combination of confidence, cruelty, and torturous devices simply yields greater sporting results.

One also can understand somehow the motivation of people who dream seriously about the Olympics and inexorably, successively and passionately torture and mutilate horses for the sake of qualifying.

Their use of torturous special equipment shows that they have gone completely mad. Psychosis reigns triumphant and an insatiable craving governs all their actions.

What they crave, in this case, is possession of ribbons, trophies, certificates and medals of various sizes, with inscriptions designating the rider's ranking in competitions.

There is no other intellectual explanation for their actions and there cannot be.

By the way, the yearning for "self-glorification" also plays a role.

Equestrianism, you see, is a such convenient thing!

One can be sickly, short of breath, fat, an alcoholic, and still be counted as a successful sportsman, pose for the television cameras, and have a career in horse sports.

Of course, the sportsman must pay for the cups, medals and ribbons... with the lives of horses and the horse's pain. Here again, equestrianism is such a convenient thing! After all, it is so very convenient to pay with someone else's life.

And the sportsmen pay diligently. This high price still has not embarrassed a single one of them, although they, as a rule, know the consequences of their amusements.

A living horse is turned into a piece of sporting apparatus, a means to obtaining medals or cups.

*Equestrian sport is possible only with full deafness
to the feelings of the horse. The more deafness, the more
insensitivity — the better the results.
All the chronicles of equestrian sport are written with the
blood of horses.*

However, it is not only the people who dream of getting into the Olympics who use all the torturous instruments for the painful correction of a horse's behavior or movement.

The motivation of this other category of torturers is, for me, an absolute mystery.

99 % of "horsemen" know that no Olympic moment awaits them, but that, instead, they will be getting together all their lives in a rented stable or traveling to wretched local tournaments. But, Lord! with what an air of importance they hook the side reins and standing martingales onto their horses, and with what laughable earnestness they select the iron!

How much droll yet horrible swagger there is in their drills and discussions... Most of all they love to blurt out something in the horse's name.

It is very funny to listen to the lady renters (of any sex): having played the sport, having bashed the horse on its sore spine with their fat bottoms and dragged it with all their might by the mouth with the iron, and finally having dismounted — they, for some reason, resort to baby talk, absolutely convinced of the horse's love for them.

They behave brutally on occasion almost as much as and as thoroughly as those who have gotten cranky about ribbons, but, as a rule, less systematically and less regularly, and they are not as qualified in cruelty itself.

But still, it is the horse that pays for their idiotic, contrived amusements; the horse pays with disability and with pain, and they persistently do not wish to recognize it, devising for themselves thousands of tales and excuses.

Let's speak first about what they all, both the first and the second variety, do not wish to know and realize. Only a very experienced master can feel a horse's pain, the more so in that the horse has a line between pain and fatigue that is very thin, almost indiscernible.

The horse, to its misfortune, has been created in such a way that it will conceal any pain, except the most intolerable, until the end, not demonstrating it in any way and striving to show almost no external change in her behavior.

Only a heightened hot temper will betray her.

To conceal a malaise is one of its most profound primitive instincts, which has not disappeared completely in the millennia of so-called "taming."

In the wild, the horse that demonstrates pain, an absence of energy or an infirmity thereby just submits itself to being eaten.

Or to move down the hierarchal ladder in the herd.

In nature this kind of behavior is perhaps justified.

But in relationships with a dumb, in principle generally deaf man, who has clambered up onto her back intoxicated with his "right of the primate," the consequences of such behavior are for the horse extreme and extremely tragic.

Man does not understand those simple signals a horse gives while trying to tell him that she is sick or in pain; he interprets these signals as disobedience, and so the beatings and use of special equipment begins.

Competition horses that refuse to jump (and they refuse it only because of the pain that the jumping inflicts), are forced to jump with a shot into the croup from a pneumatic pistol.

It is done like this: a trainer takes a position at the obstacle and, having felt that the horse is ready to refuse to jump, shoots it in the croup.

Burning with pain, the horse jumps across, since the sharp, sudden pain in the croup proves to be stronger than the nagging, aching pain in the back and legs. At the end of the training, the sportsman and trainer use a pin to pull out the little lead projectiles that have penetrated the horse's skin, they disinfect the wounds and then repeat the "procedure" the following day.

The main issue is not even in the wounds in the croup, but rather, those injuries invisible to the "sportman's" eye that have been aggravated by the jumping and which prevented the horse from jumping willingly to begin with.

A shot into the croup is not the only way, there are methods even more cruel.

And, at that, a shot in the croup belongs to the array of ordinary methods.

Any use of electricity, too.

By the way, what do you thinkis the reason that the standard frontal width of the obstacles in show jumping approved by the international rules greater than three meters and more often, all of four meters?

Why not make the obstacles about 80 centimeters wide while maintaining that same 130–160 centimeter height? Such small, economic and very effective ones instead of the present bulky, deformed, multipart and huge ones?

Well, the point is that the approved width is by no means accidental.

An 80-centimeter frontal width, or even a meter, gives the horse the freedom of choice.

Equestrian sport is fun, a game of humans who are free of the gift of feeling the horse's pain, the horse's soul. These humans are convinced with all humanlike primateness that a creature who is beneath them must entertain them simply because it exists to do so.

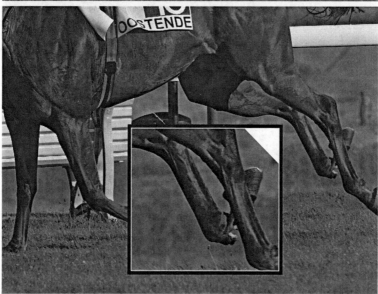

The tearing of the hind limb (in this particular case), in the jockeys'
slang, "crushing out." This can (and must) happen because of the enormous overloading of the horse's organism due to the speed and pan-
ic, and also as the result of a tiny stumble. In the photos on this page
we can see the tearing out, the partial separation of the distal epiphy-
sis, the partial destruction of the joint. The common digital extensor

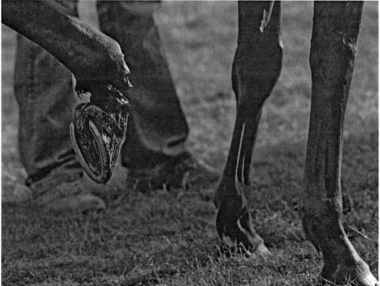

tendon is already torn, the skin and the third metatarsal bone are torn as well. The lateral collateral ligament is at the stage of tearing. The bone of the first phalanx is crushed. In the top photo we can see one of the phases of the gallop with the digging of the crushed first phalanx bone into the ground, and after that the phase of the full tearing of the collateral tendon begins.

Normal racecourse speeds are fatal for a horse. Every horse has myo-logical and physiological self-regulation laws, which always reduce the speed or even stop the horse. Even a typical racecourse speed is destruc-tive to a horse's limbs, and also leads to exercise-induced pulmonary hemorrhage (EIPH, or "bleeding") and obstruction of breathing. But

jockeys need the speed to be even faster than the normative one. Only this speed wins races. The beatings that a horse gets from the jockey can only partially switch off these security systems, covering their "protest" with hurt because of the painful burning beating and with horror during the anticipation of the next beating.

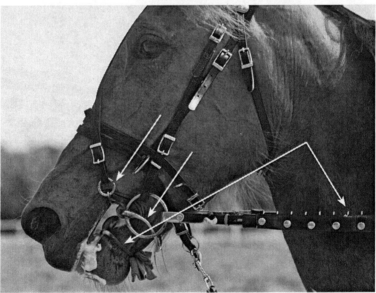

All these devices, ugly in their painful and injuring effects, are used by humans with only one definite aim — to not leave the horse a chance of successful rebellion. Check bits, bradoons, a score of different types of vicious iron, toe weights, spiked shafts, ear plugs, bound tongues and tails, turpentine and chili pepper rubbed under the dock...

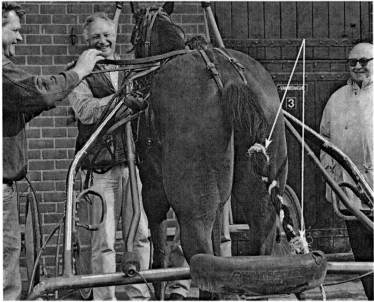

This list could be continued for pages, because the trotters are the ones to whom the demands of the humans are of the most unnatural kind. This means, that the trotters are the most difficult to subdue. So the "inventors" devised the biggest armory to... "improve the breed."

Today there are about 400 extensively used hippodromes in the world. These arenas dispose of hundreds of thousands of horses during each racing season. And for the next season the racing industry needs hundreds of thousands of new young horses instead of the ones who are still alive but can't run any more to earn its keep. The industry needs new victims to replace the ones who died on the track.

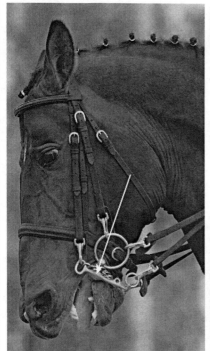

In accordance with all requirements and qualifying standards of any type of dressage, the horse is forced into false collection (with a violently flexed poll and engaged hindquarters) by means of special devices, lever force and other forms of pain. The first consequence of false collection is the full or partial crushing of parotid salivary gland.

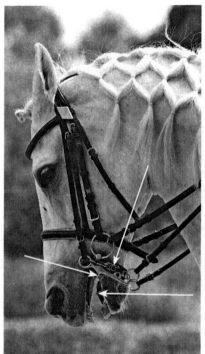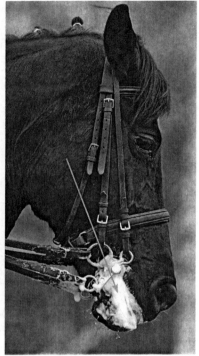

The chemical composition of saliva changes as the parotid glands — the largest of the salivary glands — are crushed and necrotized as a result of forced collection. The mandibular gland which, relatively speaking, does not suffer as severely, emits a seromucous secretion and its excess upsets the balance of chemicals in the saliva composition. Saliva tests of sport horses reveal cardinal differences between the saliva of a sport horse and that of normal saliva! Acute stresses from pain and the effect of the bit, which is unavoidable in the life of every sport horse, leads to ulcers. Gastritis, colitis, and ulcers lead to colic, which causes death.

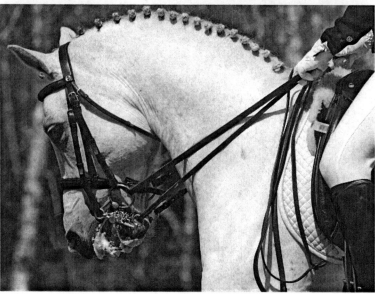

Due to forced collection, injury of the atlantooccipital membrane is unavoidable. As soon as the membranes are torn (and this is the inevitable sequel to collection) the defense mechanism that protects the spinal cord is lost.

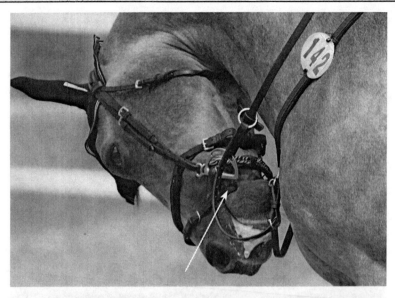

Diastema is the place which the bit effects. Here the most sensitive part of the trigeminal nerve is located. There is no submucosal layer on the diastema and the bit affects the nerve directly. The nerve is supersensitive. The bit beats and presses right on this place causing a horse "acute, burning, paralyzing" pain.

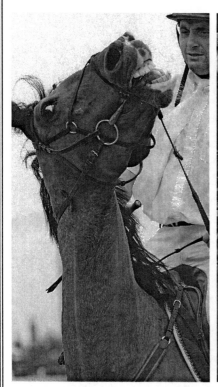

There is a great illusion that in sports, pleasure, or work, whether harnessed or ridden, the horse is controlled by the human. This is incorrect. The horse is controlled by PAIN. There are special basic methods that with «correct» application guarantee success in the business of equine sport (ES). Method N.1. For verbal clarification of the actions that are presented in convincing photographic evidence in this article, representing the primary techniques that enable the obedience of a horse in ES ; these are considered to be common practice by all criteria and are most appropriately called "NEUROCRANIALIS SHOCK" (shock of nerve system of skull). In the use of method N.1, we see a very rigid rein grab with one hand and a very strong pull by the other hand, which is so powerful that half of the bit rushes through the horse's mouth, and the rider's elbow goes back as far as it is possible. This sharp elbow movement increases the leverage force of the bit accordingly, and results in an especially severe and painful blow to the left or right part of horse's skull.

Method N. 2 represents an even sharper direct blow by the bit, over all the sensitive areas of horse's mouth. As a rule, every horse who has been forced this way, tries to weaken the effect of the blow by tossing its head up.

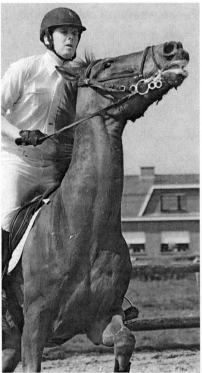

The purpose of both methods considered above, that are the basic methods of ES , is to "inflame" the entire innervational system of skull (namely, all the sensitive and "mixed" nerves from 12 pairs of facial nerves) by a sharp painful impact.

She will make the decision to jump or not to jump. She can easily "miss" an obstacle of such a small width, that is skirt it, run round it.

But you will not "miss" four meters. Four meters along the front thoroughly bars the way, the horse can go nowhere, and therefore she jumps, the more so because she knows very well how severely it will be beaten if it refuses.

The point is that the horse in show jumping is not supposed to have any freedom of choice. As is the case, by the way, in all similar types of equestrianism.

Nearly 100 % of sporting horses are invalids, that live and move in a haze of searing pain in the mouth, the back, the neck, the legs and the poll.

(The mad prancing of a sport horse, which has been let out to stroll in a paddock or in a field, is not an indicator of the absence of disability and pain, it is merely adrenal happiness which has manifested in wild movements in the moments of freedom and the absence of man's direct will, which in the horse is associated only with pain.)

* * *

Now I will endeavor to describe the mechanism of the physiological and psychological destruction of the horse by sports.

I will skip the horrific (in 99 % of the cases) ritual of so-called "breaking."

It is understood that it can cause nothing, except an aversion to man, and is equal to the procedure of branding, through which any horse goes that has been born on a stud farm.

It is when they cut the foal off from the herd, drive it into a "chute" and either with a red-hot iron or with an iron cooled in liquid nitrogen burn its back or haunch, or shoulder, in order to mark the horse for all its life with special letters, digits or figures that seem very important to man.

You can easily imagine the foal's feelings.

The cause of the pain, the destroyer of the world, is man.

It is, so to say the first nodding, acquaintance of the modern horse and with the modern Yahoo.

Don't forget that at branding, which almost always is accompanied by wild blows, roughness and the strongest painful shock, and during breaking, which at the farms, because of continuity and an "assembly line," is even more crude than branding, man becomes for the foal the main participant and instigator of the nightmare.

Breaking is the first, terrible blows with the iron along the gums, teeth and lips. Breaking is the first pain in the back.

And, this first pain is only a kind of "announcement" of sensations that are guaranteed to a sport horse throughout her whole terrible life.

Afterwards, the horse gets into sports, amateur or not very, and is subjected by now to long, systematic influences of the iron which begins to mutilate the mouth, and to the impact of the rider's weight, which begins to mutilate her back.

The "natural suitability" of a horse's back for a rider's weight is an absolute myth.

The horse has been calculated and "designed" by nature without any "growths" weighing from 60 to 120 kilograms there on her back.

And here the "growth" is shaking and bouncing.

Blows from the rider's bumping around necessitate a hard saddle tree, the basis of any saddle which partially suppresses and partially transmits these blows to the back, spine and muscles.

Even in the case when the saddle suits the horse, it suppresses at most only 50% of the concussion and stresses.

If the saddle is unsuitable, then fully 100 % of the blows and stresses that occur, even when a rider has an ideal seat, pass into the back and spine.

Only that saddle can be considered appropriate which was custom made for a specific horse, through not fewer than six measurements of the back taking into consideration individual natural asymmetry (inherent in all horses) and taking into consideration also the unique particulars of her movements.

All horses have backs which are as unique as the impressions of human fingers.

It has not been established by science that a saddle that has been sewn for one particular horse, or sewn for a certain abstract horse, ideally or even tolerably suits another horse.

The so-called saddle sizes (17, 18) have no relationship at all to a horse, they are only a statement of the degree of massiveness of a rider's bottom.

If the saddle is unsuitable for a specific horse (as in 99 % of the cases), the blows are not dispersed by the saddle panels and it does not mute them, as is thought, but instead, concentrates the impact at several points.

A poorly fitting saddle, or one that is poorly placed, is distinguished from one that fits and sits well by the fact that it does not fully mirror the shape of the horse's back and, consequently, puts too much pressure in some spots and does not make contact in others.

The blows to the horse's back are concentrated at the points of greater pressure, which quickly become centers of constant intense pain.

Thus, there appears in the arsenal of special equipment one more instrument of torture — the saddle.

True, this is the case even though the pain occurs despite, not because of the will of the rider.

The rider, being by nature blind to the feelings of the horse, does not sense these problems, and, worst of all, doesn't even conceive of them.

The horse's irritation, which has been caused by the pain in the back, is assessed as disobedience or a demonstration of his "rebellious" nature, and the beatings begin for the purpose of pacification, or the tortuous special equipment is used.

The matter, it is understood, is not only in the saddle, although that is certainly part of the problem too.

Even a correctly chosen saddle will not rescue a sport horse from torment and rapid disability.

The training methods themselves and the preparation of a horse for sports are organized and undertaken without consideration of the horse's feelings and sensations.

These methods have been decreed, as you remember, by the sportsmen themselves, that is, by the same people who in their make-up can not "hear" the horse.

They are not sadists, not beasts; they simply don't get it.

The man who is keenly conscious of the horse, who hears both her joy and her pain, will never be involved with equestrianism. He simply will not be able to physically tolerate it. The torments of the horse, and the very fabric of equestrianism has been woven of them, will be too unbearable a torture for him, inasmuch as he hears the horse distinctly and comprehends her feelings.

Equestrianism is feasible only with a determined deafness to the horse's feelings and sensations, and the greater this insensibility, the greater the deafness, then the greater the sporting results.

All the chronicles of equestrianism have been written in equine blood, you see.

I understand the gravity of my words extremely well.

In which connection, these are not accusations. They are a statement, nothing more.

Naturally, evidence is needed.

As you like.

There is a magical thing known as computer thermography, which allows the diagnosis of the presence of any problems of a horse's spine, neck, croup and legs with one hundred percent precision.

The secret of computer thermography is very simple, it captures any inflammation and pain with breathtaking precision and absolute clarity.

The thermal recorder, while building a thermal picture of any part of the horse's body, "sees" and shows the places of inflammation, injury, tension, and spasm beneath a horse's skin — damage that is invisible to the eye.

My wife, a professional hippologist and thermographist, a scientist, and a member of the American Academy of Thermography, examines several dozen sport horses every month.

Of the three hundred horses examined in the last year alone, only one turned out to be healthy, in the relative sense of this word.

The horses examined demonstrated problems, most of all, of a behavioral nature, and the most severe injuries of the spine, which the owners or sportsmen did not even suspect, were revealed with thermographic diagnosis.

One must understand that only very expensive prospective sport horses are examined, inasmuch as the procedure is not cheap.

Regarding what happens with the backs of the horses of non-wealthy amateurs, who torture horses with no less passion than the sportsmen, one can only guess, although, judging by the statistics, there are no healthy ones among them.

Here are the very graphic pictures, the computer thermograms (see table 4).

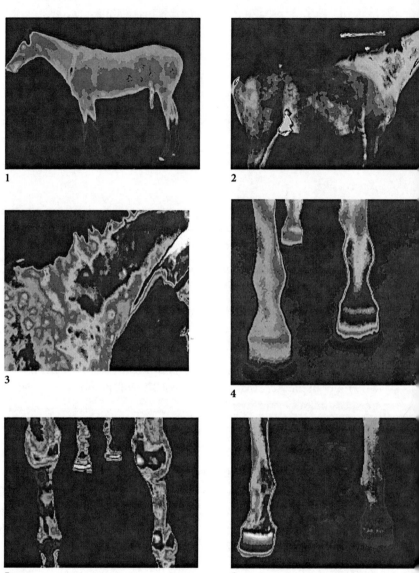

1

2

3

4

5

6

Table 4

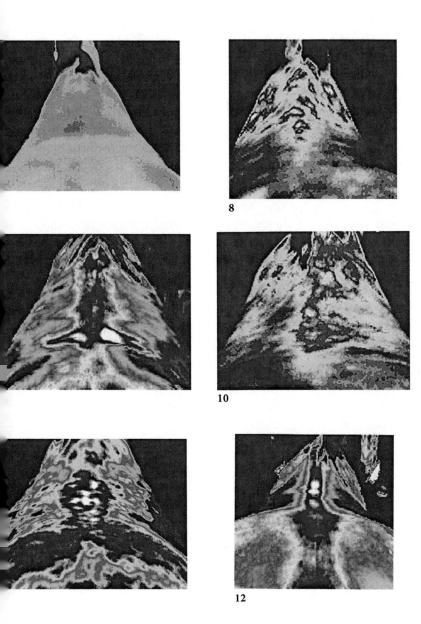

8

10

12

The Horse Crucified and Risen

The thermographic image of a healthy horse, with a perfectly even temperature of the skin on the neck, back and croup, and with legs even cooler than all the rest of the body which is normal, opens the gallery. The exception is the small point of increasing temperature in the region of groin, which is normal (see table 4, 1).

Thermogram 7 of this table is an image of an ideally healthy back. There are no painful spots, no areas of inflammation. In this case it is the back of a five-year-old Nevzorov Haute École stallion, who is worked correctly three times a week, mounted for not more than 15 minutes a day.

And this is the thermogram of the back of a sporting horse which is mounted by a sporting master in dressage (8). The numerous injuries to the muscles of the back, the keenly painful inflammation of the trapezius muscle and supraspinous ligament are well and very graphically seen. The muscle spasms and interruption of the blood supply are obvious.

Another back of a sporting horse (dressage, again) (10).

There already is total disability here. Multiple injuries of the soft tissues and spine. Injuries to the spinous processes of vertebrae, kissing spine, which have occurred as a result of an excessive load on the spine from forced collection.

Both these horses are considered absolutely healthy at their stable, have been taken to competitions and performed in them.

The changing behavior of the horses has put the owner on her guard, they have been turning more and more excitable, "stern" and nervous with each passing day. The owners have not examined the backs of these horses, they have looked at their legs, which also, by the by, are totally stricken. The other images of backs show the typical "wrecked" backs of sporting horses that experience pain from any movement, which is absolutely hidden from their riders.

Fig. 11 shows typical "jumping" injuries: inflammation of the back, loins, lumbosacral joints (abarticulation), and also displacement of the sacroiliac ligaments, which have been confirmed by veterinarians. The pain in the lumbosacral junction (roughly speaking, a joint between the loins and croup) must be hellish. (The following day after making the thermograph, the sportsman owner performed on this horse in some kind of minor competition. He considered the injuries as irrelevant. He jumped. The horse balked, so he was beaten.)

Thermogram 8 shows the inflamed back muscles of a dressage horse with injuries of the trapezius muscle, injuries caused by the use of a very narrow saddle, which was placed, as it is accepted in dressage, on the withers. It is very difficult for the horse to move around with such injuries, but, nevertheless, they saddle it with the very same saddle every day and the horse works under it for two hours.

Here for comparison (thermogram 4) are a horse's healthy leg and an afflicted one, with a severe inflammatory injury of the coffin joint as pictured by the thermograph.

The healthy leg is evenly blue, there is no inflammation.

The afflicted one has the characteristic crimson-orange color of an intense chronic inflammation.

In thermogram 5 are the broken joints of the left leg of a young sport horse. (This horse, by the way, continues to be trained and to perform.)

In the other images, the legs are affected to a certain extent, in particular by navicular disease which is practically the most severe incurable disease of 70 % of sport horses. The horse experiences intolerable pain, and at the same time the disease is never detected by sportsmen, since it often happens bilaterally and the horse limps on both front legs.

In thermogram 3 is the neck of a dressage horse with the cervical part of the spine affected; there is extensive chronic internal inflammation, injury of ligaments and pinched nerves.

The neck is typical for 100% of competition dressage horses; it gets that way from forced collection.

This horse is continuing to perform and train.

These are the legs of a jumping horse (6): periostitis, an inflammation of the periosteum as a result of being struck with an iron shaft, is well evident. (The shaft is used so that the horse pulls up her legs higher and does not knock down the colored pole; they beat the horse from below.)

Thermogram 2 shows injury to the muscles and the spine of a troika horse.

It is possible to take any sport horse, a completely healthy one in the opinion of its trainer and riding master,[b] and see the inflammation in the caudal part[c] of the spine as a result of violently forced collection, as well as inflammation of the shoulder muscles, "thermal amputation due to vasoconstriction" (as a consequence of pinched nerves of the cervical part[d])... and so forth, ad infinitum...

And, of course, in each horse, without exception, is deep, chronic inflammation of the periostitis of the gums and the whole surface of the oral cavity from iron.

I haven't exaggerated in the least, when I say that 100 % of the horses in sports are absolute invalids, forced to move with elevated paces, or to jump, while in excruciating pain.

The pain of deliberately applied force, in order to be effective and compel the horse to fulfill the rider's instructions, must considerably exceed background, chronic pain from numerous injuries.

Man, by the way, doesn't set such goals for himself straightforwardly.

As a rule, he simply doesn't think about that.

Simply, all means of coercion, both iron and accessories, are designed so that the usual pain in the back, neck and legs from blows to the trigeminus nerve or to the gums are forgotten.

There is one more secret. The horse never gets accustomed to the action of the iron. What does such an acquired tolerance mean, anyhow?

Acquired tolerance is an adaptation of living tissues to an action on them. That is, to that which in Russian is called by the word "mozoli" — calluses.

But calluses aren't formed on the mucous membrane, this is a law of physiology.

And the mouth is completely mucous.

None of the three hundred horses diagnosed would even attempt to jump across 1.3-meter high painted poles or carry a rider of their own accord; generally they wouldn't even budge from the spot.

But all these horses, the thermograms of which are cited in the book, and now, probably, wheezing, lug the ladies in hats (the horse nuts) or the men in velvet riding helmets.

Whips thrash the horses' croups, all their muscles are infused with fierce pain, and the iron beats at their inflamed gums. (Meanwhile, the "horsewomen", are more worried about how, at a critical glance from the side, their bottoms lie in their saddles, and whether their breeches are wrinkling.)

But barely 1 % of those involved in equestrianism are genuine sadists.

All others either do not know what they are doing or are afraid to think about it.

For, having thought about it, one has to change.

So what compels all these people, the so-called "horsemen," to torture, beat, and torment horses with iron pieces in the mouth? Just what motivates them?

Besides a passion for collecting pieces of cardboard with ribbons and different sizes of medals?

A staggering answer suggests itself — love for the horse and bearing a grudge against the horse.

As a rule, the greater the love, the deeper too the grudge, which develops into a pathology.

At first, they all really love horses.

It is a special love.

Invincible, dictated by a special personality pattern, when the heart stops from one look at a horse, at hearing his snort and smelling his smell.

When there is a mad, awful desire contrary to everything to be together with it, on it, to feel it, and to smell, see and hear it. When the word "horse" and "happiness" become absolute synonyms.

I'm not joking.

In reality, all these people who are almost totally preoccupied by horses, love horses painfully, passionately and to the point of stupor.

Riding is the realization of this love (even without special Freudianism), a normal act of unity, which the beloved always attains.

But their problem is that their love is unrequited.

And they all know and feel it in the depths of their soul.

At first they comfort themselves with stories and tales about how their horses rejoice at their appearance. They deceive themselves into thinking that a certain kind of relationship exists between them and the horse.

Of course, they never bring themselves to test this relationship, but for a while they console themselves, mistaking begging for a relationship, and then, naturally, that is the only thing they know how to train a horse to do.

But the oafish, dilettantish delights pass quickly. Baby talk in the stall is one thing, and the reality of the manége or field is a completely different affair.

At the same time, almost everything the "horsemen" do damages any possibility of a good relationship with the horse. They shove an instrument for the infliction of pain into its mouth, they beat the horse when he does not obey because she is ill or in pain, or their attempts to explain to the horse what it is they want from her are awkward, clumsy, unclear.

Gradually, the horse, refusing to perform for these idiotic and destructive demands, turns into an enemy.

And it begins to evoke the usual hatred and desire to squeeze out of her the desired result, large or small, at any cost.

100 % of sporting horses refuse to voluntarily perform for the riders' demands; if it were otherwise the horse's iron would be abolished for lack of need.

These people are somewhat ashamed and depressed in the depths of their souls.

They understand that they are doing some kind of very foul thing.

And that this thing has nothing in common with that sincere love which at one time attracted them to the horse.

And then for themselves and others like them they devise comforting terminology like, for example, that the horse is supposed to "chew the bit" well — I mean with satisfaction — that very implement of torture which they have forced into her mouth and which they have firmly affixed with straps.

By the way, as regards "chewing." Do you suppose the horse, when she is wandering about a meadow, hunts for timothy, alfalfa or bluegrass, or other grass? It's possible.

But according the logic of the sportsmen, she hunts for iron, and having found it, begins to chew it and masticate it greedily, flooding her mouth with saliva.

Why doesn't someone speak the truth? Why doesn't anyone "tell it like it is?"

Namely, that the horse does not "chew" the iron, but is trying to free herself from it...

By any means whatsoever. And that all the horse's movements with the lips and the tongue are, figuratively speaking, like the movements of the Count of Monte Cristo with his home-made blade, trying to break through the endless passage to freedom from the dungeon of Château d'If.

But... the "horsemen" do not wish to understand this. It is an unpleasant problem.

Okay, they don't believe me, let them open some books.

There are dozens of them.

For example, "Equine Dentistry." This is a handbook of articles of the most famous professors of modern times in this area, from G. J. Baker to Derek S. Knottenbelt...

Here wherever you turn... "Scission of the lips may be linked to injuries from bits," "Injuries occur on the bars, where the bit lays."

Ulcerations rostrally to the premolars and sometimes injuries which are found beneath the mucous membrane of a sequestra originate often as a result of injuries from iron. More serious injuries, fractures of the upper and lower jaw, also occur from the use of iron.

Serious cuts, scissions and even cleaving of the tongue are not exceptions and occur for the same reason.

Right there in black and white are details of injuries to the tongue and palate, and of splitting of teeth.

About the fact that the famous foamy saliva of dressage horses, which is considered normal, is a severe disease of the oral cavity, which is caused by iron, also called ptyalism.

Fractures and microfractures of the lower jaw also have been written about — about pieces of periosteum, which are broken off from the lower jaw, which decay in the gum — as an everyday occurrence...

Even in "Bits and Bitting," Elwin Hartley Edwards' handbook of sporting bit, which every sportsman is obligated to know (if, of course, he knows how to read) almost everything is explained.

It is explained that the bars are so damaged from the iron's action, that remnants of food collect in the gum cavities and promote infection.

And it is explained that the action of the iron not only damages the periosteum, but also smites to smithereens the bone surface which is covered with mucous.

And finally, it even is explained that all a horse's tongue actions are an attempt to protect itself from the iron.

Any authoritative and specialized periodical like "The Horse" (USA) persistently publishes articles of the "Pain in the Mouth" type.

There is objective veterinary evidence in these materials: "Injuries occur, such as scission, edema and hemorrhage (a bruising wound) of the horse's tongue, diastem and upper palate."

"Past traumas to the horse's mouth force the horse always to resist the bit.

If the mouth is damaged, it is damaged forever."

"Mandibular periostitis develops in horses from the action of the bit when the diastem bone is inflamed by the injuries and it hurts very much. Mandibular periostitis requires surgical intervention."

The famous veterinary surgeon, Robert Cook, a professor at the American University of Veterinary Medicine, has been publishing numerous works for a long time, in which he scrupulously and academically shows the origin of diseases of, for example, the horse's respiratory and digestive systems from the usage of iron.

The Nevzorov Haute École Hippological Scientific Research Center has performed a number of scientifically conclusive experiments which demonstrate visually that a child's simple pull of a rein connected to a snaffle bit puts a 300 kilogram load on a horse's mouth! Think about that number! The research was performed by serious specialists, professors of medicine and United Nations academicians. See the Appendix 1.

All these conclusions of the professors of veterinary medicine about the injurious role of iron is not news.

One may open the 1851 "Handbook of the Horse" and discover in it all the same information, only it is told in the style of the 19th century, in other words: "The mouth piece's curb bit's pressure on the jaw, which is pulled by the mouth piece curb bit's chain, causes not only wounds in the gums, but also even caries themselves in the toothed area of the jaw, with decay and bone fragments emerging from the wound…"

"The injuries that occur on the tongue are: wounds on it which occur from bits. It happens as a result of similar wounds in horses and that almost the whole half of the tongue crumbles or after an incorrect adhesion it obtains a warped shape and impedes the horse in chewing…"

As early as 1823, in the well-known "Weekly for Hunters of Horses" was published a work of the greatest veterinarian of that time, the German G. Rolves, "Experimental Treatment."

And everything already had been said there, too: "When a bit lies on a horse's tongue, it causes wounds which appear in the middle of the tongue or along it's edges. There even are examples where half the tongue has been broken away by the bits."

"Even the jaws themselves are damaged by bits, which cause conspicuous wounds on them. Sometimes the damage is so severe, that the bone itself is broken, in which case the wound itself must be examined diligently and, when bone fragments are found in it, they must be carefully removed..."

And what is there in the "Handbook of the Horse," by Rolves, or the newest research? Nothing new — only the fact that the need to stitch together horses' tongues which had been torn by iron was described as early as Pelagonius, a 4th century Roman veterinarian.

Everything was known ages ago and had been explained.

It is impossible to chalk up the ignorance of the tragic role of equine iron to some kind of backwardness; there is simply too much of this scholarly information, verified and supported by all the world's veterinarians.

And it is so distressing to know that 99% of the "horsemen," even if they accidentally find out about it, will keep pretending that they don't know.

They fully realize that they know how to cope with the horse only by causing the horse great and constant pain.

They are unfamiliar with other methods.

The acknowledgement of an obvious thing, the unconditionally traumatic and torturous role of snaffle, curb and Pelham bits, instantly transfers them from the noble role of "lovers of horses" to the ranks of either sadists or idiots.

They are sadists, if they know and understand everything about the role of iron, but continue their amusements; idiots, if they do not know such obvious, most important and top priority things and do not understand, as a matter of fact, what they do.

The "equestrian public" is not ready for either role.

Extensive knowledge of the role of iron by those who are accustomed to using some kind of baby talk about "love for the horse," places them in an extremely awkward position and somewhat overshadows the satisfaction from the amusement they have come to love.

The most comfortable and simplest thing in this situation is to make believe that everything is fine and that there is no fundamental problem with the iron.

In addition, there is a very influential "livery stable stratum," all the people who frequent public barns — trainers, horse-owners, stable hands — people who are united by a dearth of "equestrian talent" and their complete inability to hear the horse or establish a relationship with her. People who hypnotize each other with fantasies that any other way, besides the painful, does not exist, or that the horse, for example, "loves to jump."

It is as it was charmingly stated in the old cookbooks: "The carp crucian loves to be roasted in sour cream."

And, again, why not tell the truth, why not say that jumping across painted poles is impossible without painful compulsion and that show jumping itself is a form of horse torture.

Or these very people deceive themselves and each other with the comforting story that they only use "Soft bit!"

"Soft bit" does not exist in nature. Except perhaps mercury, from which you won't make a snaffle or curb bit anyway. Iron is iron.

(It is thought that the thicker the mouthpiece of the bit, the "softer" it is. This is nonsense. In reality, with thick, plump mouthpieces the painful action on the lips is weaker, but it is stronger on the tongue, that is, on the lingual and sublingual nerves, since with the greater thickness comes greater volume, so that the iron occupies more space in the mouth and painful pressure is put on a greater area of the tongue and palate.

Of course it is understood that all deep wounds and injuries of the mouth described by ancient and modern veterinarians do not occur every second with every horse.

True, they are possible at any moment and to one degree or another are unavoidable for every horse which has had dental or trigeminial action iron pieces shoved into her mouth.

One simply has to understand that the logical development of that painful exposure, which the horse experiences every second, results in serious wounds and injuries.

The so-called "gentle touch" or "soft hands" is merely the knowledge of how to inflict a paralyzingly strong pain in the horse's mouth, without inflicting particularly deep wounds or inflicting them only rarely.

No more than that. But, that does not stop horse "enthusiasts" — even the rankest amateurs on the outer fringes of the equestrian world — from deceiving themselves and others with nonsense about "soft bit" and discussions of the "gentle touch" and "soft hands."

Time passes, representatives of the "livery stable" stratum wear the ridiculous helmets and trousers in good faith, mutter about "chewing," "jumping" or "collection." They worship those who with candid sadism have constructed for themselves a road to the Olympics, they beat and torture the horse in imitation of their idols, and they all wait for the time when the horse will reciprocate their "love."

Later they begin to be convinced that the relationship they dreamed of does not exist, that the horse either hates them or is afraid, or simply totally alienated.

Having done everything to turn the horse into an enemy, they are offended by the fact that the horse does not wish their company and always frees itself from man whenever a convenient opportunity arises.

They are offended, as old scoundrels are offended when their kept women do not give shags or give them without passion.

They are offended, but they continue to love!

They just want unity!

At any cost. By any means. (We already know what the means are).

* * *

In a dimly lit, huge sporting mánege are three or four steaming horses, beneath riders.

Dead eyes. Foam on the "bit," neck and breast.

There are people on them with whips. They are driven by... love.

How strange to be without any desire to hear the one you love.

It somehow reminds those who know films of the horror movies which show the scum of a villain raping the beaten, half-dead, dazed victim he has dragged into a spider-filled closet, bound tightly and whom he... "loves."

* * *

Just like equestrianism.

If one were to study the people involved with flat racing, steeplechasing, or harness racing thoroughly, everything there would be almost the same.

The same deafness of the people and the same torments to the horse. The same beatings.

By the way, there are, in principle, more beatings at the races since the jockey has a right to beat a horse publicly, as much as he wants. There are no limitations on the number of blows.

Incidentally, in sports, they beat the horse before the competitions in order to "liven it up," they beat it during the competitions, and they beat it in the stalls, at training sessions, during loading into the horse trailer and during grooming. 100% of sportsmen practice horse beating. The Nevzorov Haute École Hippological Scientific Research Center has performed a scientifically conclusive experiments which demonstrate the effects of permissible beatings of horses in equestrian sport. The results can be seen in the Appendix 1.

True, they replace the word "beat," as a rule, with the comfortable word "discipline."

Races for the horse are somewhat scarier than show jumping or dressage and yet, also, somewhat easier.

Easier, for the horse's fate is sealed more quickly and the sorrows are not spread out for years. Two to three racing seasons and 97 % of the horses are complete, absolute invalids.

This is in the best and most favorable case.

If a horse is very lucky, there is a quick death on the race track.

Racing (of all kinds) is, per se, an occupation intimately connected with the making of the well-known Tatar sausage.

However, since I stipulated in the introduction to this book that I would like to remain in company with normal people, who either understand or honestly want to understand the secret of a relationship between horse and man, I will not allow myself to discuss in this book the technology of trotting, flat races or the details of making sausage from horses. These are equal abominations, and all of them are too disgusting to delve into.

* * *

Russian troikas merit a separate conversation; they are a most impressive and primitive symbol of torture, the uncivilized invention of drunken coachmen, born of a cruel competitive struggle for a passenger, who had to be soundly impressed.

It is no longer possible to determine who first came up with the degenerate idea of making it standard procedure to fold the necks of the off-wheelers sideways — a procedure with dire consequences including fractures of the cervical spine.

The long and short of it is, it is impossible to think of a more unhealthy and subtle torment for the horse. Neither knowledge, talent nor great intelligence are required to invent troika, so it was fully within the means and mind of the illiterate alcoholics who roamed the old high roads of the "Russian Empire" or, as they would say it, "Raissean Enpayre."

And again, the simplest and 100% accurate evidence of the damage troika does is: the thermogram (see table 4, **2**).

This is the neck of a very young off-wheeler. Here there are no longer "merely" injuries and ruptures of the muscle tissue, there is cervical vertebral STENOSIS, or, to put it more simply, narrowing of the spinal cord in the neck section of the spine.

Because of the constant fixed abnormal position of the head, the vertebrae are being deformed, pinching the spinal cord.

Physiologists characterize the pain resulting from this as practically unendurable.

After the thermograph was made, the horse was once more harnessed to a sleigh by the self-satisfied fool of an owner and sent to take the public for rides.

She did not know how to scream.

She held this pain inside herself without shouting out, she was not even able to burst into tears. This horse was unable to ask for mercy or pity... She was very frightened.

She remembered the taste of the iron and the whip.

By the way, she knew that not long remained.

The crippling of horses in Russian troikas is the standard from the very first minute. There are no exceptions here.

* * *

A special story is the circus.

Oh! It really is a completely special story...

In brief: there is all that same special equipment that there is in sports, all that same stupidity and cruelty, but...

The circus is a different world, one that is secret and closed. It is a world in which even the air, it seems, has a fundamentally different chemical composition than everywhere else.

The circus is for the fool, for the lout, for the reporter who has been permitted to look a little into its behind-the-scenes womb, and it keeps in readiness the clown's blessed smile and a few old yarns about horses.

The circus knows everything about itself and knows how to defend itself against unnecessary eyes and ears.

The defense has developed over the centuries.

The fool will sit and look at what the insiders show him, and go away, assured that he saw the circus from within.

It is a delusion and a lie.

Only the insiders, those who make up the circus, see the circus from within.

Only they can see themselves and their kind as they really are. Only with those who, like themselves, are bound by the 13 meter ring in the "big top," can they cease feeling shy and secretive and stop lying.

In order to see the circus from within, in order to know the circus, one has to undergo a certain transformation.

One has to become part of the circus.

As long as this transformation has not occurred, nothing will be seen, noted and understood.

The transformation consists of the fact that a multitude of common human concepts must undergo a mysterious change.

First, good and evil trade places, then they are refined into a third something, which combines these two concepts in itself.

Tortures, human or animal, stop seeming to be tortures, and they begin to look somewhat fresh, healthy, and cheerful.

There are many surprising metamorphoses!..

And do you know how they get horses into the pesade?

Well, with their fingers crossed, they make a horse rear.

It is very simple.

They bring the horse.

They hook her up with a long rope to the iron in the mouth. To the right or left ring of the bit, it isn't important.

They extend the rope upwards, beneath the canopy, in the darkness, where they throw it across a pulley. That pulley, with which they safeguard the trapeze artists.

They draw the end of the rope, which already has been passed through the pulley, into the arena in front of the horse or behind it.

Three to four circus workers who are somewhat huskier, all in gloves in order to not burn their hands, grab the rope.

The trainer makes a smacking sound with his lips, cracks his lunging whip (kravasch)ᵉ and the trio in gloves yank the rope toward themselves, downwards, jerking the horse across the big top's pulley by the iron in the mouth until she has been lifted fully vertical.

From behind two more flog the horse on the back as a preventative measure in order that she not move backwards and not fall back.

The trainer thrashes her from the front so the horse doesn't even think of dropping down.

The horse's mouth in such an undertaking usually is torn until it bleeds.

The most powerful horse lips do not survive the jerks, and the blood-covered eyes pop out of their sockets.

A common trainer joke afterwards (while laughing): "Put her eyes back."

It is not addressed to anyone in particular, neither to the assistant nor to the one holding the horse.

Most likely it is to a god, to that helpless god of horses who, while seeing all, already awaits the soul of this circus horse.

And, I forgot: when it all ends, they shove a carrot sliced into rings into the torn mouth of the trembling, wet horse.

The carrot, covered in blood, falls out at once and tumbles around the arena.

Let this scene come to mind the next time you take your nephew to the circus!

Here, for example, they train the horses to poop without fail before going into the arena. Exclusively so that it doesn't happen in the arena, in front of the public, since the dung spoils the presentation.

How do they teach her?

It's simple, they beat her in the stall before making her appearance.

In the beating process, the horse, who understands nothing and knows exactly that she isn't guilty of anything, begins to be awfully nervous and excited, a consequence of which that she defecates.

Everything is very simple.

The "baboons" — which in the language of the circus is what they call those who in the programs for the public are designated "horsemen"(Dzhigit) — practice this method almost universally.

And here is one more classic characteristic of the circus.

I had an extremely funny instance, where it was necessary to prepare a horse for a photo shoot, in which he was supposed, while attacking me, to bare his teeth ferociously and lay back his ears, as any strongly incensed horse does.

I had taught him rather quickly to bare his teeth (rather, to grimace).

The attack, generally my favorite subject, is one of the main games that I immediately teach a horse so that he understands there are no problems with it.

But this stallion, that had been training with me and treated me in a very amicable manner, was fully certain that we were just playing (as it were), and did not want to lay back his ears for me at all.

But the ears were supposed to be absolutely laid back in the episode.

I called my friend, one of the most famous circus artists in the world. A venerable master.

I told him the situation. I asked his advice. I listened to his answer: "Pierce his ears, put a piece of clear fishing line through the holes, and have your assistant pull the line while standing behind. Then the ears will lay back…"

* * *

A stupid question occurs, "why?". Why doesn't anyone, except me and five or six other people, see all this? Don't they want to see it?

For it's all so strikingly obvious. And, unfortunately, completely unambiguous.

I would be terribly glad if someone would at least utter something distinct about the painful role of iron.

It would be a miracle if just one person were able to refute all the data of equine dentistry and trample the hundreds of scientific works which detail the enormous problems of horses from the usage of iron...

It would be even better if thermography, ultrasound, radiography and all the other diagnostic "tricks" would be declared a delusion and charlatanism.

Well okay, the circus is one thing with its secret semi-mystical processes in its darkened womb, where people and horses boil and intermingle amid clownish insincere laughter.

We don't see the genuine circus, it is deliberately hidden from public view and always sprinkles the pool of horse blood in the arena with glittering confetti, and even dances and juggles in this pool, so that the louts will not understand anything and not catch sight of the blood, but see only the sparkles and the clowning around.

But equestrianism in its common form happens right before everyone's eyes!

Imagine for a second that a group of people, decked out and all dolled up, has gathered publicly in company in order to publicly, openly and solemnly cut off the paws of a kitten or to poke out the eyes of a goat!

And they have gathered not simply to cut off a kitten's paws, but to compete in speed and purity of the cutting.

Or they would arrange a competition for the swift tearing off of a spaniel's ears... Certainly a difficult business, by the way! Just imagine again, the pulling. One can also declare this a type of sport.

It is understandable that normal people would gather and thrash these folks for a long time, and afterwards have them locked up.

But, in truth, we see the very same thing at any equestrian competition, the torture of strikingly noble and strikingly defenseless beings, called horses, done for the sake of amusement.

One need simply observe attentively: look not at whether the horse has jumped or not jumped the painted poles, look instead into the horse's eyes, look at her mouth.

In order to clearly see the torture behind the tinsel of the competition, one must simply switch attention from the activity... to the horse itself. It isn't difficult.

Equestrianism... Horses, generally, are not involved with sports.

But even by the most stupid and traditional human measures, equestrianism per se cannot be considered an actual sport.

Yes, sports are about records and victories, but in a real sport the records and victories are purchased at the price of one's own sweat and health, one's own blood, and by overcoming oneself.

And equestrianism (if one looks into it) is man's parasitism on the physical capabilities of another being, a being that absolutely is not willing to be involved with sports and that is forced into them with pain and beatings.

What the hell kind of sport is this?

Why do the chunky aunties in caps like those worn by old undertakers chatter so impertinently for the television camera? Why do federations of this "sport" exist openly... why are the competitions broadcast?

It's a travesty!

Of course it is understood that one cannot quickly eradicate the habit of torturing horses, but the torturers should know their place; if they dare to congregate at all it should be only in secret somewhere, behind rubbish heaps, and while shuddering at every policeman's whistle.

* * *

Now and then I am able to visit the sports stables.

Any of them.

Both the wretched and the very gussied-up ones.

It is always the same everywhere.

Previously I had walked quietly along the stable aisles, simply trying not to look into the eyes of the horses.

I had satisfied myself that the horses I, or people like me, train — horses which do not know beatings, iron, punishments, gadgets — horses with open minds that understand everything completely and correctly, are somehow special.

I had supposed that the horses trained by me (or people like me) make up an almost unique caste in the equine world, and the unfortunate horses in the sporting stables are completely different horses, whose minds are not open and that have been turned into idiots, into pieces of sporting equipment.

It is very convenient to think this, but it is absolute stupidity.

It is also the arrogance of the humanoid primate, who believes that hundreds of hours of association with him changes qualitatively god's creation which is striking in its perfection.

Every horse has an open mind and each one understands what is what in this world and what a horrifying catastrophe man — with his stupidity, cruelty, arrogance, and his sadistic devices — embodies for each of them individually and for all of them collectively, for the giant, worldwide herd.

And each horse, whether jumping, trotting, racing, hitched in a troika, each one of them knows precisely the extent of human stupidity, knows that for all these 3,000 years that horses and people have spent together, everything could have been different.

And they wouldn't have had to change for it.

In order to love and be friends, they would have had only to remain horses.

It is we who would have had to change; it is we who have to change.

By the way, the era of the Yahoo's unlimited exultation is ending.

The years will pass and mankind will remember with embarrassment his wretched, savage amusements like show jumping or eventing.

Man will remember equestrianism with the same embarrassment, as he now remembers the slave trade, cannibalism or the concentration camps.

He will forget, like a nightmare, the troikas and the horse races, all the human amusements where the horse's submission was based only on its pain or on the fear of pain and beatings.

The change is already beginning. Even now, it has become painful and disgusting to look at the primitive amusements of sportsmen and lovers of troikas or races — at least for those of us who know what equestrianism costs the horse, who know that, no matter what words have been spoken and no matter what excuses have been contrived, it is all achieved by torturing the horse.

What a genius was Jonathan Swift, who wrote of his Yahoo!

And now… the era of the Yahoo is ending.

While in earlier times evil and stupidity ruled completely, sealing the fate of each horse, today opposition is already occurring.

The conflict of good and evil already has begun.

The conflict of two completely opposite views of the horse and its relationship with man.

We are at the very beginning of this conflict, the outcome of which, thank goodness, has been predetermined.

It is only a question of time.

For no matter what the genius Jonathan Swift wrote, man and the Yahoo are nevertheless completely different creatures.

---

[a] Steeplechase — a race with obstacles.

[b] Riding Master — a person who thinks he is teaching a horse something.

[c] Caudal Part — from the Latin Cauda — the tail; the part closer to the tail.

[d] Cervical Part — from the Latin Cervix — the neck, the part closer to the neck.

[e] Lunging Whip (kravasch) — a long whip with a long lash on the end.

EDUCATION

Chapter Three

Morning.

An enormous training manège with a high vaulted ceiling.

The early morning sun assaults the Gothic arches of the walls and stained glass of the windows.

The chubby sparrows that inhabit the manège have settled down.

In front of me is a black, four-year-old stallion.

Slender, shaggy-maned, passionate, equally ready either to fall in love or develop hatred.

He is very fussy, very cantankerous, but not by nature or by make-up, but because of the delicate circumstances of his extremely young age.

He is teething and of course his whole mouth burns like fire.

A big lateral incisor grows from an inflamed gum, shoving out the baby tooth by its action.

There is a terrible temptation to help the incisor, to pull out the tooth with my fingers. I see that this stupendous stallion, if I don't mess up, if I don't make a mistake, will be an enchanting steed.

I'd really like to pull out the baby tooth and keep it as a souvenir. I laugh.

Having stretched, he stands in front of me and bellows at the top of his lungs. Despite his extreme youth, his life has been difficult.

On his gums are barely healed sores from iron.

It seems they tortured the young one.

He bellows, addressing it not so much toward me as toward the huge space of the empty manège, which he has entered for the first time.

The armor on the walls, the arches, pillars, stained glass windows, the lurking twittering sparrows, the rays of the sun, the shadows, the huge mirrors and the smoke of my pipe… nothing frightens him.

He is a brave lad.

Besides the history of his teeth and sores on his gums, he also has had a prolific sex life.

At only four years old he has already had two offspring!

Some fools at the collective farm stable, delighting in his stature and color, bred him time and again with all that were still able to take on the stallion.

Two were foaled.

It supposedly wasn't even very important, but they enticed the boy into the joy of sex.

At any rate, having arrived yesterday and seeing our mares for the first time, he went into long, joyful hysterics.

Computerized thermography, which allows seeing any very small inflammation in the skin, beneath the skin and in the muscles, has found signs of recent beatings with a whip on the shoulder and croup.

Surprisingly, the blows were heavier on the shoulders than on the croup. Usually it happens the other way round.

Even without the thermography it was possible to know.

It is understood that they beat him.

Kaogi Ich-Ichaga.

That is his new name.

When I get a horse, I always give him a new name, just as in any monastery or with any start of a new life. The old name is forgotten along with everything that had taken place before the horse's appearance in our manège.

Kaogi Ich-Ichaga is "enchanted raven" in translation from the Lakota.

He is very similar to a coal-black crow.

He bellows, scowls at me and paws the ground.

He approaches, sniffing the smoke from my pipe, scowling yet again.

Earlier the sparrows had felt more at ease, their chirping had become more deliberate as they discussed something among themselves. It was not that common twittering, but a quite distinct sound.

I'm still laughing.

I wait for what will happen when the black urchin sees himself in the mirrors.

So far, he hasn't looked into the mirrors, he has been studying me.

But with an astonishing, movie-like tossing of his mane, he discontentedly shakes his head and whole neck, and for a moment his eyes catch his own reflection in the closest large mirror.

Bang!

Oh-ho!

Suddenly it is no longer the human — a revolting but commonplace annoyance — that requires his attention.

It is now a fierce and impudent black steed that lives here.

This steed is angry and fusses about, extending his neck in an invitation to combat.

And the young Kaogi begins the fight.

Lord, great god of horses, just how courageous he is, this youngster!

Not once did he attempt to buck! It all was with the forelegs (a very good sign). He thrashes with those forelegs, he rises on his hind legs, he bellows.

The manège sparrows are struck dumb in total terror, nervously clinging to the pock-marked arches.

Thank goodness the mirror is so high that Kaogi cannot reach with his hooves and teeth the stallion that lives in the Gothic manège. But Kaogi can reach the wall. And when he does, the black, insolent stallion turns out to be a coward — he disappears. Without a trace. Where is he?

The young Kaogi's eyes glare angrily, attentively from beneath his thick forelock.

But the mirror is empty.

The manège proprietor has concealed himself, the coward. (The mirror, as I have said already, hangs rather high up on the wall, and, when my fierce boy approaches the wall beneath it, his reflection disappears.)

If he jumps closer to the middle of the manège, the impudent steed is reappears in the mirror.

And Kaogi drives him away again.

Even more confidently.

The sparrows clearly are on Kaogi's side. They begin to chirp a little, softly, but briskly.

The black stallion appears again in the mirror.

Kaogi rears upwards, attacks, crashes against the wall with his hooves, and the impudent horse disappears again.

When for the third time the insolent fellow appears again to threaten and then retreat as soon as he is approached, the young one is no longer interested.

He thrusts out his rump, squats and triumphantly urinates on the captured ground with a thick, most powerful stream which penetrates the manège sand to Hell knows how deep.

Now this manège, these pock-marked arches, the rays of the sun and the stained glass windows all are his.

The sparrows are clamoring with notes of obvious delight.

In the meantime, it all makes me fully contented.

I know that now, inspired by victory, the young Kaogi definitely will begin to deal with me directly.

In principle, having seen such a black glaring beast like the one which ran away from the mirror, the young Kaogi would be obligated by all the rules of decency to run up and, having tilted his head, show an ingratiating half-smile, tightly and precisely drawing back his lips so that only his front teeth are revealed; heaven forbid he show any more teeth than those.

This ingratiating, foolish expression indicates a desire to "fall into line" immediately and completely.

Any colt in any herd is supposed to put on such a face a hundred times a day, just to walk past any of the older ones, even his own mother, without causing a "scandal."

I know something about the herd in which Kaogi grew up. The late chestnut mare, Chimera, ruled it and was an authoritarian figure.

A very attentive lady when it came to observing the rituals within a herd.

Kaogi's mother, the bay, fat-flanked Dinastia, never even became an aide to Chimera.

She was able only to watch emotionally as Chimera "disciplined" her son, who was not to run there, not to go there, not to lay down like that, and so forth.

One was not supposed to raise objections to Chimera.

What is all this hot air about, then?

It is because youthful Kaogi's courage is unusual.

Usually only the offspring of the dominant mares, who really are permitted more than the others in the herd, behave so bravely.

There is nothing in this youngster's dull, oppressed childhood that would lead one to expect such a valor in the four-year old.

But facts are facts, the urchin is awfully courageous and insolent.

I understand how funny it sounds, but my immediate task is to evoke the very same sweetly foolish face of respect toward me that Kaogi, as a foal, directed at the late Chimera.

And I have fewer means than Chimera had, god rest her soul.

I can't hit him.

Unfortunately, I can't bite him or jostle him with my chest or croup.

I will never put a bridle onto a horse so that the pain from the iron puts him in his place, the place of a slave.

I will never, for any reason, even in jest, hit him with a whip, because I know that is a road to nowhere.

I have only a dry twig from a hawthorn shrub and some knowledge of how to win the hearts of horses.

That is all.

But I need a lot — I need the horse's completely sincere and voluntary recognition of me (an absolutely wretched being, from his point of view) as an older brother and a friend — a friend who is a bit more domineering, perhaps, but not boring.

Everything on which a human prides himself is worth absolutely nothing in this situation.

The gaze of the horse's large, watchful, but sorrowful eyes from beneath his forelock instantly devalues by 99% every vanity of which man is made.

Titles, names, money, cars, scientific degrees, politics, property, religion, orders, participation in special operations, the conquering of space — all are just so much crap in the eyes of a horse.

No sane horse ever recognizes your seniority based simply on the fact that you are a man, that is, someone from the order of primates, the sub-order of anthropoids.

There is simply no basis for it. Your vanities are admirable qualities only in the eyes of your fellow primates; your thoughts of entitlement are shared only by others of your kind.

The trainer (belonging to the sub-order of anthropoids) who overestimates his position will make any serious relationship with the horse absolutely impossible.

Being left alone with the horse, whose soul you want to win for yourself, (because it is impossible to train and teach the horse otherwise), you must go back.

Calmly go back several million years, to an absolutely primitive physical state, where your status is simply that of a living creature who wants to be with another living being with whom he has much in common.

At the same time, one must remember with what these millions of years were filled, and the well-known last 3,500 in particular... One must always remember the mistakes, and be ashamed of belonging to the race of developed primates which made those mistakes.

It also is very useful to remember the stupidity and cruelty of the representatives of your species and the guilt of your species for its behavior toward the horse.

True, if you keep all this aforementioned nonsense about primates and guilt and metabolism in your head, nothing will ever happen for you.

A great modern-day rider, a genius stunt man and horse trainer, my teacher Mario Luraschi said: "Either you are a horseman, or you are not. If not, training is useless."

Well, it seems my turn has finally come.

Having finally driven away the insolent one in the mirror, Kaogi now summons me to battle.

The apparent delight of the arch dwellers is boundless. (Kaogi still doesn't understand their duplicity and absolutely greedy intentions.)

Cheered by his victory and the flattering chirping of the chubby manège sparrows, he advances.

He does it, true, not so much like a mature stallion, but more as a colt.

He pounces with abrupt shakes of his head and neck, and they are so abrupt and broad that he can barely maintain his balance.

I personally do not intend to disappear in the mirror, as oh how I need this fight!

I happily egg on Kaogi into the skirmish, impudently snapping the twig of the hawthorn in the sand of his manège.

But my cheerfulness and calm put the young stallion on his guard.

It's just as though I am fighting, but somehow I'm too calm and cheerful.

The young one stops in the light of a large sunbeam, begins to ponder, becomes frightfully agitated, and, as a result, suddenly dumps a huge, steaming pile.

And here is where all the duplicity of his "support team" is revealed.

The chubby manège sparrows didn't care about the beautiful Kaogi, they didn't give a damn about his victory.

They were waiting for the warm, damp manure.

The "adoring" chirping ceases, the whole swarm of sparrows is already in the sunbeam and well into the dung — dividing up the pile, pulling it apart, pecking at it, digging in it while it is still warm.

I take a step forward, threaten and lash the twig in the sand.

And then I just step back, for I have played this "part" many times in my life and I know it by heart (I too am a horse).

Kaogi rushes, still surprised, without spite, assured of a very easy victory.

I: Flick the sand. Take a step forward.

Kaogi: Rises on his hind legs and makes the grunt of a stallion. He makes a nominal rush at me. He bullies me.

I: Another flick, and another. I advance.

Kaogi: He jumps aside, rousting the whole swarm of sparrows from the steaming dung. But all at once he turns on his hind legs, and, having scattered five of the flying sparrows with his head and chest, again brings himself up with teeth bared and stands for a long time in the ray of the sun, shaded by whirling feathers and fluff.

I: Another flick of the sand. I have to lure him from the sun and provoke him from a distance, without any threats, into coming right at me, until he touches me.

Kaogi: He raises and swings his forelegs. While I am about five meters away.

I: Flick the sand again and make three abrupt steps toward him, flicking the sand in front of him, and I back off.

Kaogi: Rushes and rushes, he has been lured out of the sunbeam! Leaping forward, he rises up so that his hooves are somewhere over my head, and again with all the power of his long, black neck, strikes at me with his head, with his teeth bared while chattering noisily. He wants to bite me, which is understandable.

Kaogi — first meeting

I: Dodge. He's young and teething, of course, but he already weighs about 500 kilograms.

Kaogi: Another pass at me! A very violent one, he's grunting and trying to smack his hoof into my forehead.

Stop! Here I, having driven the stallion back into his sunbeam, praise him and try to reward his fury with oatmeal treats.

I praise him — in Spanish, in French and in Lakota.

I praise him confidently, in the voice of an elder: "Nata'n'pi! Chiye chik'ala. Nata'n'pi!" (He attacks… little brother attacks.)

I praise him sincerely for a long time as though he, the courageous young Kaogi, had carried out my very important and difficult mission.

And so it goes: he attacks, I praise him and finally it does the trick — he begins to take the treat.

He attacks — he receives.

He is awfully nervous, he plucks at the treat and my fingers as well, rolls his eyes, stomps and flares his nostrils, as if he had finished a three-kilometer gallop.

But he takes the treat.

It becomes clear that he is still awfully ambitious. He doesn't begin to fight again until he has heard all the praises.

And I too silence my teasing twig, and begin to click it in the sand only after ceasing my praise.

Kaogi waits for the praise to end, he waits for the flicking of the branch, and once more he wages war in good faith, but now he no longer targets me — instead, he designates me as his opponent in this "war game."

He somehow suddenly casts aside his tiger-like bared teeth and furious attempts to bite me. He hardly clicks his teeth at all.

The confused sparrows have settled down around us, in the sand, dumbfounded, having removed their dirty beaks from the dung (their confusion is hypocritical, for they have seen this process more than once).

What started as a battle of two stallions is turning gradually into a ballet, where Kaogi immediately demands praise and a treat for each furious pas and amboite.[a]

The reality is changing.

Gone are the stallion and the primate with nothing in common, gone are the strangers, fearsome and terrifying to one another, who clashed on an early August morning in a huge manège with Gothic arches.

The young Kaogi hasn't even noticed himself that we have begun to train him… and that his teacher has appeared before him.

Very little time will pass before relations with the youngster become completely different. I will play other games with him, and with those games I will draw the stallion into ever deeper and deeper relations with me.

They will be different games, completely fantastic at times, but he and I never will forget the first game on that dazzling August morning, a game which the grey-headed horse whisperers on the prairies called "Nata'n'pi," "the attack."

"Nata'n'pi," it is understood, is choreographed and refined; any part that adrenaline plays must disappear from it, so that it becomes simply a means of communication between two creatures who were very different in the past, but for whom, now, things are bad when they are without each other and amazingly happy when they are together.

The point is that if there is a common game, there is a relationship, and if there is a relationship, there is everything. And if the relationship is built skillfully, so that it is of value to both sides, there is friendship. (I completely understand the conditional character of this term.)

And if there is friendship, there is the horse's voluntary, conscious desire to recognize seniority, since every friendship is naturally hierarchical. (True, sometimes the horse takes the lead in such a friendship. But this is a question of the trainer's knowledge and talent.)

And here — here something completely astonishing is revealed.

Any means of coercion or painful control are made absolutely unnecessary in the presence of a true relationship with the horse and all "High School" stunts and figures become possible.

Already, and not even six months have passed since Kaogi Ich-Ichaga placed his hooves on the ground of my manège for the first time, the young one lies down easily on request; he sits at a whistle, he is starting to carry a rider, to do the piaffe, the terre à terre, pirouettes, Spanish walk, — and all of it completely free willingly, without, of course, any bridles or similar crap.

And that is certainly primary and most important.

The work of a horse that remains free is not extreme and exotic. It is the only way not to make him an invalid.

I don't force him; in fact, I cannot force him to do something that may be painful or injurious since I have no means of coercion.

He always has the right to refuse that which seems to be uncomfortable or unhealthy for him, and that could, during a forceful repetition, lead to those terrible consequences characteristically suffered by horses in sports (see the thermograms in the previous chapter).

Right now Kaogi is happy.

He studies and trains very diligently.

It goes without saying that the veterinarian's knife has not touched his pride and joy, his huge black testicles. He is still very, very interested in the lassies. But somehow within the bounds of propriety.

Previously he had conducted himself like a drunken sailor.

What was most important was to climb on — and only afterwards get to know onto whom he had climbed, if such a need arose at all.

But now his style is that of a dandy on the boulevards of Paris.

He stands in his splendor, exchanging glances with charming females and only occasionally points his "lorgnette" at one a bit longer than the traditions of the boulevard demand.

His baby tooth, which my hands had so itched to pull and preserve as a keepsake, had dropped out by itself and was lost.

It was either in the sawdust of the stall or somewhere else.

It would have been rather simple to take advantage of his luxurious, black, powerful and violent body.

By having him castrated.

By hooking on the iron and harness and taking up the reins for work in hand, the most degenerate and sadistic of all the ways of increasing the painful action of the iron by hundreds of times.

By sitting on him, repressing his unwillingness to be together and his indignation with the skillful infliction of pain to the mouth, the poll, and in the neck...

But that would be just mastery of his body.

A ho-hum rape.

I wouldn't want to discuss such "training" methods in this book. It isn't training at all, it is ordinary brutishness. We shall leave that to the sportsmen.

But for me... "Shunk-wakan kile nagi-ki uachi elo" — I need the soul of this horse.

So it has transpired that with the light hand of today's Haute École masters, particularly mine inasmuch as I am seriously involved with Lakota, that this dying language of the North American Sioux tribes (Teton-Lakota or Teton-Sioux, Oglala-Sioux, Minneconju, Hunkpapa-Sioux, Blackfoot and Itazipco) has become the main language of the school, and almost all the terms, with the exception of some unavoidable French, Italian and Spanish, are Sioux Indian words.

Possibly this happened because the North American Indians used a language that is striking in its ancient savage sound and energy, a perfectly existential language (phonetically speaking) that horses understand best of all.

There is not even anything especially mystical here, there just is that arrangement of vowels and consonants that a horse masters more easily than words in Russian or German or English. (On the other hand, the reason for this may be the very persistent and charming myths that exist about the Indian horse whisperers, in which I force myself to believe.)

By the way, the whole training process also has a Lakota name, "su-ichago-pi" (the literal translation is "sprouting of the grain"). There also is a French term that is rather precise, "L'education."

So, the games have been and remain the best beginning, the best method of establishing the relationship between man and horse.

The perfection of mounted work, the horse's readiness to carry out any difficult elements without a bridle, all this begins with the games and the establishment of correct relationship.

All the hierarchal refinements also are established in the games.

Since man, like it or not, stands out anyway as the "one who pays the piper" it is he who "calls the tune," meaning, it is he who decides when such an astonishing thing as the game begins and ends.

I just don't know if this needs to be mentioned, or if it goes without saying, but, of course, one must never strike a horse, not under any circumstances, not in any situation.

For various reasons.

Let's begin with the technical reasons.

The whip, lunging whip, switch, twig, chambriere and large chambriere are actually the most shrewd instruments for correcting the lifting height of the legs, the position of the body, the degree to which the hind legs are positioned beneath the body, the height of the chest, and other similar subtle nuances of the horse's position and movement during its training, especially if it is being trained to perform difficult movements and figures.

The touch of the whip is supposed to be used with such judicious tenderness, such delicacy, that the horse wouldn't ever suspect that the whip has some other moronic sporting purpose.

The whip is always an aide, a prompt, a devilishly sympathetic training accoutrement, from which there is no reason to expect pain or meanness.

A single instance of infliction of pain with a whip (by hitting) instantly brings the whip out of the status of a certain friendly thing.

Two or more instances and the horse learns to fear the whip, and the trainer thereby loses his primary instrument.

Simple examples.

When I am teaching the horse "from the ground" to do the terre à terre, I am obliged to guide the height the chest is lifted, by ever-so-lightly flicking it with the twig. If I don't convey to the horse that it has to get its chest up higher, then the terre à terre will turn into only a series of little pesades (small risings onto the hind legs) and the horse won't be able to make the movements with its hind legs that provide forward motion in this figure. I won't reach the chest with my hand because, though the horse is moving in very short steps, it is at a gallop.

The twig is at once a guide and a prompt.

It is the same story when training the passage, piaffe, douze or practically any element from the ground.

If the twig or lunge whip are used just one time to inflict pain, everything would go kaput, be lost, and the horse would begin to fear the whip's touch, its shape and its crack. I wouldn't be able to control the horse's movements any longer. Only an idiot or a man who doesn't want to teach a horse anything can whip a horse.

Pluvinel was a genius.

One day the king and some nobles were visiting his manège to observe the great master's work with a horse.

Pluvinel, standing alongside a chestnut Andalusian mare being held by an aide, was teaching it to do the piaffe.

In each of his hands was a chambriere (a small long-handled whip with large switches), at his feet lay freshly cut branches of a hawthorn, and the aide, standing alongside, held the larger chambrieres and a lunge whip.

The mare was poorly disposed to perform the piaffe, she first had tried to bite Pluvinel, then she reared up, then pushed forward and then she reared again.

At all attempts to explain to her the need to dance with her croup, while lifting her hind legs a bit higher, she, as they say, struck back (in universal translation, she attempted to savage the whip with which Pluvinel lightly flicked her about the hooves).

And so it continued for a rather long time.

Pluvinel, whistling but unruffled, continued the flicking.

The horse frankly was behaving outrageously.

The king exchanged the most puzzling looks with the other royals and winked at one of them, silently pointing at Pluvinel.

The latter approached the master from behind and whispered to him what he had read in the king's eyes: "Why don't you give her a good beating?"

Pluvinel didn't even turn his head (the master did not deign to respond to just any royal).

He continued the flicking.

The mare continued to roughhouse somewhat.

The king rolled his eyes. He made a puzzling gesture with his silk glove to his retinue and walked up to Pluvinel himself: "Why don't you hit her?"

Pluvinel, holding whips in both hands, turned his head toward the king and replied: "I have nothing with which to do that."

Once Antoine de Pluvinel was forced to put down rather abruptly a king whom he had taught the art of working with a horse.

The king had tried to whip a horse. Pluvinel flicked the king on the hand with the very whip he was holding — as I understand it, hard.

"There are many ways to train a horse to hate man. This method," and he indicated the whip in the king's hand with his eyes, "is the easiest."

Thereupon Pluvinel explained (I quote): "I maintain that you mustn't under any circumstances hit a horse, not at the beginning of an exercise, not in the middle, not at its end..." (Pluvinel generally was the first of the great masters who forbade his students to hit or punish a horse.)

The term "flicking" originates from middle and old English and means "a light, quick touch." It is the closest English translation of the Russian term "tushirovat" which itself originates from the term that was introduced in the 17th century by the haute école founding fathers and originates from the French word "l'attouchement," which means "touch," and "la touch" is "pushing a button."

In other words, a whip is a kind of conductor's baton, with which it is forbidden to hit under any circumstances, since a change of its status will create irresolvable problems in training and instruction.

Even with the worst manipulation of a whip above its head, ears, in front of its face or beneath its body, a horse must react, in the worst case, with absolute indifference, and, correctly, with affability, interest and good humor.

This is the technical side of the issue.

There is one more side.

The relationship.

If you become friends with a horse, become his defender and protector, then any blow, being ordinary treachery, will destroy that relationship altogether.

The relationship is the foundation on which all else rests, particularly if the horse is being trained "nakedly," without any special equipment, and when he has only a cordeo on his chest. The cordeo, a thin braid, a freely dangling thong, is purely a symbol of the lesson. When positioned and used correctly, it is impossible to hurt a horse with it. You cannot use it to turn or restrain a horse.

The cordeo, being tightly sewn into a ring, cannot be either a choker or a means of control. The cordeo is only an indication for the horse that play time has ended and the time now has come for a serious exercise.

The horse is equally free, whether or not there is a cordeo on his chest, and any blow will evoke from him a desire to get some safe distance away. It is unrealistic to restrain a horse using a cordeo. It is like trying to restrain him by holding onto his mane.

And, the horse's burning desire to always be alongside, together, close by is a most important factor, since nearly all the training process occurs "in hand" (as it is called) when the master is not mounted, but on the ground, alongside the horse.

That desire is lost if the horse is hit even once — and it is thanks only to that trust, connection, and the desire to be together that anything at all can be undertaken.

For trust and a desire to be together are fundamental and basic prerequisites; only with them is the correct training of a horse possible.

The horse that a man strikes will not want to be together with this man; that is certainly understandable.

Much, it is understood, has to be tolerated; much patience is required. Young horses are awfully predisposed to frolicking and biting.

Teething (and the canines are growing in, for example, until the age of five, and the molars until five and a half) provokes a young horse to continual outrageous behavior with its mouth.

With a trainer's slightly ironic reaction, both the frolicking and biting pass rather quickly.

True, at times one has to squeeze out of himself a slightly ironic reaction through tears of pain from an especially successful horse bite.

Though "bite" is an incorrect term. Young horses more precisely "pinch". If a horse actually bit you, then half your palm would easily be taken off.

As a "child," one of my mares, the thoroughbred, Tashunko-Uashshta, consumed my hands with such passion that I could not endure it and I spent the exercises wearing the steel gloves belonging to a knight's suit of armor. She, having scraped the steel with her teeth several times and discovering that it was absolutely uninteresting, soon gave up the habit of biting.

In general, the desire to bite, more accurately, to pinch, is a normal prank, a normal desire of a growing foal to provoke a happier situation.

You pinch, jump away and they start to chase you!

Great!

In the horse's opinion, this is an awfully good game.

One must understand and respect such things. Any vigorous (even well-intentioned) reaction of a trainer to a pinch is evidence for the horse that a game has begun.

Only absolute calm and imperturbability and the trainer's composure are signs that he isn't playing this game.

But enough with distracting tangents; let us end with the subject of beating, such an indisputable norm in the world of "horsemen."

One may conceive of innumerable synonyms for beating, both vulgar and convoluted.

Here many terms are used, from "punishment" or "bringing to one's senses" to completely candid terms of the type "laying on of the whip" (popular in competition and meaning a sharp blow on the croup with the whip, which forces the horse to leap across the painted poles.) Most used, though, were, are and will be the various obscene substitutes for the word "beat."

They beat horses most of all during the instruction and breaking process in particular, when they thoughtlessly are trying to explain to the horse just what is demanded from him.

The sportsmen are awfully cunning and wretched.

Take jockeys, for example. They believe that they have the right to beat a horse with all their might in public as much as they want. The racing regulations do not stipulate the quantity of blows allowed during a race (or, as in some countries, the quantity of blows are regulated, but plenty of them are allowed).

But that's seemingly not enough for those sons-of-bitches; a special type of whip has been invented with a battery in the handle and wires in the whip which, in addition to the usual blow, also can give a very strong electrical shock.

The capacity of the batteries allows shocking the horse 10 to 15 times. (In 1999, Billy Patin, in the Arkansas Derby, was caught by chance using such a whip and in 2003, Aaron Yugovich. These are only the official, juicy scandals; thousands of similar cases remain secret, although everyone knows about them.)

I have to stipulate at once, my training, or those methods about which I speak below, have nothing in common with so called "breaking."

Breaking is considered an abusive word and rightly so.

In fact, it is only the development of automatic reflexes in response to painful or arbitrary gustative stimuli.

The place for breaking is in the circus and in sporting dressage, which, by the way, also is called "dressage" as an Olympic sporting event (that is, the most primitive training, without any exceptions).

As I already have said, there are exceptions in the circus. But there the people are a bit more talented and bit more artistic than in sports.

At any rate, the most prominent circus horsemen have some awareness of the shamefulness of the term "breaking."

I remember one famous French circus artiste.

At a certain question of mine about breaking, he blushed and drew me through the black womb of his circus in the Boulogne forest, through the wings saturated with sawdust, past the shampooed elephants, past the stalls with Akhaltekes and Friesians, past a circus-owned covered wagon in which he himself was born and which has carried him for 50 years already.

I was led into the arena.

They were just assembling the daytime performance which started with a carousel of wooden horses, on which his assistants mounted and showed something very sweet and pathetic.

In short, having dragged me to the center of the arena, he outlined the wooden horses with his palm and said with charming simplicity: "These are the only broken horses in my circus!"

Aha, of course…

I had watched his rehearsal many times. I always saw the tightly fastened side-reins (those very ones by which a horse's head is drawn fast to its chest); I saw how, at the sound of the chambriere, all of the rehearsing horses' stomach skin flinched and the ears laid back a little. (They well know what the striking power of the chambriere is.)

I consider the charmingly spoken phrase about the wooden horses empty words. The circus is the circus.

A horse's intelligence is not in any way required during breaking.

And the trainer doesn't require great intellect, either. Only the knowledge of where to hit, where to push and when to compliment are necessary.

The horse, being phenomenally intelligent by nature, accepts this scheme of relationships too. Gritting his teeth, but he accepts it. (After all, what else can he do?)

Let's take teaching a horse to lie down at the trainer's (or breaker's) request as a simple example.

In the circus and in the world of stuntmen they teach lying down using the straps of a special system of ropes and hobbles which are worn on the horse's legs. They use these to repeatedly force the horse down and, having pulled him down, give him something to eat in order to get him into the habit of lying down on command.

If there is resistance, they beat the horse dreadfully and stop the beatings only when the horse performs what is demanded of him.

I will not describe the technique in its disgusting detail, but the essence of it is simultaneously pulling the horse's legs with the ropes and unbalancing him using iron in the mouth.

So, roughly speaking, some men pull on the leg ropes while another compresses the horse's head and neck with the bridle. This requires from three to five men, depending on the horse's strength, weight and temperament.

Not all horses by any means overlook this point. The wretchedness of the method sooner or later cries out, and the horse refuses to lie down at a most inconvenient time. (Without exception, all horses who have been taught to lie down using force, that is to say by hobbling them, have — more than once — pulled fast ones on their trainers in grand style.) My intimate knowledge of practically all the famous horses of the circus and of the cinema allows me to confirm this.

Usually these "fast ones" occur in those cases where the horse knows precisely that the primary method of persuasion, brutal beating, is impossible at a show, on a movie set, or in the circus arena — that is, in public.

The horses evaluate the situation perfectly well, with 100-percent precision, while sizing up the emotions of the man they understand the best of all those present, and they reach very precise conclusions.

Having sensed that the man is not able to hit them, having understood his weakness, and having ascertained that the tormentor has no primary means of action, the horse immediately sends the man to that place widely known as hell.

The reasons for such behavior of the horse are understood and worthy of respect.

But what do you want? The horse has disgusting memories of how he was forced down the first time and he persistently associates this action with pain, fear and discomfort.

And finally, the horse comprehends that human beings humiliated him forcefully time and again; he comprehends what, overall, the action of being forced to the ground means, in his understanding, particularly as the action was committed by those who had no right to do so.

I shall explain.

If a casual acquaintance or someone hateful and strange has driven a long needle into your back, your normal reaction is rage, pain, resentment, opposition and a desire for vengeance.

If someone who has the right to do so pokes that same needle into you, a nurse for example, you even will help her, relaxing your muscles at her request and adopting the most comfortable position for her.

It is exactly like that for the horse. He is ready to fulfill everything, but only when you, from his point of view, have the right to order and control his actions and movements.

The request of the leader, an elder friend, is essentially just and, therefore, not to be opposed.

The horse is a wise being, but with somewhat crazy ideas of hierarchy and sociality.

Speaking honestly, knowing a little about the world of living beings, I cannot name anyone with such an acute sense of fairness as the horse.

And in understanding the horse, the breakers or sportsmen are most likely the ones who try to control him with no right at all to do so.

The ability to beat and inflict pain is not any right of man, it only turns him into an eternal enemy, and never into a leader.

After a sportsman or circus artiste has exhausted a horse with straps and lines, which the horse now associates with paralyzing pain, then he organizes the so-called "obedience lessons" to show the horse who is in charge. He wishes to show the horse who's in charge, but he is gravely mistaken when he assumes that he attains authority or certain rights to seniority in the horse's eyes.

The kind of submissiveness that a horse shows as a result of the application of such methods, can gladden only a creature with the brains of the sporting horseman.

Nothing has happened.

The horse simply has understood the degree of pain which man can inflict and, in order to avoid this pain, puts up with it temporarily. The horse has evaluated and memorized perfectly well the array of devices that cause pain, and he has complied with them, not with the oppressor who wields them.

That same oppressor, if he tried to fight the horse honestly, without any of those devices, would instantly be thrown and, I hope, killed and trampled.

If something from the arsenal of the oppressor's special equipment is broken or lost at a decisive moment, he is doomed.

It proves the most obvious thing, man has not attained any seniority, any authority or any rights to command as a result of his repressive actions.

There are a million such examples.

I will cite the most vivid and the most intelligible.

The Greeks, the Sarmats, and the European knights, all the public that practiced combat while riding and the very many who sentimentalized in prose and verse their union with the fighting steed, surely secured the rein, that went from the iron to the hand, with metal (chain or plate), which did not allow an enemy to hack this rein in two. They knew: the hacking or cutting of only one lousy strap and that would be it, the horse would be uncontrollable and the battle lost.

The year is 1258. Honored for his bravery, the king of Aragon is fighting the French on the fields of northern Spain.

He fights furiously and successfully.

And here some kind of French smart aleck cuts the king's rein in two with a blow from his sword.

The king's horse begins to dash about, trampling its own infantry and, frankly wishes to bolt even further away with the brave king on his back.

If all the royal armor-bearers had not hung onto this horse and had not reconnected the rein, restoring control over the horse, then the King of Aragon would have been thought a coward. The steed would have carried him off the battle field.

Examples from the English medieval era of the War of the Roses are well-known, where the enemy cut the reins of the knights' horses. Whereupon, their own crossbowmen shot the knights' uncontrolled horses in the stomach with their crossbows or they chopped off their legs with partisans [b] so that the horses wouldn't carry the knights sitting on them right to the enemy, where they would be captured or killed.

In the very thick and chaotic combat situations that were characteristic of the inter-city wars in Italy during the 15th and 16th centuries, it was enough just to grab an enemy's fighting horse by the bit in order to take it and its knight out of the skirmish. They were supposed to operate with the protection of five pikemen, which did not allow the knight to attack the one who had grabbed his horse.

Similar cases have been recorded too during Bajamonte Tiepolo's revolt in Venice (1310), and in Genoa, during Fieschi's conflict with the doge, Doria.

Besides the direct participants of these conflicts, this method was widely used by the law enforcement agencies of the time, the mission of which was to separate the warring clans, taking the ring-leaders of the knights out of the skirmish (the clan wars in Capua.)

It is known that savage Samogitians killed Ulrich von Jungingen [5] himself, master of the Teutonic Order, during the Battle of Grunwald (the First Battle of Tannenberg) in this particular way. Having seized his steed by the bit, they deprived the master of any maneuverability.

Then they pulled him to the ground from the halted steed and having searched calmly and thoroughly, found all the chinks in his splendid armor, where they began to poke him with the crooked knives they kept in their boots until the master died from indignation and, probably, tickling.

Of course, countermeasures were undertaken.

The branche of a medieval combat bit was fitted all around with bristles from dozens of thorns which were positioned in such a way so there was no way to seize the bit (see tables IV, **6a, 6b**).

It would take too long to list the sportsmen who have lost control of a horse because of a broken bridle strap or rein.

However, let us return to laying down a horse.

When I need a horse to lie down, I will never put him down using force.

I can't.

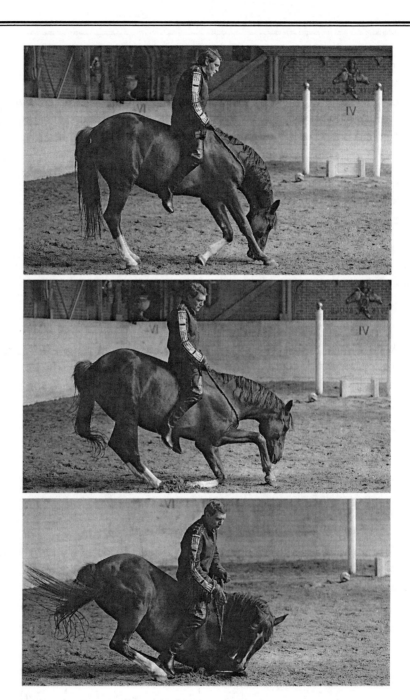

3 phases of a horse laying down

I don't have the devices (ropes, straps, iron pieces).

I only need to teach the horse to understand me and to perceive me as the absolute authority and a being who understands him.

Horses understand everything instantly, with astounding speed. Being somewhat younger and a bit more vain, I demonstrated this point quite often when, after two-three hours of dialogue with a horse, I would touch him on the leg with a switch, and he would lie down in front of me, quickly understanding what, in particular, it was that I wanted.

This always produced a shocking effect, but there was nothing supernatural about it.

Generally, the discussion about laying down is not casual, it is a very important moment in a horse's training.

My task consists not simply in getting the horse down onto the ground, but to have him understand that I am asking him to lie down and that I have the right to ask this.

I play with the horse; by establishing my own seniority in very extreme games, I will show him that I have a right to be respected.

I begin with the easiest exercises in the physical sense, such as fetching, relaxing the poll willingly, stopping when I whistle, putting his feet on pedestals, and so on.

I will carefully, in a most tender way, convince the horse that my desires are manifold, at times strange, but always rather acceptable to him in principle — and I interrupt the exercises for a very pleasant game.

Friendship is always a difficult task.

As is known, one quite often has to put a lid on one's own desires in the name of friendship. If you do not create friendship, if you do not patiently weave its fabric, tailoring thread upon thread, then nothing will turn out.

Friendship with a horse is an even more difficult task.

But the results can be stunning.

There are other training systems in the world. However, even those effective ones such as accepted at the Vienna school, or Saumur or the Royal Andalusian

Games

Games

Academy, are systems, that although enlightened, are nonetheless extremely cruel, only one step removed from those accepted in the 16th century. They are based only on breaking and consequently, they are a dead end.

Those minimal attempts at understanding the horse and teaching him to understand man freely and with satisfaction, as there were during Pluvinel's time, have remained the same and have not developed in any way for the past 400 years.

One can admire the work of these schools only when one doesn't know the suffering the horse endures to pay for all this art.

Such as at the Vienna school itself.

And I can only say for the Royal Andalusian Academy that the serretas, side reins and terrible iron used there are the absolute training standard, and any Spanish training, even in the uncivilized times of the 18th century, was considered openly as butchery. As it has remained even through the present day.

Tauromachy, a corrida horse craft of the gold-embroidered boys, who sacrifice a horse in order to kill a cow in public, added its abominable specific character to the style of the Andalusian Academy.

There is no need to examine it in detail.

Essentially, that's all.

I am not leaving out sport, it is beyond good and evil. It is beyond the ability of a sane mind to understand.

It is useless to stir up the past.

The ancient Greeks had an ideologue of early "horsemanship," Xenophon, a very wise and gentle tutor to the horse, whom all of ancient Greece did not heed. Having abandoned in military and civilian use the famous spiked iron and awful masks, they increased the action of the iron and the fashion of horses.

Xenophon was generally the first man in history who was aware of the need for collection (or its like) and instructed the ancient Greek riders in the method of positioning the horse's hind legs beneath his body.

How he advised they do this is another question…

In order to observe the "haute école" tradition of high regard for Xenophon, I will not quote how he proposed to do it.

He also taught the horse to get down onto his knees (the carpus), for the rider's convenience in mounting. No valuable ancient Greek writings (except Xenophon's) or at least some references on the subject of training a horse using science have been located.

Scythians, Sarmats, Antes, Persians and similar "equestrian" peoples never left behind any written evidence of their own training methods.

The Persians, however, left very conspicuous iron.

I turn once more to iron, because one even may assert with full authority that their training methods were extremely primitive based on their methods used to control the horse, and no one even guessed at the existence of a soul, a mind, pride and the desire of the horse to be friends.

One can judge much based on Scythian bits "with the barbed psalia" and on the first premolars of Scythian horses from the Pazyryk barrow, that now repose in the halls of the Hermitage in St. Petersburg.

I had an occasion to examine them, and there, where I succeeded in turning back the skin of the lips which had been stiffening for 2,500 years, I looked closely at the teeth.

The teeth of riding horses were so wrecked by the iron (characteristic injuries, make no mistake) that everything about Scythian style of riding was immediately clear, and it wasn't necessary to trouble myself searching for ancient training methods of Scythian horses.

Incidentally, they don't exist.

The only thing that is known is that the Scythians were the first who began breaking a young horse with lavish bloodletting. They calmly emptied about five liters of blood and then broke it, usually without any special drama and problems, since the great loss of blood weakened the horse and suppressed its craving to resist. They broke it at the time of the last snow, that is when it was completely exhausted by winter's hunger and immediately after agonizing castration. (The Scythians castrated their horses by smashing the testicles with special hammers).

Those remains of the Pazyryk horses are evidence that even foals were saddled for actual heavy work and for war: the joints, spine, and bones have the characteristic pathological changes which are particular to horses that were burdened blatantly from infancy when the skeleton still was not fully formed.

I have preserved Scythian foal bits from the third century B.C., which were found in one of the Crimean graves together with the bones of a foal. They are 6.5 centimeters wide, whereas the standard width of an adult's Scythian "iron" is 13 to 13.5 centimeters.

As soon as they had the horse under the saddle, they cut off the mane which, in principle, could interfere with shooting from a bow.

And again, Roman iron testifies to the Roman training traditions with absolute eloquence (see table I, **3**).

The Greek and Persian thorns disappeared, somewhat, in this form, but a certain trick was added that provided for breaking a shank at a right angle and, correspondingly, increasing the impact on the mouth. (It is understood that extremely little authentic Roman iron was left in the world, and I have preserved only a version which pertains to late Rome; theoretically these are Egyptian excavations from the times of Marc Antony). There likely were other examples, including those with spines.

At least the poet Virgil advised riding horses using a curb bit with a high port and long shanks, with discs and thorns on the mouthpiece.

The only thing that relates indirectly to training and education is evidence that they trained horses with a normal diagonal pace to amble by tying the required pairs of legs together (front and rear) and forcing them to run. It was done for the rider's comfort — ambling is actually a more comfortable gait for one sitting on a horse than lively correct diagonal gaits.

Medieval Europe in its Gothic era and later continued the traditions of the Romans, Greeks and Scythians.

Laurentius Rusius, a very fashionable author at the end of the 15th century, advised in his work "Hippiatrica sive Marescalia" to apply a scorching piece of iron beneath a horse's tail in order to train the horse to move ahead swiftly.

The book was republished many times and was an absolute bestseller.

Frederico Grisone, whom you already know well, went to the limits of idiocy. In the very same book that evoked the Vatican's delight and the official benediction of Pope Julius III, he writes: "Place a man behind the horse. Tie a wild cat with ropes tightly to a stick, with its stomach up. The cat should be tied so that its teeth and claws are free. A man should hold the cat on the stick to the horse's legs from behind so that the cat can bite and scratch with all its might..."

All this horror with a cat was supposed to be carried out only to force the horse to bring its rear legs in deeper beneath the body.

It is very amusing. Something like 400 years passed and they replaced the cat on a stick with electroshock which has a similar impact.

A new era (the 19th and 20th centuries) gave birth to a host of technology charlatans who, once more, looked for a powerful answer to the secret of the horse's soul.

The task was exactly the same as thousands of years ago: achieve the horse's absolute obedience and "perfection" in it's movements, that is, extravagant, light and impressive.

When you seriously get to know the thousand devices that were invented in the 19th century, each of which was a sensation and a hit, you understand immediately how the consciousness of the inventors was directed and mainly, by what it was directed (see table 5).

For each of those who passionately invented one sadistic thing after another, it most likely seemed that it was enough to contrive something unthinkably cruel and highbrow, difficult and mechanical, so the horse at once would become something else.

They all looked for a certain secret button to push so that the horse would begin to make friends, begin to be sincerely obedient, benevolent, industrious, graceful and strong.

They sought the button everywhere.

By the way, not only in the mouth.

There are memoirs about special anal plugs, which, in the mind of the inventor, were supposed to "improve the horse's nature... Since a loud passing of gas makes horses nervous and works them up, on hearing a horrific sound from behind and finding no explanation for it, they lose their head and bolt..."

Some idiotic jack-of-all-trades actually developed a special plug which was fastened by a complex system of straps.

But it was only a curiosity, while the majority of the inventions were not curiosities.

During training they put cruel wooden and metallic frames with "horns" from 40 centimeters to 1 meter onto the back, through which a mass of small straps was passed which controlled the position of the head in deadly fashion via a special switch.

Methods of tying the tail to the head were invented (!)

It was thought that the tail being in such a position influenced the horse's nature (for the better!).

Systems were created in which all four of the horse's legs, were brought to certain puppet-like actions with the ropes through pulleys, locks and supports. (Lifting of one leg caused the higher lifting of the other leg and so on... That's how they taught the piaffe.)

Mechanical blinders (eye flaps) would appear which operated on the shutter principle, which one always was able to open or close from the saddle or the cart, and could inflict a certain shock for the horse, as their inventor writes, "both opening and closing them with force and quickly about 15 times."

Automatic iron, "Britt's Automatic Safety Bit," was invented which changed the configuration in the horse's mouth with the aid of spool pulleys while simultaneously squeezing the nostrils and smothering the horse, thanks to a system of noseband straps (see table 5, 1).

Rubber blinds served that same purpose, when at the necessary moment the horse's nostrils were covered by the force of special actuators (see table 5, 5).

All this was in Europe and Russia.

And on the American continent the romanticized cowboys gave vent to their feelings. For example, they taught the well-known cowboy method of neck-reining, when the horse turns from only one application of the rein toward the neck: they hit one side of the neck with a hammer, after which they turned the horse the other way and hit it on the neck again with hammer.

America itself spread around the world an absolute innovation, the "horse training machine."

The machine consisted of a narrow, hollow box, which was fastened to a platform that turned at high speed, causing dizziness in the horse.

When they retrieved the dazed horse from the box, it really was very obedient, for some time.

The machine spun using steam power.

Straight-jacket belly girths appeared (!) (see table 5, **8, 9**) and Count Keller's surcingle (see table 5, **13**), about which the inventor himself wrote with sorrow, that its use "may have nasty consequences, and in particular, fracture the nasal bone."

Today, from the lofty height of the 21st century, one is not especially justified in giggling at anything. The collector who acquires everything that really operates today's sport, also will have a very impressive collection (see table 6, **1**). This photograph does not show even half the present-day devices; there are no electrical shockers, electrical whips, pneumatic equipment, or the railroad ties used in show-jumping training for those horses who are careless and know that it is easier to knock down the lightweight, colored pole is than it is to exert themselves and jump high. For these horses the extremely heavy railroad tie, which is painted the same as the pole, is inserted in place of the lightweight pole.

The effect, I assume, is understood.

Toward the end of the 19th century training masters appear who operate totally in synch with all these inventions. Each of them considered it their duty to publish some kind of trashy book.

Generally, a huge quantity of garbage on the problem of training horses was produced at the end of the 19th century. Musany, Baucher, c Comminges, De Mauleon, Count Lancosme-Breves, Fillis... there are too many authors of garbage to count.

It is noteworthy that the ladies who rented horses in those days learned this garbage by heart and they worshipped the authors.

James Fillis became the most worshipped idol of the rent-a-horse ladies — who were not necessarily female, and not necessarily of the upper strata of society. Fillis was an ideologue of overt and very aggressive sadism, who ultimately instilled in the brains of his followers that a relationship with a horse is the same as with a biological mechanism which is turned on for use only by the strong blow of a spur.

I quote Fillis: "One must pour on blows with the spurs as drum sticks beat a drum-roll. No horse can withstand the blows of the spurs which are poured on in a torrent near the girth. If you are in no condition to work for long with the spur, then take the whip or stick, or call someone with a whip, or order the horse burnt with fire. When the horse begins to be obstinate, I myself usually strongly and roughly, but conscientiously, descend upon it... When the horse begins to be obstinate, the rider must attack it with all his strength..." Good Lord, what a sick person!

And not only Markir, Jerminal and the rest of his horses paid for his stupidity and lack of talent, but another few generations that grew to respect Fillis and his moronic methods trained horses who suffered as well.

Thanks to those such as Fillis (and there were a lot of them), man again ended up with the fools, and for a long time. He had to again (and again and again) for a long time and nauseatingly force an open door, looking like a beast and an idiot simultaneously. They showed him the way to the next dead end again, and they pointed it out with inexpressible importance in the manner of prophets.

The naïve trebuchet and coquille of the "haute école" founding fathers were just kid stuff in comparison with the inventions of the 19th century.

From the moment when the cold, worn Louis d'or coins covered the eyes of the fat Gueriniere, the last of the Haute École fathers, at least 300 years had passed!

During this time, hundreds of Fillises were born and died, and anal plugs and rubber shutters and electric shockers and chambons were invented, but not one step forward was made in the establishment of a real relationship with the horse.

The inquisitive and aggressive being from the order of primates desired a result, sincerely desired (which is staggering!) friendship with the horse, but instead of simply and honestly peering into the horse's eyes and trying something totally different, he piled on stupid and cruel inventions, made a fuss over sadists and contrived new methods of humiliation while moving in the exact opposite direction of where he wanted to go.

Different wise men, such as the "haute école" masters, philosophers and writers, hinted at this direction for mankind repeatedly and very authoritatively.

The ancient Chinese elder, the great Taoist and philosopher Zhuangzi, subtly, but absolutely distinctly suggested the correct way.

Antoine de Pluvinel, tutor to the kings, who had the nickname le Rustre (Boor) at court, suggested it.

And the canon of St. Patrick's Cathedral, Mr. Jonathan Swift, no longer suggested it, but yelled about the true and only way.

But the Fillises turned out to be stronger.

By the way, the Fillises always carefully avoided the subject of laying down a horse, since they never conceived how it was done; however, life around them swirled about this subject with a particular passion.

Nearly half the devices of the 19th century were devoted to getting a horse to lie down.

An apparatus was invented by Hamilton for Messrs. Raabe and Liznel, which was an ultra complex straightjacket for a horse, as well as a host of rope and belt mechanisms.

One can look at these pictures (table 5, **15–18**) in order to understand that the mechanical means of pulling down or laying down a horse were a special foible of inventors and horsemen of the past.

The horsemen of that time, thank goodness, were not Fillises and not all of them trusted in only the spur and sadism.

While absolutely not understanding the horse, they had a vague feeling that the laying down of the horse was a certain key to its submission, and they wrote a lot about it. True, they didn't imagine that there are no mechanical methods.

They were partly right, of course.

A horse that is lying down is absolutely defenseless, which she herself understands well. So, a horse's readiness to lie down voluntarily in the presence of

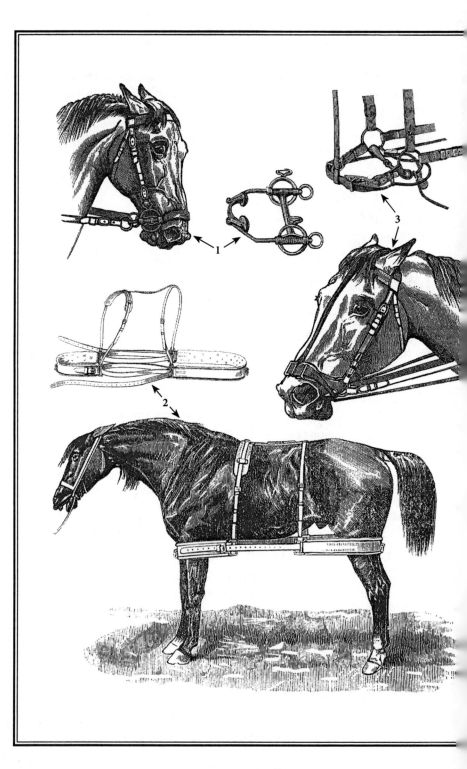

Table 5

Instruments of mechanical impact on a horse

Britts Automatic Safety Bit; **2** – Humility Horse-Collar; **3** – Swedish Asphyxiation Apparatus;
4 –Felling Headcollar; **5** – Bridle with Rubber Blinders;
6 – Mechanical Blinders

Table 5 (end)

7, 10, 11 – Head Fixation Apparatus; 8, 9 – Humility Girths;
12 – Piaffe "Trainer"; 13 –Earl Keller's Girth; 14 – Binding a Tail to the Head;
15–18 – Laying Down Apparatus

man is a manifestation of complete trust in him, as well as recognition that man represents security and protection.

But! Any usage of any mechanical or auxiliary systems, the straightjackets of Messrs. Raabe and Linzel, circus or cinema straps, a cluster of ropes for pulling them down such as veterinarians use, and even ordinary roughness, beating on the legs or coercion, negate the primary purpose of laying down a horse in the first place.

The technologists of the middle and end of the 19ᵗʰ century hopelessly confused reason and consequence.

One is not to lay a horse down for the sake of training and relationship, but to establish a relationship in order to lay the horse down. (Damn it! This resembles something and, certainly, not by accident.) While laying a horse down is important, one should not be obsessed with this for it is absolutely not key to the real training of a horse.

So, the training. Genuine and pure training of a horse and turning it into a friend is absolutely not difficult.

My way.

As you recall, the games are the basis for any relationship.

First it is "nata'n'pi" and later a ball game.

They are tough games.

Rather extreme, but I have special goals.

From the very first minutes of relationship with a horse I try not to lose the slightest part of her natural energy.

I cultivate conceit, spirit, and courage in the horse, and I look upon these qualities as the greatest treasure.

They in particular allow me to train and teach the horse.

Being very well acquainted with the thermographic studies and modern veterinary practice, I know that miracles do not happen, that an apathetic or drooping (the so-called "tranquil") horse is simply to a greater or lesser degree a sick horse.

Tranquility, depression, the indifferent acceptance of any actions are a direct and unerring sign of illness, a sign that the horse's primary strengths are going toward overcoming internal pain or other physiological problems.

Look at the urban horses that are for hire! So much more tranquil and submissive.

Their submission and tranquility are the result of some physiological problem that makes them half dead, and they end up where they are only because they have been completely destroyed by sport or by pulling wagons for amusement.

Life as an urban hireling is no life for a healthy horse. You don't lift boozy newlyweds or a five-year-old child onto the back of a healthy horse that is full of strength.

So:

Any healthy horse of any breed is always full of energy and always ready to romp and play.

The North American Indians called playing ball with a horse "tkh'an."

I have consciously not written anything about the training methods of the Native Americans, since there are not any kind of documentary sources.

All memories are very ephemeral, based on the oral tales of the elders from the reservations, and there is nothing so concrete or so defined that it can be cited in a serious work.

You must rely on what you feel, and what you feel will be what you need. There is no direct instruction — you must feel the game.

With great difficulty I extracted memories of the old Comanche games with horses from an alcoholic and not very handsome elder with a crew cut, Joshua Piia-Khutsuu (Joshua Dirty Bird), who earned his living making and selling souvenir feathered dreamcatchers[d] at a rodeo in Texas, in which I took part because of my youth and stupidity.

It is well-known that hair or leather balls were once used for "tkh'an," so I use a common volleyball, deflated a little bit so the horse can grab it with its teeth but not enough for it to lose its bounce or ability to roll.

The game consists of very energetic, happy fights to get the ball away from each other. I can kick the ball to the other end of the field or manège, and expect the

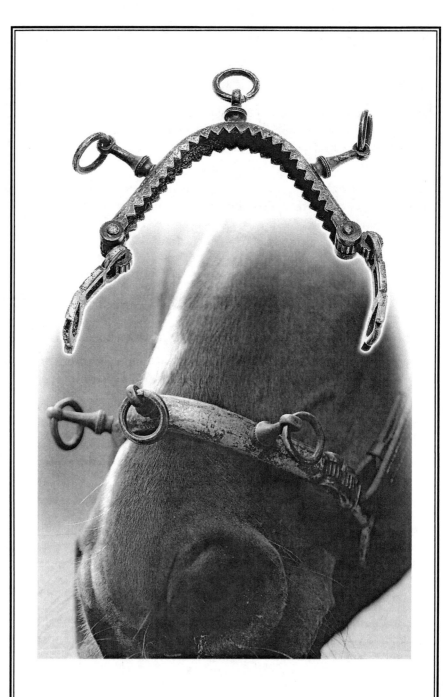

Serreta

Table 6

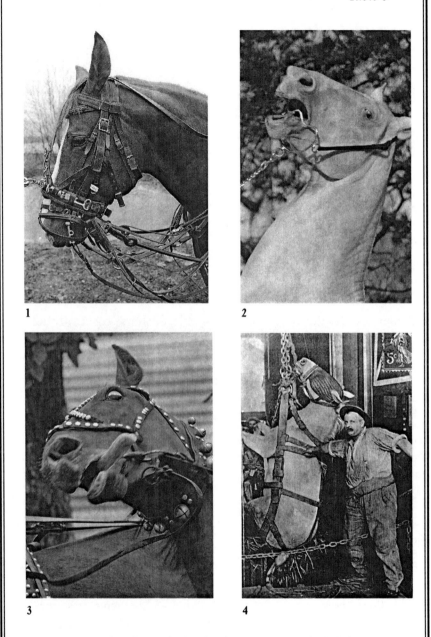

1 — modern devices for "teaching"; 2 — anti rearing bit "Chifney";
3 — convoluted head of a sidehorse in Russian troika;
4 — lowering a horse into a mine

horse will smack it back and forth a few times when he catches it, then grab it, and at a gallop or a quick trot bring it to me, where he surely will lay it into my outstretched hands.

Without slowing the game's pace, I am supposed to immediately scamper off in gratitude, having hidden the ball behind my back.

Having gotten off my guard, I lose the ball, which the horse will then easily snatch. This is not so acute and effective as "nata'n'pi," but it is awfully cheery.

The horse's desire to play with you, to play enthusiastically, to give his all, is his first recognition of man, if not as an equal, then at least as worthy of attention.

As soon as the trust and disposition won in the games stabilizes and the horse begins to understand that man is a main event in his life, and this "event" has been accepted, one may transition to real, true training and education.

The elements of this disposition are very simple: the horse constantly desires to be together with the trainer.

The horse calmly walks or runs alongside you, he stops when you stop, he rears if you suddenly get it into your head to make several steps backward, he runs up at your whistle, and with a light touch of a switch to the sand beneath his hooves, he will lie down at your feet and then sit up.

He is supposed to perform all the actions I have enumerated either completely on his own or with a very light touch of a small strap laying loosely on his shoulders.

The strap is called a "cordeo."

I have already mentioned it and in enough detail. One more element of the horse's disposition is his facial expression.

The more the horse is indifferent and hostile, the more severe, indifferent and uniform his face.

The more he is drawn into a relationship with man, the richer and more expressive his facial expression. The first grimaces, rolling of the eyes, good-natured showing of its teeth, rotating of its ears, smiles and also some grunting, pinching with the teeth, all of these are very good signs that indicate that the horse is paying attention to the man, is well-disposed toward him and accepts him not as a torturer and enemy, but as a friend.

Naturally, if one wraps a horse's face in straps, there will be no facial expression, and for the horse it will become impossible physically and psychologically, but I have already said, and I am ready to repeat, that with real horse training there are not supposed to be any systems of forcible restraint at all, such as the bridle or halter.

Being alongside the human is supposed to be a free and conscious choice for the horse. Otherwise, not a damn thing will happen.

If a person begins a serious training process before the very minute the horse constantly wishes to be alongside him, then the very first minimally difficult exercise for the horse will cause him to want to bolt and no longer come close.

It is most definitely not by chance that I am talking about the horse's desire to be close.

All initial training work is done on the ground, alongside the horse, or to put it the old way, "in hand."

The success of the whole training process depends on how much the horse is ready always to be nearby, in the necessary position.

The readiness of the horse to lie down at your request and his indulgence in the fact that you can lie on him from above, also is a necessary confirmation, a certain certification of the unlimited trust that the horse puts in you.

It is easy to lay down and sit a horse down.

Laying down of a horse generally is not a problem in the presence of trust and your ability to be understood. Several flicks with the switch in the sand near the horse's hooves and the horse is already lying down.

It is a bit more difficult if the horse is sitting on his rump.

If you lay a dry and calm horse onto ground that is not very alluring for him, then there are no problems as a rule. But if the horse has been warmed up with a game or an exercise, then, having lain down on the cool sand of the manège, he almost never is able to overcome the temptation to roll about, vigorously rubbing his back and sides in the sand, thrashing his legs in the air, spinning and turning around.

His conscience is absolutely clear throughout.

You had asked him to lie down, and he lay down. But you hadn't explained what else to do. Well, he does what seems to be most pleasant, scratching a body that itches from open pores and sweat.

In this case, as soon as the horse lies down for the first time, I immediately sit on his shoulder. Very lightly, so as not to frighten him, but also very authoritatively. And I begin to fawn over him and converse.

As experience has shown, in such a situation, the thought of wallowing about doesn't even enter the horse's head.

Another of my methods consists of asking the horse to lie on his back as soon as he has lain down; I then sit on his chest, explaining in that way that the game is by no means over, but is only beginning, and that even in the lying-down position he is supposed to understand both discipline and my seniority.

Horses are strikingly intelligent and comprehend immediately what is going on.

In addition, a horse that is lying down is fully relaxed. This exercise doesn't cost him even the slightest effort. Lying down is pure delight for any horse, if it is done without force and with trust.

When a horse consistently and willingly lies down at the first request, both with a rider on his back and while simply alongside, and when he lies down for as long and as often as required, and he tolerates his trainer lying across his recumbent body, then it is possible to teach the horse to sit down. It is completely simple when the horse is really amenable toward you.

It is necessary that the horse, while lying down with you or at your request, experiences such comfort and satisfaction that he does not desire to stand up.

And when you "lift him up" or persuade him to get up, he will obey, but wants to extend these seconds of happiness, light-heartedness and satisfaction so much that he will not leap up quickly, but half rises, is slow in standing, is cunning and, as a result, half sits, proposing to you a very attractive compromise from his point of view.

The cordeo is a good aid, but you don't need it to keep the horse from standing (anyway you can't keep the horse down with a mere strap around his neck), but just the opposite — to encourage the horse to rise when he does not really wish to get up.

Passage and lying on the back

Persistence is needed here. It is impossible to damage relations with the horse in this situation, thank goodness.

You have to persist and ask the horse to rise ever higher and higher.

He has to be "lifted" with light oscillations, while flitting the cordeo. Signal with the cordeo, but don't pull, of course.

And then, unwillingly and "doomed," the horse begins to rise up ever higher, thrusting his forelegs into the ground.

At this point, which is a point relative to a full, high seat, one must cease manipulation of the cordeo and compliment the horse.

The high, straight, classical sitting, the way my horses sit, is not achieved immediately.

But it will come with time. (For hygienic considerations one generally can allow mares to sit on their hips, and not lift them further and higher to the straight sitting position.)

There is one danger that one must remember well! Sitting mobilizes a mass of muscles and stretches the nuchal and supraspinous ligaments which are necessary for collection (the international definition, the French word is "rassembler"), and develops the croup's muscular system. By means of regular, correct and measured sitting, one can very thoroughly stretch and strengthen the muscles of the back, loins, croup, which are responsible for fixation and bending of the spine, the positioning of the rump that helps a lot later on and for organization of correct collection, and for a good Spanish walk, and for pirouettes and for caprioles.

But!

As with any difficult exercise, in the beginning sitting should be strictly measured and minimized.

The slightest excess, literally for a second, and the muscles will be badly fatigued or injured.

To play it safe, the horse must get up practically immediately for the first two to three months.

Generally it is easier to teach the horse than to teach his muscular system.

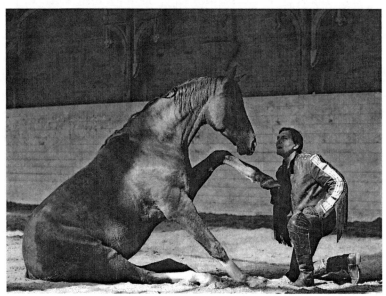

Crunch and sentado

The horse will understand mentally almost in a moment, but his muscular system takes much longer to understand. It gradually grows accustomed to new and unknown loads and is developed and built up through these loads.

The horse listens well to his own muscular system and obeys it.

And it is a keen and very capricious adviser, the human trainer's eternal antagonist, which instantly recalls pain, numbness and intimidation at any excess in efforts or any forcing in general.

Without any pang of conscience the muscular system can "condemn" whatever element of training resulted in its being overloaded or unduly stressed.

And the myological memory in a horse is just as strong as his ordinary memory.

And an exercise, even the most pleasant one, having once begun to cause pain, loses all its fascination for the horse and turns into punishment. As a result, the horse will not love it. And the horse will never carry out well an exercise he does not love.

It is really no joke about the horse's myology; the most insignificant excess for the trainer may ruin any training element, even if he started it well and the horse demonstrated an absolute desire to fulfill it and astounding capabilities for it.

I know what I am talking about, for I had occasion to ruin the piaffe this way in a horse that was very well disposed to it.

Since then, I feel as if I am in a mine field when in the myological field, and, to insure against the danger of causing a problem, I shorten individual elements of power exercises by half and even by two thirds.

And, in general, I am constantly flirting with, and looking for the goodwill of the horse's main adviser, his muscle system.

Friendship with it is just as important as friendship with the horse himself.

A heap of endurance, tact and absolute knowledge of a horse's anatomy and biomechanics are demanded from the trainer.

Besides sitting and lying-down, there are at least 30 more elementary exercises that prepare the horse for the serious, power part of his training and education.

Any of them is suitable in order to secure one's own capability to understand the horse. It isn't necessary to teach the horse to understand, he understands everything splendidly. Man is the one who must learn.

Pluvinel even explained to his royal student that it is necessary to break (he used this term) not the horse, but the rider. He was right, man needs to learn how to understand the horse. In time man will acquire the horse's language, and he will understand any new horse that comes to him for training almost immediately.

There is a multitude of simple, but completely obligatory elements for training that do not present difficulties either for the horse or for his muscles (exercises such as: crunches, [e] placement of the feet on a pedestal, fetching of objects, games, lying down, reverse pirouettes on three legs and pirouettes on crossed front legs, normal pirouettes backwards and forwards at liberty, backing up at the sound of the voice, approaching backwards from a distance to his calling trainer and the like. But, the Spanish walk should be mentioned separately.

The Spanish walk has an absolutely natural origin.

The North American Indians called what was named the Spanish walk in Haute École the "Shunk-bloka o-ali," which literally means "stallion's walk."

One who knows the natural herd behavior of horses has observed numerous times how a stallion will, at first still politely, use this movement — high and aggressive extensions of the forelegs — to drive off an invader after his mares or his territory. (It is the first warning to the invader before any pesades and fights).

The Spanish walk isn't so much a preparatory exercise, but a real, educational, purely "haute école" movement.

Much in the horse's further training depends on the correctness and purity of the Spanish walk — for example, the passage, Spanish trot and true collection.

The secret of the Spanish walk's effectiveness is that you deprive the horse almost totally of the front legs as a means of forward motion. They are too occupied in fulfilling the effective, very high picturesque movement, and the horse is forced to learn to work with his hind legs and to concentrate a greater part of his equilibrium in his hips.

The second great effect of the Spanish walk is in the development of the shoulders. I shall explain. The horse's forelegs participate in movement hardly at all (except for a measured, light push for their own lifting), but the "half sleeping" and little used muscle groups are mobilized for their deflection and lifting.

A good Spanish walk is done only "in hand," on the ground.

It is unnecessary to touch the horse's legs — neither with the switch nor with anything else.

In the first moments of training, one can provoke angry and puzzled striking-out, but then also merry trampling, with flicks in the sand ahead of the hooves, but generally it is better never to resort to all the provocative methods, as they draw out the process of teaching the element for a long time.

The horse, like man, is an extreme creature of habit. And provocative action is for him an intrinsic component part of this element, where at times the provocative action and the movement itself merge into a single whole, so that the horse simply does not realize they are separate.

It happens very often that the horse already performs the Spanish walk well, but does not agree to carry out this element if the provocative actions are not generated.

It is best to teach the Spanish walk by using a game.

Explain the need to lift the legs with the aid of one or two shorter switches in the sand.

And then, propose to the horse beside you that he move ahead, but don't let him — by keeping your palm on the chest.

The horse will be surprised.

Already having been taught to move ahead, he doesn't fully understand why this is being proposed to him, but not permitted.

It is okay if by this time he doesn't know the passage, piaffe or terre à terre, because if he knows these elements, he offers them all.

The phenomenally quick-witted horse understands that there is a certain condition for moving forward and begins to conjecture just what this condition is, offering his versions of the answer to the riddle.

If the horse knows only the angry and merry extension forward, there is 100-percent probability that he will offer exactly that. And it will be the first step of the Spanish walk.

The horse will have to solidify and develop the movement, all the while observing the greatest care, bearing in mind the myology.

In about two months of exacting exercises, the horse will be able to do a full-fledged Spanish walk perfectly.

Generally, the greater the "myological thoughts" in the trainer's head, the faster it will go and the more splendid the result will be.

The Spanish trot is a very energetic, extremely effective movement; it is the direct consequence and continuation of the Spanish walk. The training procedure is identical, but time must nonetheless be spent, either with the cordeo or fully at liberty, polishing the movement to impart impulsion and the correct extension. Once that has been achieved, the Spanish trot should be carried out only while mounted.

In addition to its significance for shoulder development, the Spanish walk is the key to the passage and piaffe.

We shall begin with the passage.

François Robichon de La Guérinière gave the simplest, but also most precise definition of the passage: "The passage, from the Italian word, 'passeggio,' means literally 'a promenade.'"

It really is a casual gait, very easy for the horse, less effective than the Spanish trot, but also less onerous.

In and of itself, it is merely a very short and rhythmic trot in absolute collection with suspension of diagonals and with a distinct lifting of the legs.

The passage has to be taught to all non-Iberian horses (it is natural for the majority of Iberian horses and is done surprisingly easily).

It is very simple to do. The Spanish trot, which any horse makes in semi-collection with a nearly freed head, has to be shortened slightly (so that less ground is covered per stride) and the horse asked to collect himself fully. A very high and good quality passage is obtained almost at once.

It is even easier with the piaffe; you ask the horse to do a passage, but either not to move from the spot at all or to move insignificantly.

Spanish walk

Spanish trot

Both of these elements are "set up" either in hand or simply completely at liberty.

I will not repeat any more that nothing should be on the horse's head, that goes without saying.

But in the case of the piaffe (and the passage), even though in the early stages it is simple and primitive, everything is nevertheless in absolute, correct and harmonious collection.

Right here we come to the most savory moment.

Up to now I have managed to bob and weave, artfully bypassing some school secrets that I don't have the right to give out.

Now it is significantly more difficult for me to do so. It must be said, mystery and the love of secrecy are not my invention, but a tradition that I follow owing to my membership in the School.

I am also a heretic of this School and have been going my way for a long time already.

I despise iron, bridles, standing martingales, halters and any forceful or painful means.

Be that as it may, I fulfill the "haute école" elements that the Haute École masters taught me, and I also observe the "haute école" traditions. Knowing and remembering well the shameful pages of the School's history, I also know that it was the only school in the world from which comprehension of the horse's soul began.

The masters at almost all times most rigorously guarded the secrets of working with horses by which, as they say, "progress was made."

Only the bloody, brutal secrets of work with the horse were discovered, which the specialists shared at all the fairs and in hundreds of books, from Rusius to Fillis.

What is curious is that only the secrets of tenderness, the secrets of reaching into a horse's soul, and the mysteries of the surprising and rare contacts of man and horse were piously preserved.

They went the limit, to total absurdity.

In eastern England and Scotland at the end of the 17th and beginning of the 18th centuries there existed a certain "Horse Brotherhood," real magicians. It unified English masters in working with horses. Secrecy was primary.

Gatherings took place on rare occasions, at night. Strange letters with the hair of a stallion included were in vogue for the initiated and those letters said a lot. Those selected received them by mail both in England and throughout Europe.

Ritual invocations and expressions were developed with the subtlety and awareness of a shaman's tricks...

In particular it is well-known that members of such an English "Horse Brotherhood" vowed: "I of my own free will undertake not to disclose the secrets to anyone... I also vow to come to the aid of any of the brotherhood members within an area of three miles. Justification for refusal can be only a wife or a mare giving birth."

The initiation ceremony took place at a cemetery.

They sent a lad there at night to find a horseshoe or whip on a grave. When he found what he had been looking for, a hand thrust out of the earth, grabbed and pulled him, and someone said in an eerie voice: "Brother, brother... Do not disclose the secrets..."

All this is very nice, but the members of the "Horse Brotherhood" overdid it.

They really hid all their secrets, unfortunately.

Even today we do not have any authentic information about what they really knew how to do.

What evidence exists of the exchanges at these nighttime gatherings regarding "power over the horse" is fragmentary and hit-or-miss. To this day we do not know whether the brotherhood members actually knew at least something, or if it all was pure, empty mysticism and an excuse to "hang out."

There was a ceremony in Cambridgeshire "for attaining authority over the horse."

It consisted of catching a toad, killing it and burying it in an anthill.

When the ants had exposed the toad's skeleton properly, it had to be removed from the anthill and taken to a stream at night (during a full moon, of course).

The toad's skeleton had to be thrown into the stream.

One bone was supposed to separate from the skeleton and float against the current (the very pelvis bone that is similar in shape to a horse's frog).

The pelvis bone was fished out of the water and assured authority over the horse.

There is evidence that the "initiated" went completely out of their minds, were shot or disappeared.

And when a man demonstrated to people any sort of talisman that "proved" he was talented in relationships with the horse, they said that "he was beside the river," implying that the man practiced Satanic rites that gave him magical authority over the horse.

In short, what the members of the "Horse Brotherhood" did cannot be explained clearly; however, the existence of this brotherhood is an indisputable fact. (One may read further details about secret "horse societies" in the splendid research of Clive Richardson, "The Horse Breakers.")

The "Horse Brotherhood" again flickers on the stage of the universal equestrian historical theatre toward the end of the 19th century.

The equestrian hero of that time, John Solomon Rarey, about whom it is difficult to speak seriously, since nothing except legends and myths about his work with horses has been preserved, easily rocked all European and American society.

He boggled the minds of his contemporaries with his ease of communicating with the most difficult horses.

John Solomon began his "horse whisperer" career when, at the age of 20, he broke two elk with which he appeared at local village fêtes. (This is reliably known, together with the fact that he was the eleventh child in a poor farmer's family.)

Having become famous in the region, he undertook conquering the world and by age 38 he had fulfilled his mission completely.

Russian Tsar Alexander II, Napoleon II, Lord Dorchester, Prince Albert and Queen Victoria are only a small part of his client list. He travelled throughout the world and huge lines of owners with "difficult" horses queued up before him.

If one is to believe the sources that don't agree with each other very well, Rarey rather quickly and very gently corrected the mental state of even the most problematic horse.

He had a collection of ropes, with the aid of which he laid down a horse, and then did with it, as his enthusiastic contemporaries wrote, "everything that he wanted."

He shocked Queen Victoria, opening an umbrella in front of a horse and "even beating a drum while sitting on its back." (Frankly speaking, no great shakes.)

So John Solomon kept his secrets for a long time, but then demanded from his aroused public 250,000 pounds via the press for disclosure of part of his secrets.

The times were crazy, the insanity for any type of secrets of training a horse were almost a mass epidemic. A company of "cavalry generals and wealthy horse owners" was quickly formed who collected this sum by subscription and were prepared to award it to Rarey.

But then the most curious thing happened.

On the very day when the company of generals and horse breeders proclaimed that the necessary sum had been collected, letters arrived both at the company's office and for Rarey himself in which there was nothing, except a hair from a horse's tail, torn in the middle.

Notably, they had sent Rarey the hair of a black horse, and to the curious generals, a grey one.

All of this was simply ridiculous, but, as luck would have it, having opened the envelope, the famous horse whisperer John Solomon Rarey, a healthy guy only 38 years old, suddenly died of a stroke.

A coincidence, for certain.

There are even more intriguing versions and variations of this story. I have deliberately cited the most banal and prosaic. But, most likely (I hope very much), all of it is simply complete nonsense and myth.

— The Horse Crucified and Risen

The point is that the main secret of a special relationship with the horse, which imparts to man the astounding abilities to educate and train him, consists of the fact that there is no secret.

More truthfully, there is, but it is so unpretentious, so unspectacular that I am somehow uncomfortable even to mention it.

When you meet with a horse, when you know what you have to do to train him, to teach him and connect your life with him, you have to know distinctly just what it is you personally love in this horse.

If you love only his form, his powerful shoulder, his hefty croup and the legs with their clean sinews… then nothing will happen.

You will be traveling the very same dismal, banal route that thousands of "sportsmen" have traveled before you.

You will thoughtlessly take advantage of this croup, the sinews, the legs and neck, forcing them to carry out your whims in pain, until you either stop your "game" or you destroy all this splendor.

It is also possible that all this muscular splendor, having rebelled against your stupid and unthinking dominion, hauls you along the wall of the manège or breaks your spine, having thrown you in the fields.

Whatever the outcome, you always will be the horse's enemy.

If you love the abilities that the horse provides: the ability to earn a ribbon in the competitions, the ability to lose weight, the ability to assert oneself and brag, the ability to become aware of oneself as a conqueror of a huge, proud and most perfect being, the ability to imagine yourself (thanks to the horse and your position on it) as a certain romantic personage, so to say, a rider, then you also don't have a snowball's chance in Hell for anything to turn out well.

You will be the horse's enemy and you will never hear him.

And the horse will remain your enemy. Beloved, adored, but an enemy nonetheless, for the subordination of whom devices that inflict strong pain always will be needed.

The secret of relationship with the horse is to love his essence as you look at him.

Sense his pain, fear and discomfort as your own. Love his strange, from a human point of view, view of the world, and whenever possible, share that world view.

You need to respect the horse's total defenselessness and to recognize his right to be dissatisfied.

You have to renounce the stupid primate haughtiness and realize that belonging to the suborder of higher humanoids gives you no claim at all to any sort of supremacy.

The secret of the horse's soul is that the horse does not owe you anything and is not obligated to obey you.

You need to earn and win the horse's obedience by making yourself understood, by proving your love in your actions, and by your absolute willingness to understand the horse and become part of his soul.

It is not the horse's neck or sinews that you must conquer, but something else.

The old horse whisperers of the Lakota prairies stated this something else remarkably, "Shunka-wakan kile, nagi Ki uachi elo..."

Only in this case can something begin to happen.

So, the literary and lyrical digression has ended, let us return to the business of training the horse.

Collection is the most important point of educating and training a horse.

Collection is a condition of the horse in which he assumes a certain psychological and muscular concentration, fully ready for movement or for focused absolute immobility.

An external sign of collection is the powerful positioning of the legs beneath the body and lifting of the poll.

An internal, unerring sign of collection is the concentration of the greater part of the horse's weight in the hindquarters, loins and the croup's muscular system that is felt by the rider (and during work in hand, too).

Collection is what the "haute école" founding fathers desired so passionately, because, in their opinion (and they were right), it enables a horse to sustain a rider on his back without injury to his health.

Without collection a horse's movement with a rider on his back pains and cripples him.

The huge weight of the stomach and its contents pulls down the spine, part of which is burdened by the rider's weight.

Among other things, collection mobilizes the horse's abdominal muscles, shifting to them some of the burden of carrying a rider.

We are analyzing only voluntary, natural collection, not that which is developed by a nudge from the rear (with a spur or whip) and restriction in front (iron or serreta or restraining halter, etc.).

Collection must be voluntary so that the horse, having perhaps felt pain from the extreme muscle tension, can at any moment get out of this condition, relaxing his neck and back muscles, and even the hindquarters, at his own discretion.

Forced collection cripples the horse.

Five minutes of forced collection creates serious problems in the neck, back, spine and croup, problems that require treatment for more than a month.

Twenty minutes of forced collection does permanent damage — damage that will affect a horse for his entire life, causing him pain and ultimately destroying his soundness. In that sense, forced collection makes a horse an invalid for the rest of his life.

In his natural condition, the horse often collects on his own.

In a fight between stallions that occurs mainly on the hind legs, the freedom to strike the opponent with the front hooves comes only when the haunches are very well positioned, that is to say, steady, and easily maintaining equilibrium on the rear legs alone. (A well conditioned Haute École horse should do the sentavo element easily, that is make five to six steps on the rear legs even under the weight of a rider; without a rider, 12 to 15 steps.)

It is unrealistic to be steady and maintain equilibrium on an "immobilized" rump, so consequently, the hind legs should be positioned well under the body. The further under the body they are, the higher the horse can rise (absolutely vertically).

And the higher the lift, the greater the advantage in combat — the possibility may even arise to strike downward from above with the front hooves.

The poll becomes the highest point in natural combat collection for two reasons.

Piaffe on horseback and in hand

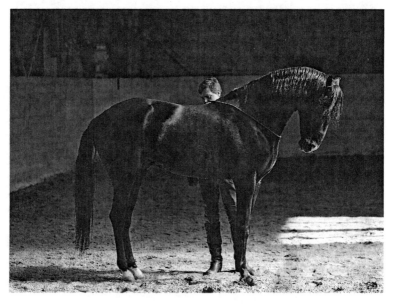

Teaching collection and collection at liberty

Collection while mounted

The head is lowered to press the jowl onto the neck in order to cover it and protect the jugular vein, which an enemy always tries to bite through.

The head is lowered also in order to engage a certain general bodily muscular ring and assure absolute maneuverability, and springing of the neck, shoulder and hip movements.

A stallion while enticing a mare demonstrates his collection to her first.

He does it for various reasons.

Collection is an absolute status symbol.

Something like the epaulettes of a general.

The one who has never fought and mated cannot brag to the young ladies about the fabulously developed rectus capitis ventralis which accounts for flexing the atlas-occipital joint and lowering of the head.

Development of the poll is a sign of an experienced lady-killer and victorious warrior.

A low ranking stallion, having once been put in his place and, therefore, deprived of the ability to participate in the fights, and not "given" mares because of his low status, goes around jaded all his life, looking up into the eyes of real stallions or dominant matrons. His own rectus capitis ventralis remains underdeveloped and such a stallion will never demonstrate good collection during courtship.

Of course, he will go through the motions, he will "drop," grunt, and flex the poll, he will mimic something and tell lies, but a mare will see immediately the absence of authentic, splendid skill in collection, which is natural and faultless evidence both of a high status and competence in love affairs.

As one can surmise, the finest nuances of the quality of this collection, completely invisible to man, are as obvious to the mare as the difference between a cigar and a spacecraft is to you.

She certainly is no judge of dressage, so you cannot trick her with a forced bulging of the neck.

The mare well knows what is genuine collection and what is counterfeit. (But, all that does not absolutely imply that it is obligatory on a mare's part to dismiss the stallion of low status. The mare may even "give in" — it depends on the degree of the mare's desire, or on a great love; that is, when there is no one special from which to choose and one has to marry).

Collection for love is somewhat different than collection for combat.

There is less threat and defense than in battle, therefore, pressing with the jowls to protect the jugular is almost non-existent.

But there is a bit more spirituality and facial expression, which generally is very rich in horses.

True, the wealth of expression rarely manifests itself in the horse's communication with man (as a rule the horse doesn't even want to communicate with him) during sporting, renting and stabling. (If one looks at photographs from concentration camps, the faces of the prisoners there also are practically without expression, eviscerated and apathetic.)

In collection for love there is not such a clear-cut positioning of the rump, since the horse generally is very open, demonstrably open, in order to allow their own groins to be sniffed.

True, when the act, as it is called, "pans out," and the stallion feels that it is on the point of beginning, a very good positioning of the rump immediately appears.

The stallion warms his loins, which have to do some serious work, and gets ready to penetrate.

And in order to penetrate accurately and copulate, he has to possess the same freedom of movement on the hind legs that is there in combat. With the same equilibrium and the same power.

After only a second the stallion is mounted, holding the lady with his forelegs, and at the critical moment, everything happens only on the hind legs.

Quite a bit depends on balance, equilibrium and confidence.

Mares, as is known, are of various heights and builds.

Stallion dilettantes or debutantes, who come down on a mare right away, also frequently "fumble."

Of course, besides fights and love, there are a multitude of situations where natural collection appears, but we have examined the main ones. I presume it is enough.

The haute école horse is supposed to collect voluntarily, which is a consequence of his awareness of all the advantages of being able to precisely control his haunches and relaxing his poll.

The horse, as I have been saying, is incredibly intelligent and sensitive. He quickly understands all the advantages of voluntarily positioning the hind legs well beneath the body and relaxing the poll.

The horse easily feels all of this.

The movements, unstable and creeping, are nevertheless flooded with life and volatile energy.

Collection at liberty is achieved rather easily, but this "easily" is based on two difficult things.

First, one must know how to appeal to the horse's intellect, to his phenomenal ability to learn and understand.

Second, the hind legs, croup and loins should be at least as well-developed as those of a horse that lives free.

A horse living free has frequent opportunity to use his hindquarters energetically and freely.

I shall explain.

In nature, in natural conditions, there are a great many situations when a horse stands on his hind legs, putting weight on them, and using the loins and the muscles of the croup.

During boisterous and adolescent games, in fights, during flirtation and the act of love, while intimidating or welcoming, being surprised or angry, the horse stands on his hind legs, performing what, in the "haute école" register of exercises, having been transformed somewhat, are called the pesade, mezair, levade, sentavo, etc.

Depriving a horse of these natural opportunities terribly weakens both the hind legs and the muscle system of the croup and the loins. (And it robs a horse of his natural ability, his natural strength. In all types and varieties of equestrianism, from show jumping to trotting races, a horse rising on his hind legs is considered threatening, a rogue, a calamity, extremely dangerous. So these barbarians deal with rearing using all sorts of barbaric, neanderthal means: iron, blows to the head with rubber cudgels, special devices like the standing martingale, and similar stupidities.)

A horse standing up on his hind legs is absolutely uncontrollable for a sportsman.

"Bucking" for the most part evokes terror, it is considered as something outrageous, and it is evidence of the horse's terrible nature.

Special "anti-bucking" iron has even been invented (the inventor is the English jockey Samuel Chiffney (1753–1807), which is used even to this day (see table 6, 2).

As early as the 19th century, idiotic methods were being invented which taught to flip a horse onto his back if he should dare to rear up on his hind legs.

In truth, it all is the other way round.

Movement on the hind legs is natural, harmonious and necessary for the horse.

If a rider is afraid of that moment when his horse stands up on his hind legs, then that rider has no business being on the horse's back. The position "on the hind legs," properly speaking, is the pesade, which is natural, indispensable, and necessary for the horse's normal physical development.

For this reason, all movements on the hind legs that occur randomly in the first stage of training, in games and simple exercises, are welcomed and encouraged.

Haute école training without them is unrealistic, since a large part of the figures, elements and exercises are based on the croup, loins and hind legs being fully accustomed to great loads, roughly speaking, on this part of the body being "pumped up."

One can see such "pumped up" haunches in herds of stallions that fight and mate a lot.

In the beginning of manège training, the horse is taught to rear up for 1 to 3 seconds in the pesade for development of the croup and loins, first unmounted and then with a rider, gradually transitioning to the sentavo in which he advances on its hind legs.

This is done very simply. Standing up on the hind legs is encouraged and complimented and, having been elicited first in games, is then formalized with a vocal request and a slight movement of the cordeo.

The first time, the horse, having risen up, will "paddle" with his forelegs as he searches for his equilibrium.

He can be prompted with the switch that he should not do this. However, one may not have to prompt him at all, but just be patient until the rump has swung for a while and then the ideal equilibrium will be achieved. The random waving in front will cease on its own, and the forelegs will be positioned correctly, bending at a right angle at the carpi.

Here it is all about the trainer's patience and his terrible fear of somehow insulting the horse.

It is not by accident that I have cautioned about flicking. The pesade is vigorous and jerky. Flicking may turn out to be too much for a sensitive horse rushing upwards out of your hands, reaching three and a half meters in height, with forelegs thrashing in the air at the same time.

One must take care of relations with the horse, for they are of much greater value than the speed of teaching a figure or element.

I, for example, always wait when the horse is in a pesade, even a very high and very jerky one, for him to settle down by himself.

A bit later I will turn to the subject of working "above the ground," as Pluvinel said. We have to finish with collection first.

There can be no good collection without activation of the croup and the loin muscles.

The hind legs "tie up," stiffen, and one cannot compensate for this with any work with the switch while mounted, or any jumps across the painted poles.

How to teach collection.

If the horse has been sufficiently exercised by work on his hind legs and absolutely understands the trainer while going through 20 to 30 of the simplest exercises, then one can begin to teach collection.

A "naked" horse is taken, one that wears only a cordeo on his shoulders.

A cord is fastened to the cordeo.

This is done only to assure that the horse moves in a consistent correct circle.

A large chambriere is selected. (At this point, no matter where the horse has come from, nor how somber his biography, he must understand that the whip, be it lunge whip, forpaeche, or chambriere, represents no danger and that there is absolutely no need to fear it. The horse will be fine because he has learned in the games and exercises that all these thingamajigs are simply part of his friend.

If the horse isn't the least bit afraid, but simply is still a bit apprehensive about the whip or the chambriere, then it is too soon to begin to teach collection.

The trainer asks the horse to make a circle around him at a trot.

As a rule, the horse does this at the beginning with a completely lowered head and neck, dragging his feet, with absolutely no sign of collection.

The task is to prompt him to relax his head, raise the base of his neck, flex his poll, begin to step under with the hind legs, and to attain grace, power and confidence.

For this the chambriere is introduced behind the horse's hind legs and begins to follow the horse, moving along on the ground.

The horse should either not pay any attention to this or view these manipulations with good humor. When I say "good humor" I mean a state of mind in which the horse, while still not understanding what the trainer wants, begins to look questioningly — indulgently and in expectation. The horse's state of mind remains very good and he continues to like everything. It is the trainer's obligation to understand virtually all of the horse's condition, mood and heartfelt gestures. If the horse does not like you, he clearly will not learn. Teaching an angry or enraged horse is a total waste of time. The foundation of training is the knowledge of how to impart to the horse great satisfaction with the act of learning and the mastery of very difficult tasks and elements.

Let's return to the meandering chambriere.

After some time, the chambriere's tail is moved closer to the horse, nearly beneath the rear hooves. The horse begins to feel it, and inasmuch as the chambriere is a certain part of his trainer, he treats "him" "with kid gloves," trying to lift his hind legs a bit higher so as not to step on "him." In doing this, the horse

Teaching sentavo

Mounted sentavo

does not move faster, but maintains the very same pace, of which the measured clip-clop is like a metronome; the trainer's subtle quivers of the cordeo in time with the hoofbeats help the horse maintain the rhythm.

The subtle quivers are provided by the movements of the cord attached to the cordeo.

The chambriere becomes more insistent, the thin tip of the tail appears ever more frequently beneath the hooves.

The horse lifts his hind legs a bit higher more often, and at some moment pushes himself with his rear legs for the first time.

This is the most important moment, which must be reinforced with extravagant caresses.

After this moment has arrived (still not understood and or even noticed by anyone observing), remove the cordeo and begin the unbridled games, so cheerful and so loved by the horse.

If he likes the ball, get a ball, three balls, even ten balls. And play like crazy.

If he loves "nata'n'pi," let him begin the attack, you have to be the one doing the evasion.

It is important to celebrate this moment. By any means.

The next day, when repeating this easiest push with the hind legs, you have to compliment and caress the horse again, scratch his withers and give him a treat, but continue the exercise, up to the moment it becomes clear to the horse and to you that the chambriere's tail behind him is being used as a recommendation to use his hind legs to move forward.

When the pushing becomes a habit, the horse will carry himself.

And as soon as the horse engages what is called in its entirety the "hindquarters" the head will get into the correct position by itself.

The horse can release between the atlas and the axis, the two upper vertebrae, and he sometimes can release not the head, but the neck between the third and fourth vertebrae; there's nothing written in stone here.

It is no big deal to achieve release of the poll between the first and second vertebrae; it is a big deal to do the movements with grace and intensity. The horse himself will choose how in particular he should flex the neck and poll.

The main thing is to explain to the horse what magic advantages he gets in collection.

Once collection becomes known to the horse, it is possible to show him the full advantage, as you teach him the piaffe and passage (see above).

I assure you, afterwards there will be a big problem in convincing the horse to run at least ten rounds at the usual slack trot, as he will much prefer collection — not from a desire to gain your favor, but simply having adapted for his own convenience.

It is more difficult to teach a horse to walk in collection, but if everything has turned out well with the trot, it will also work out with the walk. The method is the same, the only thing is that the understanding of collection that the horse has during a trotting movement is at first missing.

At a walk, collection is more likely to be a difficult job than to give the horse satisfaction, which is why I first teach collection at a trot, and only later at a walk.

It is about the same story with the canter.

The task of collecting a horse that is cantering at liberty is supposedly completely unrealistic, but after several months of exercises at liberty and "in hand," exercises which are reinforced under saddle, the problem disappears.

Of course, I have explained only the primary principle of teaching collection to a "naked" horse.

It takes me from one to three months to teach a horse collection, but I, as already has been mentioned above, don't rush it.

I strongly fear a very capricious, but absolutely justified reaction of the muscle system.

Everything that I have described for making a horse sit down holds true for training collection, too; the same millimeter increments, the same excessive desire to play it safe and the same fear of inflicting the slightest muscular discomfort.

An exercise the horse does not like makes not the slightest sense to me.

The horse really understands the advantages of collection, which I teach at liberty, when a rider sits on his back.

At that moment, the horse easily comprehends that only collection makes it possible to bear a trainer's weight on his back without pain and discomfort that is severe (let's be honest) for any horse.

A horse that I train begins to love collection since he has no concept that collection can be forced upon him.

I don't bend his poll, I don't draw his head toward his chest, I simply make it possible for the horse to satisfy himself that the position of collection is the best one for him. And he, being a creature with a phenomenal mind, understands this very quickly. Moreover, he remains free and can relax at any moment, and I am obligated to respect that right.

Which I do.

Collection never lasts long and cannot last longer than the horse wants; it becomes his personal business. (Hence, his love for it.)

But just what happens in sport? Collection is achieved with a painful action from the rear and a very painful limitation from the front. Any attempt by the horse to get out of collection, and he wants to do this only when his neck, poll, back muscles and croup can no longer stand it, is prevented at once by the iron and the spurs.

There is no genius in this world who, in a split second, can feel precisely the fatigue in the horse's muscles, immediately comprehend the reason, and then stop using the iron. Aversion to collection is imparted at the very early stages of teaching it when iron is used.

The primate, essentially, is not a very sensitive creature and is very hot-tempered, and furthermore is convinced of his right to command the horse, so, the horse's lot is abuse by collection — abuse by the renting "dummies" and Olympic champions alike.

I have performed an appropriate experiment.

A horse that is collecting well without any iron (willingly learned collection) can be collected not more than 45 to 50 seconds at a time in the first year of training.

In the second and third years, continuation of a voluntary stay in collection can reach a minute and a half, on the condition that the horse has been perfectly developed athletically.

Only in the second year does the horse begin ideally to maintain voluntary collection beneath a rider in small voltes, pirouettes and difficult elements.

Here correctness of the rider's seat still plays a huge role.

Of all the types of seat I recognize only the "haute école," with the leg as straight as possible a little ahead in the stirrup as long as possible. The passé school seat in particular most of all is suitable both for the field and for the manège, and, as experience has shown, such a seat in particular spares the horse's back most of all and provides the greatest freedom for his movements. A good seat, by the way, is possible only in a man who absolutely does not think about how he looks on the horse, but adjusts himself, his weight, and his position only with the horse's movement and rhythm, trying to minimize his own presence on the horse's back.

Salomon de la Broue, one of the haute école founding fathers, while listing the components of a good seat, mentions a "straight and unbending waist," "legs, extended and straight, as if you were walking on foot."

Pluvinel offers his own characteristic, believing the best position of a rider on a horse is that "which allows absorbing the horse's roughest movement, while maintaining gracefulness and elegance."

Pluvinel, judging by everything, was very profoundly tormented in defining seat. Besides the fragment quoted, while he wrote quite a bit very ornately, it was not entirely distinct.[6]

Takuan Soho, an enlightened Zen monk, described a good, ideal seat most brilliantly of all in his book "Writings of the Zen Master to the Sword Master" in the chapter "Zen and Horse Riding."

The history of this famous definition goes like this.

Takaun Soho, the 17th century Zen monk, calligrapher, artist, poet, master of the tea ceremony and creator of a recipe for pickling radish, very cheerful and brave, who subsequently became the central cult figure of Japanese Zen-Buddhism, was provoked by his dreary friend Yagyu Tajima, who was speaking to some extent about a mountain, to the top of which led perhaps 50, maybe 100 stone steps.

Moreover, Yagyu talked a lot of nonsense to Takaun about the famous rider of the past, Magaki, who at one time had galloped alone up the steps on a horse.

Yagyu intended to repeat Magaki's achievement, and invited Takuan to be his witness. The mountain's name was Atago, if I am not mistaken. Takuan and his friend Yagyu reached the mountain, but as soon as Yagyu saw the steps rising sharply upwards, he lost heart and put his plans on hold.

Takuan sat on Yagyu's horse and very nicely, thank you, galloped up the steps... then he turned around and galloped back down, "as if it were a smooth clearing."

Yagyu was numb.

Takuan explained, giving rise at the same time to determination of a rider's good seat which is unsurpassed in its precision and simplicity: "In order to gallop up the steps, one has to realize that there is no rider in the saddle and there is no horse beneath the saddle."

According to the age-old Zen commentary, mastery begins only when we achieve the ability to not recognize ourselves in the saddle and the horse beneath the saddle.

I don't like anything mystical and related coincidences, but there is something mysterious here.

Takuan Soho was born and lived practically at the same time as Antoine de Pluvinel.

When in March 1608, Takaun becomes the 153rd abbot of the Daitoku-ji temple, Pluvinel is named France's ambassador to Holland and becomes a member of the National Assembly.

The years of Takuan's career and spiritual blooming in Japan happen to be the years the haute école was established in France.

But guess what, "Rustre" Pluvinel didn't even know that somewhere in the north of someplace called Japan, about which he had only heard, in a darned grey Zen frock, in an absurd hat of bamboo leaves, among the black garden of stones, stood, slyly smiling, the inventor of the fundamental laws of the "haute école" seat.

You will agree it is all strange, although it has no special bearing on the matter.

It would be possible here to malign as much as one likes the apeish seat of the jockeys and competitors or the wooden and pompous, thoroughly false seat of the dressage queens who think not of the horse, but about the impression they make on the judges and spectators. But we have already stated that we are not analyzing pathology or stupidity.

And, anyway, enough space and time were allocated to both of them in the chapter about equestrianism and iron.

And, by the way, about stirrups… They are considered the greatest invention, although their significance for arranging the correct seat is quite overstated.

Who invented stirrups is the greatest of mysteries, the answer to which will be clear in about 150 years, when all the possible archaeological discoveries which still have not happened will be made, all the results of the diggings for the last 200 years compiled and the undisputed timeline of the exhibit exposed in a strictly scientific and archaeological way, and consequently, also the credit for invention will go to one or the other people.

At the present time, I know of approximately 18 existing versions of the invention of stirrups in which the inventors are variously said to be the Celts, Chinese, Huns, Sarmats and Alans, the ancient Hindus, Romans, the Syanbi, and even Altai Turkic peoples.

But who invented them isn't all that important.

The reason for their invention is much more interesting.

Military historians, who in the best case may have sat on a rented horse once in their lives (whereby they immediately lost their pince-nez and berets and afterwards went around in the kind of haze that happens after an event like giving birth to twins), zealously allude and agree to the impossibility of the ancient riders being able to shoot, hack and stab without anything on which to rest their feet.

Supposedly these specific necessities of fighting provoked the invention of stirrups.

What a lot of rubbish!

Some fool dreamed this up a long time ago, and the rest repeat it like parrots.

It is certainly possible to fire a bow without depending on stirrups.

"Hacking" and "stabbing" without stirrups also pose no problems as long as there is a very high degree of true control of the horse (to the millimeter). This has been proven by me, as well as by very many stunt people who go to war on horses in the movies without saddles and stirrups.

I shall explain.

The success of the blow, whether chopping or stabbing, depends only on how precisely the horse is controlled, whether he is able to pass an enemy at a gallop at a "hand and blade" distance. (I am simplifying it somewhat in order not to beat around the bush.)

Simply put, if the horse were to get too close to the enemy, maintaining a distance of just half a blade length, or about 50 centimeters, the blow will not work out.

If it has taken an extra 50 centimeters the other way, the blow also will not work out.

If the horse were to be too frisky and break out of the requisite correct, measured gallop, it would be impossible to strike the blow. Similarly, if the horse were a bit too slow there also would be no result.

So, the secret of delivering a good, effective blow lies not in whether or not there are stirrups, but in the control of the horse.

Generally, stirrups have nothing to do with that.

And they weren't invented for easing the soldier's labor, either.

Stirrups were unable to ease anything, because a jaded horse cannot be controlled. By "jaded" I mean a horse not in collection, one for whom positioning his hind legs beneath his body and releasing the poll have not become a habit and standard for movement.

Furthermore, the Huns, Turks, Celts, Hindus and the Syanbi were all separated from the main haute école invention by at least eleven centuries. So it's not a matter of stirrups, and there was no "stirrup revolution," about which today's historians, who have no notion of what a horse is or how to control him, love to write.

Curiously enough, it's a different reason.

And it's not even that it wasn't very convenient to climb onto a horse.

Hippocratic evidence has been preserved that the Scythians and other peoples who were accustomed to riding for a long time suffered from the worst edema, tumors, and inflammation of the legs because their legs were in a hanging position for a very long time, and the blood supply infracted the feet.

Not having colluded with Hippocrates, the Roman physician Galen describes approximately the same symptoms in Roman soldiers.

The doctors were not wrong this time.

Being still young and very stupid, I decided to test Hippocrates and Galen's assertion for myself. I ascertained, that in reality, it took not five or six hours, but only three hours of riding without a saddle with my legs hanging free like spaghetti, and already my legs were swelling and growing numb.

This was, probably, the main reason that prompted riding man to invent some kind of support for the feet.

As regards a seat without a saddle, riding bareback is a special matter, a special pleasure, which, unfortunately, it is easy to abuse, since a saddle most of all protects a horse's back and spine from the rider's weight.

During a ride without a saddle the horse's spinal processes are under steady pressure from this weight.

The saddle tree has an arched curve specifically for their protection. It is possible to allow oneself to ride without a saddle from time-to-time, but only on a horse that is perfectly healthy, with a "blue" back, as the thermographists say.

Despite the seductive allure of bareback — its ease, freedom and comfort are everything — it should be indulged in only very rarely.

At times I almost have to force myself to saddle a horse. *

Spurs are another story.

In particular spurs, the pieces of iron attached to the boots, have long been canonized by mankind as the primary symbol of riding, as a sign of a rider's mastery, and as the first and most romantic token of belonging to the horse's world.

---

* *Editors note:* now Alexander Nevzorov fully rejects horseback riding. This realization is based on the results of long term research. Precisely this chapter allows the reader to trace the way of School growth, its evolution. For the attentive reader who follows the School steps it's truly important to understand the transformation of Nevzorov's views on a horse.

School gallop in hand

School gallop under saddle

A spur cult has existed and continues to exist. (Pluvinel and Guérinière mandatorily hooked spurs to their jackboots.)

According to the old haute école canons, they occasionally prick affectionately or stick a horse's side in order to make his movements more acute and excited, and in this way add a neural zest to the "haute école" elements, which imparts, it is thought, a special chic and a certain aesthetic.

In point of fact, the spur, in its most noble variant, is little distinguished from the twig, it only suggests a degree of emotionalism to the horse and the need for fulfilling one or the other element. Nothing more. (I don't even want to talk about the degenerate use of spurs by sportsmen; it is ignorant, extremely brutal and thoughtless.)

I, too, once saw the spur as an indispensable, sacred thing, the holiness of which had been confirmed by centuries of riding practice, the more so because the number of corrections to a horse's movement during training of difficult elements or during their fulfillment is so great that it would be difficult to do without the spur.

To position the rump, assure high lifting of the legs, maintain the rhythm, and all at the same time, add some fire to the horse's movement using only the manipulation of one's own weight and a switch seems almost impossible.

But despite the sanctity and loftiness of the spur wearers' names, despite the absolute canonization of the spur in literature and art, it is a disgusting object, disgusting to the highest degree.

If one is to be completely honest, of course.

I have, true, always had the splendid excuse, that, because my horses work without bridles, iron, and halters, if I overdo it or am rude with the spur, they will tell me about it on the spot.

I have persuaded myself that my spurs are not really spurs at all.

Mine were small Portuguese les perons, effectively a Tom Thumb or European dressage spur which is attached without straps, and on which the shank is cut off and slightly rounded.

Tom Thumb spurs cannot be considered spurs when it comes down to it.

Their origin is funny.

The world history of the spur is generally not a rich one.

Only Sarmats claim originality in the design of spurs and, possibly, the Syanbi, Alans and Huns, following their example. Only, judging by the latest excavations of Samartian burial sites, their spur was a wide bow with thorns and two shackles which were attached to the rider's shin with thorns on the inside (see table 3, **1**).

Such a spur "operated" constantly, every minute, as long as the rider was on the horse.

Of course, the small Samartian horses, burdened with the heaviest horned armor and heavy riders, eternally underfed, with legs that were fractured (which the arthritic and arthrosic joints of the horses from the Pazyryk burial site confirm) and with sore backs, required not only the sharpest, but also a steady painful stimulus in order to move.

Hence, the barbaric form of "permanent action" spur.

The Romans, Greeks, and Europeans before the 12th century knew well enough the traditional shape of the spur, more or less pointed, a bit shorter or a bit longer, with a larger or smaller rowel, but it was a common spur all the same with which, of course, one could make a lot of trouble, but not immediately.

The Crusaders brought the style for spurs with a goad in the form of a straight or crooked thorn 30–35 centimeters long from Palestine.

Such a spur, which was used in Europe for a long time, was still called "Arabian" for a very long time.

As did the Arabians, the knights made direct use of it.

Myths that they stabbed through a thick horse blanket with a similar spur are absolute rubbish. Not one horse blanket with holes from spurs or traces of spur have been preserved in any collection of hippic antiquities.

Moreover, if a thick quilted horse blanket was put onto a horse, then somewhat larger "window-like openings" would have remained beneath the spurs.

The side was stabbed, and it was stabbed very deeply, the blood on the horses' sides being a sign of a rider's bravery and daring.

With knighthood's absolute inability to control the horse, a similar spur at least solved the problem of how to break abruptly into a gallop, and, again, as in the Sarmatian variant, only it was able to force an overloaded and, as a rule, ill horse at least to move somehow.

The haute école fathers at the end of the 16th and in the 17th century again affirmed the common spur as the only feasible one, not the "Arabian."

True, the rowel, a toothed wheel or wheels (they numbered as many as three per spur) was still rather large and sharp (see tables 3, **6**; V, **10**).

The cavalry of the 17th to 19th centuries, which did not require either skill or high school figures from a rider, or a special speed, overly simplified the spurs, shortening their goads, having reduced the rowels (the wheel itself) somewhat.

Spurs became an indispensable part of the military uniform, particularly in such a form.

But at balls, gallant officers with sharp toothed rowels contrived to slash the skirts of the ladies while dancing in such a way that the latter resolved to give up dancing, which they announced through their tears.

Depriving the cavalry of dances was the deprivation of any desire to continue living.

The dance, as a universal method of flirtation, was an obligatory and unavoidable prologue to the feather bed or hayloft.

The choice was distressing.

It was either barracks homosexuality and goats, but in spurs, or traditional delightful sexual banditry, but without the spurs. In practice homosexuality and goats turned out to be more terrible, and ultimately inspired the officers to remove the toothed rowel and contrive for the ballroom a certain decorative variety of spur, the so-called Tom Thumb, which was safe for skirts. In this way the presence of some kind of iron pieces on the feet, which were mandatory in uniform, was complied with, and the skirts remained intact.

The dances continued, to the satisfaction of one and all.

Thousands of discarded goats throughout Europe suffered terribly for a time, but afterwards returned to fulfilling their routine goat obligations, only sometimes allowing themselves a melancholy chorus of bleating after the departing troops.

In Tom Thumb spurs, which returned European officers to a normal sex life, there was one colossal deficiency: they did not jingle like real spurs.

People wrestled with this "problem" for a couple of decades, introducing into the hollow shank of the Tom Thumb spur different balls and bells, but then they shrugged it off and forgot about it, and the Tom Thumb spur, the ballroom spur, remained as we see it now: safe for skirts, but, nonetheless, to a great degree unhealthy for the sides and stomach of the horse.

Time passed and I began to understand that all my arguments about the Tom Thumb's "softness" were merely an excuse, in no way better than the profuse talk of the sportsmen about the "softness" of the snaffle or curb bit.

Moreover, following my own logic, any spurs, even Tom Thumb spurs, are a very eloquent sign of the rider's very low qualifications.

If I, considered a master of training horses, do not know how to convince a horse to be energetic and spirited without pieces of iron on my feet, then what am I doing for these horses and what right do I have to be called a master?

What kind of understanding of and feeling for the horse do I have? What kind of friendship do I have with the horse?

When a horse's vitality and fervor are generated by a mechanical, painful irritant, no skill is required and it is in the power of any "Fillis" to cause them.

So I mustered up my courage and told myself honestly: "It will be better for me if nothing comes of it, than if it comes only because of the spur."

And I took them off.

Forever.

Friendship is friendship. And the spur has absolutely no place in this friendship.

It is better to be reduced a degree lower in the mastery of the capriole or the pirouette than to obtain the quality of a capriole or pirouette with a piece of iron attached to the feet, in order to periodically jab painfully the one who trusts you unconditionally and completely.

Like it or not.

It will be more interesting to return to my promise to discuss those figures thanks to which haute école received its name.

The name has nothing to do with high self-esteem on the part of the haute école personnel, but rather, with the main figures and elements that were

Teaching terre à terre

Terre à terre under saddle

considered and named "high," because they are performed partially or wholly above the ground.

And that is all there is to that.

The basic, fundamental "high" figure is the pesade. Though I have spoken about it enough already.

The pesade has several derivatives, the mezair, sentavo, courbette, balance (on the rump), douze, levade, lancade, croupade, ballotade and capriole. The saraband and cross follow the capriole, a collection of five to six courbettes that are executed either sequentially along the same line (the saraband) or two courbettes ahead, two back, two to the left and two to the right (the cross).

Let's start with the simplest.

The mezair is a semi-pesade, a short and easy lift of the horse's forequarters, so that the hooves are raised approximately one meter above the ground, but no more than that.

A series of mezairs forms the so-called terre à terre, a short gallop in double time.

All the pirouettes are developed from terre à terres in haute école.

Limiting the height of the lift is achieved very simply.

When the horse wishes to lift himself up high and powerfully, as he was accustomed to doing in games or in the pesade, and he ignores any of the trainer's requests not to lift himself so high, I, using the fact that the horse is very accustomed to moving at my speed, begin to go a little faster without stopping to use the cordeo to ask the horse rise up.

Having been taught to move continuously alongside me and to be very attentive, the horse is puzzled, but makes the right decision very quickly.

Wishing to keep pace with me, and to rise up on his hind legs, he continues to do pesades, but because there is very little time for each one, the horse, on his own initiative, stops increasing the height of the lift, gradually transitioning to an even higher and incoherent type of terre à terre, which normalizes itself in three to four exercises, and it will be tied together from just a series of mezairs in a double-time gallop and drop down to the accepted height.

The terre à terre is requested of the horse by a light flicking with the twig on his chest, and a bit later, by a verbal request.

Later, it is possible to transition to polishing the terre à terre completely at liberty.

Completely at liberty is when the horse is wearing nothing, not even a cordeo, and is about two meters away from the trainer. The only contact with the horse is a slight flicking of the twig on his chest; this creates a spaciousness which soon elicits the horse's rabid enthusiasm for this element.

Disregard for perfecting the terre à terre at liberty may backfire, in time, with what is called stiffness of the figure, that is, the movement appears rigid and formalized.

The terre à terre, both in hand and mounted, is evaluated by its abandoned and merry energy, its freedom and elasticity.

This also applies to the courbette and croupade and capriole and balance... almost everything, really.

It is best to perfect and fully polish completely at liberty virtually any element that can be taught in hand, so that the horse experiences the feeling of "authorship" of the element, develops absolute confidence in his playing and a very sympathetic truth occurs to the horse.

At the same time, in all the exercises, whether mounted, in hand, or at liberty, discipline should be perfect, not amateurish and lax.

Yes, I infinitely value the relationship with each horse that I train.

But horses, being very wise, will also value these relationships. A plus for it all is the hierarchal system of relationships that has been built and secured in which I am indisputably senior and chief.

At liberty, the most insane gallops and games, jumps, or the performance of any element begin only at the request of the trainer and immediately end at his special whistle.

When the element has been done in hand and perfected at will, it is possible to do it while mounted.

What I have said about the mezair, pesade and terre à terre pertains to the very same degree to all similar "high" elements.

Something a bit simpler, something a bit more difficult.

The fundamental danger is overloading the horse, thereby creating in him an aversion to the element.

The courbette, a jump on the hind legs, is comprehended by the horse even more easily since it is possible to be "lashed out." There is none of the mezair's constraint and restriction.

It is not mandatory for the courbette to be very high, it is not mandatory for the horse to be in a strictly vertical position. The main thing is that the horse first lifts all his own weight onto his hind legs and then "jumps." The technique of teaching the courbette is a bit more difficult than that of the mezair, but the horse very quickly understands what is wanted.

Here the main thing is not to be in a hurry and not to accidentally insult the horse when you are striving for that takeoff, a hop on the hind legs.

This hop (the main thing in the courbette) should occur for the first time of the horse's own free will.

The trainer's job is simply to bring the horse to this point, having curtailed the terre à terre to the limit and simultaneously having energized it to the limit. Any horse wants to escape, turn back, put an end to what the trainer is urging.

But again, everything is done in hand or at liberty.

The main thing is concentration of the weight in the hips and absolute collection, from which the horse lifts himself upwards.

A skillfully executed courbette opens up an easy and rather rapid road to the capriole and croupade, and even to all school elements.

I have hardly touched on the real training technique here.

It is impossible.

The real training technique for each element would take a book, equal in size to the whole "Horse Crucified and Risen."

I have only explained the training principle for those elements in which all power, all talent and all the horse's intellect are revealed in the most amazing form.

It was by no means accidental that I chose the main theme of this chapter as training in the haute école spirit.

Everything that I have enumerated with such ease has been, is, and will continue to be considered most outrageously difficult.

Traditionally, it is considered acceptable to drape kilometers of straps and shove a multitude of iron pieces into the horse's mouth for teaching and performance of these elements.

I do the piaffe, passage, capriole, balance and more without any of it. The horse always remains free.

And that doesn't speak to my genius or supposed talent in the least.

I believe there is or will be a master to whom I won't hold a candle.

It is a matter of the horse's genius, of his staggering capability to understand and fulfill those outrageously difficult things without compulsion and without any violence. It is a matter of how sensitive and easy the horse is in his relationship with man, when the relationship is developed correctly, with tenderness and respect.

The horse really is splendid. He overcomes that formidable inter-species barrier and makes contact.

My job, the trainer's job, is only to learn to be understood by the horse, to make this feat easier for him — a feat the horse undertakes solely out of tenderness, respect and the desire to be friends.

* * *

Sometimes the young Kaogi Ich-Ichaga, the black haute école stallion, having broken off a game or exercises, stops dead in his tracks, looking around beneath the manège arches.

There is a mocking bewilderment in his large impudent eyes.

He listens with half an ear to the cooing pigeons in the arches and the chubby manège sparrows.

I don't hurry him, for long ago I learned to respect the horse's right to stop and ponder.

And out of pure mischief I fantasize the face and eyes of Antoine de Pluvinel. Then my imagination finishes by drawing between us the elder Zhuangzi and everyone who is dear to me in the story of the horse.

Courbette. The first stage — rising and aspiration upwards

Courbette. The second stage — separation

The living and the dead.

I fantasize the hushed steps of Pluvinel's soft suede boots, his dry calloused hand as it touches the cordeo on Kaogi's shoulders, and the man's puzzled eyes as they are drawn to the stallion's lips, to the mouth in which there is no iron.

And then, the tears of joy in the eyes of Pluvinel…

The arches explode with pigeons, and suddenly Kaogi trumpets furiously, as if the dry hand of the long-dead great French elder really had touched his coal black neck.

* * *

In concluding this chapter, I would like you to imagine the horses that I train; they are shown demonstrating the Nevzorov Haute École elements in the photographs.

You are already acquainted with the first one, the black stallion Kaogi Ich-Ichaga. His mom, Dinastia, was an English Thoroughbred, and dad, Ararat, a Russian Riding Horse. When I finished writing this chapter, news arrived that two sons had been born to Kaogi almost simultaneously.

The powerful chestnut mare, so strikingly demonstrating collection and courbettes in the photographs, is Lipisina, a Russian Riding Horse, third daughter of the famous Chimera, who died under a Gypsy's knife (i.e. was slaughtered) the year before last.

Lipisina is a very sly, very affectionate, very capricious and violent horse with a florid temperament.

The bay mare demonstrating passage, Spanish trot and the like is the English Thoroughbred, Tashunko-Uashshta. She had been galloping at the horse races from the age of a year and a half. She was removed from racing because of her "terrible nature," went to the breeding facility of a horse farm where she was supposed to give birth, in the muck and while starving, to the end of her days, but she ended up in St. Petersburg by some strange fate, and then with me.

Well and finally, the brown, very powerful steed is Perst, in whom are mixed the blood of Arabian and Don horses.

Up to the moment he reached me, his fate had been monstrous. To his misfortune, he was very beautiful (as he is now, by the way), but violent and unconquerable.

The sportsmen tried to get the better of him, but he broke someone's legs, kicked someone in the stomach and they began to hand him over from one to another as being uncontrollable.

There, where I found him, they were struggling with his unruly conduct. They hadn't fed him in months, hoping that starvation would correct his nature.

And he really quieted down for a time, kept a low profile and for two whole months didn't kill anyone.

Then I got him and he ate to his heart's content and again became violent and got into mischief. And then... and then we became friends.

He was and has remained a hooligan. But he is a hooligan with a golden heart.

* * *

The year 2008 was a turning point in the history of the School. This was the year that we fully rejected horseback riding.

The horse is not intended for riding even in the slightest degree. Not physiologically, not anatomically, not psychologically.

I had to come a pretty long way to have this realization, and it is based not only on my feelings but first of all on the results of long term research.

I understand how difficult it is to accept this fact. But the ability to abandon horseback riding is a guarantee of a true, high relationship with the horse.

Today horseback riding is a turning point of our history.

Now we comprehend and bring into this world another beauty — the beauty of a conversation with the horse as an equal.

---

[a] Amboite is a very difficult and rare haute école element. Effectively, it is the very rhythmic and "propagated" movement of an "attacking" stallion, that throws one foreleg high in the bounce from a trot. The amboite is understood as a natural movement here.

[b] A partisan is a spear with a broad and long tip.

[c] Baucher — in 1855, as Baucher intended to sit on a horse while in the Napoleonic circus arena, a bronze chandelier fell on him. The horse, remarkably, was not injured. Baucher never appeared in public again.

[d] A dreamcatcher is a special Native American talisman that filters dreams in a magical way, screening out those that are bad or troubling.

[e] Crunch is a gymnastic exercise that consists of a horse's voluntary deep bending (see photo on page 175).

WAR

Chapter Four

T he Hermitage in St. Petersburg.

The Scythian Halls.

There is no one here, thank goodness.

There is a smell of mummies and it is cold here.

A chestnut Scythian steed lies in a square glass coffin (there is an inscription in purple ink on an old piece of cardboard: "Horse Remains Number 10.")

Two and a half thousand years ago he was killed over the coffin of his Scythian master, both of them unnamed. Killed along with his master's wives and servants.

He lay for a long time in his deep grave made of logs until the barrows of the Pazyryk Valley tract of the Great Ulagan valley were discovered and excavated.

And now his final home, his huge luxurious barrow has become the imperial Hermitage in St. Petersburg.

No one disturbs the nameless steed, not even with a glance.

His Scythian lord is alongside, but in a more modest glass coffin.

Black, to be sure, somewhat thin and hollow-cheeked, with a rag barely covering his privates and the characteristic grin of a fully happy mummy.

Typical dead guy.

For some reason, the museum's old women call the dead one Andrusha. If someone even wanders accidentally into this cold, Scythian hall, then, being unable to resist glancing beneath the rag to learn what happened in two and a half thousand years with Andrusha's penis, he would move away, not even having noticed the steed in the glass coffin.

The chestnut steed, crowned with golden deer antlers and in a felt, embroidered mask covered with Persian gold, was brought to the crypt with the king's body in an as yet not understood Scythian funeral ritual.

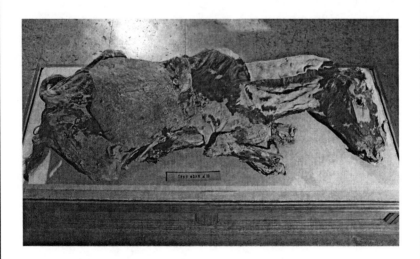

The mummy of that chestnut horse from Pazyryk

In its skull is a single hole from the blow of a bronze ritualistic spike.

The Scythian funerary horse killer probably had a firm hand and plenty of skill.

The heads of about 17 wives and servants were pierced with that same spike.[7]

In all of this there was no more intended cruelty than in the accurate packing of a suitcase for a vacation.

They had prepared the Scythian chief for a journey.

And he needed a horse in that black country where he was going.

And it was supposed to be as dead as he himself in order to easily and reliably put its hooves on the black earth of that land.

The ancient Jews conducted themselves significantly worse.

The Bible describes without any reservations the following custom of its heroes and prophets.

Having once more conquered someone (either the Syrians or Moab), the holy, divinely inspired forefather, prophet and king David, the poet and writer of Psalms, ordered the cutting of the hamstrings of practically all the captured horses.

A horse crippled in this way is fully deprived of the ability to move and in about ten days, awaits its death in inexpressible torment, having half squatted in the red hot sand of the biblical desert.

I am not overstating this in any way, here is a quotation: "And David took from him a thousand and seven hundred horsemen, and twenty thousand foot solders; and David hamstrung all the chariot horses…" (Samuel II, 8:4)

The holy prophet and writer of the Psalms was not an innovator.

He only fulfilled the direct instructions of the Biblical god.

The same that had been given to Joshua a little earlier: "And the Lord said to Joshua, 'Do not be afraid of them, for tomorrow at this time I will give over all of them, slain, to Israel; you shall hamstring their horses, and burn their chariots with fire'" (Joshua 11:6).

Joshua then did just that, in full compliance with the will of his god.

David was only following tradition.

It would have been good had they treated people in a similar manner, but they did not. They killed their prisoners, with enthusiasm of course, but quickly and painlessly.

The Biblical holy ones consciously subjected only horses to the most terrible, poignantly inconceivable death. The chestnuts, the bays, the blacks, the grays, all of them.

In the lifeless, dusty haze David's warriors, having seized the iron with their hands, held onto the captive horses which were harnessed to the empty chariots. Blinking in the dust, other of David's divine warriors wearing leather plated suits of armor and clean bronze helmets bustled among the chariots yelling, while hacking the hind legs of the captive horses with broad bronze swords.

Boys immediately ignited the chariots to which the horses were harnessed with long, smoking torches, shoving them beneath the planked bottoms of the chariots.

The wicker chariots of Moab and Adjara, covered with hide and parched from the desert heat, were quickly engulfed in flame, covering the backs and croups of the already immobilized horses with fire.

The horses most likely tried to shinny and creep on their forelegs in the sand, but collapsed on their carpi, tried to stand up and then collapsed onto their sides with the burning chariots.

They left those who were burning in the desert to die by the thousands, huddling in pain from their severed tendons.

Around them lay those to whom great mercy had been shown, the slaughtered men, as the chariots burnt low.

The bastard David most likely sang his Psalms, keeping an eye on what his hands had wrought.[8]

In the "enlightened" 19th century, Napoleonic Hussars had clear cut authorization for shooting captive horses in particular: "It must be shot in the head, aiming the shot so that a bullet that ricochets cannot injure any of our own."

These are the words of the great ideologue of cavalry, de Brack.

That same de Brack, summarizing the Grande Armée's authority, explains the need for shooting artillery draught horses, if there is no possibility or need to drive the captured equipment back to their own lines.

Thank you, French history, French historians and French writers of memoirs.

Thank goodness no reliable information about how this occurred has reached us.

And the English, holding forth before the whole world about their love for the horse, have left documentation about their own methods during the Peninsular War.

In essence, they virtually replicated the actions of the Biblical prophets then.

During the evacuation from Corunna, the English did not have the necessary number of ships on which to load the horses.

And then a decision was made to destroy all the horses so they did not fall into the hands of the French.

The English, having driven all their riding horses (several regiments, nearly two thousand souls) to Corunna's town square, began to shoot them with rifles and pistols, and when the smoke had cleared, an order was issued to cut them up with sabers, stab them with what was available, slit throats, break legs, and do everything in order to kill or cripple them so completely that even if the French found the horses, they wouldn't be suitable for anything.

While three hundred English cavalrymen destroyed their horses, the rest were loaded onto ships in order to evacuate Corunna for good.

The extermination of the horses in the square and in the side streets by small units of cavalrymen was very organized, but they quickly withdrew to the boats.

They were evacuated in haste, and they did not finish off the severely injured horses. (That, by the way, was impossible, since the heaps of horse bodies on the square reached 1.5 to 2 meters in height.)

Captain Gordon from the 15th Hussars regiment witnessed the gigantic slaughterhouse in the Corunna square, unreal in scale, as the passion of the killers and the bloodshed.

And I emphasize that those they excitedly slaughtered were their own, native combat horses. Some of them already had survived campaigns and the clashes of the Peninsular War and many of them had served in the regiments for three to four years each.

Any niggardly tears on the mustached mugs of the cavalrymen, which were certainly shed there, were unable in the least to stop or slow the process of the destruction of the horses.

But there were also people there with enlightened hearts. "Sir Godfrey Webster's servant was not able to kill Sir Godfrey's horse. He dragged it from the carnage under a hail of Hussar bullets, himself being accidentally wounded in the leg and back of the head, and brought the horse to the edge of the town, and let it gallop directly toward the French."

No other evidence remained of normal deeds of the English in relation to horses during the retreat from Corunna. There probably weren't any.

It is known that in a conversation with a Dutch envoy, the French king, while experiencing certain linguistic difficulties, playfully asked Antoine de Pluvinel who was standing next to him to give him a precise translation of the word "cavalryman."

"Precise?" Pluvinel repeated.

"Yes! Yes! Yes!" the king responded in a great huff.

"A cavalry man is a person who should not be allowed to come near a horse," Rustre[a] slowly answered, stumbling for words and glancing at the decorated cypress flooring of the Louvre.

Pluvinel was right, as always.

* * *

So why is this chapter being written?

It is understood that in fights among primates, both local and wide-scale, everything was used that could yield the slightest advantage. This includes the horse.

The horse's life, his feelings, his soul are not at all taken into account, for he, "it," was merely a piece of equipment, most often used only once, his death was considered a trifle and his suffering meant nothing.

I, honestly speaking, adhere to Pluvinel's point of view and I can only repeat after him that "a cavalryman is one who should not be allowed near a horse."

But I am ready to change my opinion on the condition that the 3,000 year history of the horse, which has been inextricably involved with man's violent endeavors, will yield at least some facts that refute my conviction.

The myth about the beauty and effectiveness of the cavalry is so strong and so entrenched in human culture and history that perhaps it is worth knowing it a bit more thoroughly and looking for some kind of affirmation for it... in at least one place or at one time.

I am writing this chapter while not knowing at all how and with what I will end it.

I hope very much that it will not turn into just a list of abominations.

Don't forget that the aforementioned myth asserts, among other things, that war is one of the horse's chief callings, that all the finest things that man valued and idolized in a horse were embodied in a military horse, that war in particular engendered that most miraculous unity of rider and steed and this became a canon in art, literature and cinematography.

But as far as unity and friendship with the horse are the fundamental and chief subjects of this book, then the need arises to write some short history of the cavalry, which rests on tested, serious and characteristic facts.

Naturally, this history will not investigate the principles of cavalry formations and tactics.

I am totally uninterested in the fundamental question of the cavalry's history, the advantage of a single file formation in front of a double-file formation, a chess formation or terraced formation of cavalry troops.

I don't want to argue about the prince-electors or dispute the eternal subject of the role of the hippotoxotès (horse archers) in the Punic Wars or for the umpteenth time, on the heels of all the cavalry historians, be horrified by the stupidity of Servius Tullius, who once divided the Roman cavalry into 18 centuries.

All of this has not the slightest relationship to the horse per se.

Nor to his relationship with man.

And I don't quite intend to groan in this chapter about man's misunderstanding of the horse. It is not being discussed, for a multitude of evidence about that has been presented in the chapters about iron, sport and training. War was the apogee of all this ferocity.

I also do not intend to repeat and attempt to analyze the cavalry's history through iron.

It is understood that here, too, in the history of the horse at war, everything has been decided only by merciless painful compulsion.

These issues are no longer under discussion.

Something else of interest is that the horse and man were able to be in particularly close physical proximity at war, they were in continuous contact for years, they fought and starved together and they ate and slept alongside each other.

Did such proximity then engender at least a hint of understanding of the horse?

At least a little bit?

Is there really no cavalry in all of history that would be worth imitating, is there no useful and good experience that would assist in the matter of irreproachable contact with the horse?

At first glance it seems not.

* * *

In practically all the military cavalries of the world, from antiquity to the end of the 19th century, they cut off the horse's ears (completely, down to the skull) and they always severed the vocal cords.

They cut off the ears so the horse's eyes did not become flooded with its own blood in battle, since the cavalrymen, while waving their sabers, most often hit the ears of their own horses.

Lord Donogan finally made this a rule in the cavalry, but even before it, as you can understand yourself, preventative removal of the ears had been practiced by the time of the Greeks.

The vocal cords were severed so the horse would not give away the location of an ambush or the position of troops with its whinny.

* * *

Naturally, one would have to examine the cavalry's history, professing the main valuation principle of any phenomena, which consists of the fact that they put together both the positive and negative experience of those who preceded them, for example, Murat's hussars at Wagram carried with them the experience of the Parthians at Carrhae.

This is altogether indisputable.

True, being guided by this principle, one could have been limited by the analysis of that very de Brack, who wrote the gospel of all 19th century cavalrymen, "Light Cavalry Out-posts", but then the story loses its polyphonic diversity, cogency and voluminousness.

Here is a short collection of facts from different times and peoples, which is enough to illustrate fully the relationship of the cavalryman to the horse.

The year is 1812.

Detailed descriptions have been preserved of how French dragoons, in order to get warm, disemboweled their own horses on retreating from Moscow, in a rough and ready manner while still alive, in order to free a place in the stomach and totally (!) lay in it in order to get warm before the horse got cold.

Though the officers did it, the soldiers snatched away the warm entrails, "which they coiled around their hands and shoved them to their bosom, like a hot water bottle."

The 12th century.

The crusaders were poorly provisioned during the crusades. It was impossible to stock up on meat, since everything would go bad in a moment in the heat of the Palestinian desert.

A way was contrived for the gradual cutting off of small pieces of meat and skin from live horses that were walking behind the units. The crusaders cut off pieces of horseflesh, hastily sewed and closed up the wound and drove the horse further so that at the next bivouac they could cut off and have fresh meat again.

The year is 1793.

I quote: "The horse of a hussar by the name of von Zieten was severely wounded in the stomach. He moved to another horse and went about his business. Returning along that very same road the following day, he saw his horse lying there where he had left it, its entrails had poured out and were wrapped around its legs. He only said: 'I was surprised the horse lifted its head when we passed by…'"

The 1400's.

Tamerlane especially rewarded messengers who presented proof of how many horses they succeeded in killing by exhaustion during the delivery of his orders to the troops.

The Castilian ambassador in Samarkand (1403), Ruy Conzalez de Clavijo was astonished in his memoirs by the number of horse bodies on the peaceful Tabriz-Samarkand road, until they explained to him that messengers wishing to distinguish themselves one and all had done it all so that on the approach to the staging area where fresh horses waited, their horse would fall from pulmonary hemorrhage through the nostrils and mouth.

It was a sign of a special and exclusive zeal. Professionals of the "messenger" trade who had this distinction killed up to a thousand horses in several years while riding.

Wheezing, bloody foam and death of an exhausted horse became for them not just an absolutely everyday affair, but also a subject about which to boast.

The year is 1859.

General de Marbot described how one of his officers, a Captain Labédoyère, was angry with his own, very hot and nervous horse for its being frightened by a sudden shot. "Labédoyère jumped down from the horse and in a moment hacked its hind tendons with his saber. The horse fell down and, covered in blood, dragged itself forward on its front legs."

The 400's A.D.

The Sarmats paraded in front of each other the mass and sizes of the armor they wore on their combat horses.

Other Sarmat horses were arrayed in armor so long that it covered the horse from its head to its hocks. It is noteworthy that this armor was manufactured from horses' hooves, which were flattened using steam and very hot water, and later ground into the shape of a large fish scale.

For assembly of one set, nearly one hundred horses were killed at once or crippled so they could not move, and their hooves chopped off.

The year is 1814.

The memoirs of General Mersier: "…Many lay on the ground with their guts hanging out and they were still alive. One unfortunate horse even aroused the morbid interest of the soldiers who now-and-then threw glances in its direction and, laughing, swapped gags about it. This horse, I suppose, had lost both hind legs and sat on its tail the whole long night, in a huge puddle of thickening blood, glancing from side to side, letting out from time to time a long and melancholy whinny.

The following morning, when everyone had broken camp, the martyr was still sitting on its tail and softly whinnied behind us…"

The Third Century B.C. The Punic Wars.

The Numidians took a foal and starting when it was quite young, made incisions in his back with knives, though as soon as one deep wound healed, another was made immediately alongside or across it.

This continued until the horse was 3 years old, until the whole back was covered with a thick mesh of scars. It allowed one to sit more reliably and firmly on the horse, since a certain rough pattern had been created.

It is noteworthy that they maintained this tradition in Nigeria until the middle of the 20th century.

Russia, the 19th century.

Nikolai Volynsky, a well-known historian of the Russian cavalry, describes the traditional method breaking army horses: "They laid pouches with sand weighing from 5 to 6 poods (80 to 96 kilograms) onto a wild horse with extreme effort and lunged it until it was completely exhausted. In about two days they saddled it, threw those same sand pouches across the saddle and repeated the process. Then a rider jumped onto it and, continuing the movement, began to beat it into complete exhaustion. Precisely the same thing was continued the next day, and then the training ended: the horse was considered sufficiently laid back and sent to the front." (Approximate-

ly the same method of training was used by Genghis Khan's troops, and the Assyrians and Sarmats.)

North America, 1876.

It is known that during the battle of the Little Big Horn, the American cavalry, defending itself from the Sioux Indians, killed their own battle horses in order to use the horse's body for cover.

It is unfair, by the way, to ascribe this habit only to General Custer's soldiers and officers, for in the event of battle, the murder of horses in order to use their bodies as barricades or protection from arrows and bullets was practiced both by the ancient Hibernians and the Mongols and by medieval mercenaries.

I could continue this wild, shameful register which characterized the cavalrymen of different epochs and peoples for eternity, but, believe me, it is monotonous.

Almost always, there is phenomenal indifference to any agony of the horse; almost always there is brutality and stupidity.

That physical proximity itself of man and horse, that continued for years and which ideally should have taught man to "hear" the horse at least a little, went nowhere.

The cavalryman, as he was, thus remained a creature who should never have been allowed near the horse.

Moreover, violence on a horse, stupid and primitive, was the professional obligation for any cavalryman and he never developed an ability to understand the horse, but he was adept at violating it.

Everything is indeed simple.

Namely, the cavalryman was a human who was supposed to develop his own inability to "hear" the horse almost to the absolute.

The fulfillment of "march" or "combat" missions in any other way would have been unrealistic.

The notion did not exist in any army of the world of "arrhythmia," that is the disturbance of the horse's balance, which indicates orthopedic problems or internal pain.

Real, visual lameness was an annoying circumstance, but the horse did not leave the formation.

Cavalrymen en masse were distinguished over all the centuries by their weight and meanness in relation to the horse, which also is impossible to forget.

So what does "cavalryman" mean in translation from a lofty language? It is a military serviceman who sits on a horse. Everyone knows well what serviceman means and there is no need for comments.

For example, cases were very widespread in cavalry units where soldiers and officers injured their horses intentionally. Sometimes it was done under the cover of a battle.

Sometimes, during the march.

The advantage was very great, since an unmounted cavalryman was sent to the rear, to hide beneath the skirts of the camp followers.

De Brack writes about the methods cavalrymen used to injure their horses as follows: "Men are seen who deliberately injure their horses out of the cowardice, so as to have a pretext to go to the carts. They accomplish their purpose either by wrinkling their saddle blankets or by placing small pebbles between their folds…"

Everything is simple, it is enough to shove a stone or sliver into a blanket fold, saddle the horse and march 10 to 15 kilometers so that the spot beneath the pebble mashes into the living flesh.

It is always easy to write off a pressure sore (if you succeed in getting out the pebble) as a loose saddle tree, as a stiff blanket and a host of other reasons.

Besides this, as you recall, the chapter "Iron" described the almost universal inability of cavalrymen to ride.

The point is, riding and holding onto a horse while not falling off of it are two completely different abilities.

Cavalrymen, as a rule, knew how to stay on a horse, sometimes knew how to hold onto it, but never knew how to ride.

Many years of practice only reinforced the errors, and the inability turned into a tradition.

In the chapter "Iron," I analyzed this situation in great detail, with references and quotations, which is based first of all on the opinions of very well-known cavalry ideologues.

It is not difficult to understand the cavalry general who considered any mastery of riding a harmful overindulgence for the military rider.

Be that as it may, both the rider and the horse were mass consumables, the advanced training of which would cause postponement of a war and bankrupt any state.

General de Bohan, mentioned already, who had an academic riding education, knew of what he spoke, forbidding soldiers and officers to grasp even the basics of it.

He well knew that real training of a man in the art of riding takes five to seven years of daily intense work at a manège, and the training of one horse that would be able to demonstrate dressage skills, not less than seven to eight years.

Naturally, there were neither funds nor time for a lot of training.

And chiefly, there was no such need.

To gallop, careen, and run down an enemy in a close formation with a mass of horse flesh was the cavalry's whole mission.

The cavalry generals of all eras wrote with great satisfaction about the stupidity of cavalrymen, the so called "men," recognizing that 99% have, as de Melfort expressed, "a rather narrow mind," not capable of accepting any knowledge.

At the same time, a man in the military learned the chain of command, learned to be humble before those senior in rank and to disparage those who were lower.

The horse of any cavalryman always was subordinate to him, and therefore one could vent one's feeling onto him. (It is very funny to listen to the tales of how horses carried the wounded from the battlefield. For the horse, you see, as soon as painful control of it weakened because of the rider's physical mutilation, ran away from the battle, where it was horrible and dangerous.)

Finally, just as no horse ever had a personal interest in winning the Olympics, no horse ever had a personal interest in the fact that the side on which he supposedly was fighting could win a victory in battle, in war or a skirmish.

Bonaparte was correct, railing terribly at horses and always saying that "the horse has no fatherland and does not desire to fight for it."

Horse losses always were huge.

Let's take, for example, a small, almost inconspicuous war.

The English lost 350,000 horses in the four years of the Boer War (1899–1902).

Let's take war a bit more seriously.

Napoleon invades Russia, having nearly 500,000 horses.

These are not only the horses of the cavalry, of course, but there also were the transport, and the caissons and the guns, and the provision wagons, and the artillery horses and a multitude of services.

By war's end, he had nearly 30,000 left, despite the steady resupply of horses from France, Poland and Italy.

The figures were approximately the same in the Russian army.

Nearly a half million at the beginning of the war, and several tens of thousands at the end.

In translation from the tedious figures of history, this means that the roads and fields of Russia were piled with the corpses of a million horses.

And only a small part of these horses were killed in battles. The majority of horses, injured by ringworm, lice, mange, scratches, terrible decaying wounds from poorly fitting saddles and harnesses, took a long, agonizing time to die, in snow, rain or impassable mud, for the war consisted mainly of campaigns in mud, bivouacs in mud and similar unromantic details.

The combat losses, of course, also were huge and terrible.

These figures, the figures of the combat and so-called "fatigue" losses, usually are of no interest to cavalry historians, for they all are silent about how the cavalry horses suffered from diseases in reality. (They are silent not because of a certain conspiracy about this questions, but simply, as a rule, that it interests them significantly less than the verbiage of the generals or the color of the blankets of mounted huntsmen or arguments about where whose flank was located.

What is remarkable is that not even one cavalry historian has even considered what these horses felt and thought, how they died and suffered.

Reading the works about the cavalry's history, of which an enormous number were written, I always have been struck by the fact that there is not a single word about a horse or horses in them.

Even more so regarding the suffering of the horse at war.

They are mentioned in historical works only when they were disrupted themselves and the battles were broken off, which happened quite often.

For example, in the Krasny battles (1812). A Muscovite dragoon regiment attacked a column of French infantry, but, as a historian writes, "the horses were so ill and exhausted that on reaching a French formation, they were in no condition to go further." (Imagine how they beat them in order to force them to reach these formations). "Some horses, three meters from the enemy, silently sank into the snow and died from their last efforts without being shot.

And others stopped and hung their heads and it was impossible to move them from the position, even on stabbing them directly with bayonets."

It was like this for each war, without exception.

And it wasn't only from starvation.

Art and sculpture, it goes without saying, communicated a strongly sweetened scene of mounted duels, attacks or cavalry on the march.

And the representation of the horse at war at this time has been radically romanticized in the movies thanks to thousands of productions based on the "myth."

But at the movies we see stunt horses which really, as a rule, are in good shape and which just have been unloaded from a comfortable horse carrier or led out of a decent stable, fed and thoroughly examined by a veterinarian.

Modern cavalry shows, of the Royal Windsor or French Garde type are again the window dressing of decorative parade units which exist beneath a glass dome and have nothing in common with real cavalry units.

In reality, it all looked completely different in the real wars of all eras.

Even in Napoleon's army, for example, up to 90 % of the horses in all cavalry units had mange or ringworm, suffered from scratches, or had glanders, strangles, farcy glanders, trypanosomiasis, lymphangitis, piroplasmosis and encephalomyelitis.

Ancient veterinarians, including Pelagonius (4th century A.D.), repeatedly mentioned "scratches" which struck down the equestrian units of armies contemporary to him.

Varro (1st century B.C.) and Columella (1st century A.D.) wrote about skin diseases, lice, worms and scratches.

Mass diseases of cavalry horses were not the exception, but the rule. The idea of an "epidemic" in veterinary medicine did not exist before the middle of the 19th century and diseased horses were never separated from those still healthy.

Sick horses, naturally, could still move somehow, so they remained in the formation.

The Table 7 pictures provide insight into the real condition of combat horses.

These wounds were made now, but they were made with special make-up under the observation of veterinarians and a hippologist specialist and reconstruct precisely the main military injuries, both on the march and in combat.

1. *Scratches* in translation to what is generally understood are a very painful scab which is formed on the legs of any horse from dirt and dampness. The scab grows, it cracks, and then spreads as an infectious yellow ichor, and in the absence of a complex and long antibacterial treatment can involve almost all the horse's leg from the inside.

It is extremely painful.

Even in conditions ideal for horses and with modern medicines, treatment of scratches can take more than a month every day of soaking and rubbing off the infectious scab, rubbing in of zinc ointments and other procedures.

It is understood that during the march and while slogging through the mud and the damp, when assaulting and retreating and during similar stupidities, it was impossible to be concerned about scratches, and very soon the horse became a complete invalid.

2. *Galling.* This is the most wide-spread problem of all mounted armies of the world. The point is, even if the saddle fits the horse, which happens very rarely, then during the campaign the horse, in conditions of a fodder shortage, is apt to lose weight radically.

The saddle is changed into an instrument of torture and very quickly turns the horse's withers into one continuous bilious sore.

Our dear de Brack in his "Out-posts" recommends the following in case of the appearance of a gall: "...the surface which chafes the injured parts should be covered with a linen cloth, in order that the wool may not irritate the sore; then the saddle should be raised by half pad which will bear upon the sound

Table 7

2a

4

2b

1

3

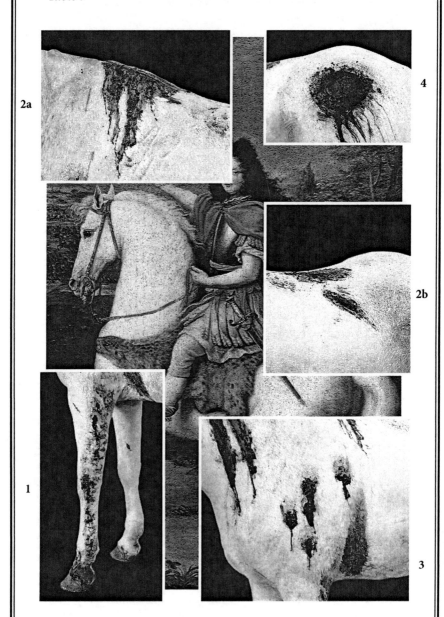

1 – scratches; **2 a, 2 b** – galling; **3** – saber woundsk;
4 – wounds from large caliber weapons

surface, without touching the sore, so that the horse may be cured while marching…"

In the other pictures are combat wounds: grapeshot wounds in the shoulder, saber wounds in the neck and wounds in the croup from large caliber weapons.

Except for a wound in the croup, not one of these combat injuries was considered disqualifying.

The neck was sutured with thread, the pain from the grapeshot wounds was treated with sharp blows of the spurs, the iron on the teeth or blows of the scabbards on the head, croup and hocks.

No one paid any special attention to scratches, galls, and chafing of the flesh from the girth.

Equally so, no one seriously diagnosed internal diseases. And they did not treat them.

Simple examples.

Upon the manifestation of an intensively bloody urine, the cavalry's diagnoses was: kidney bruise.

They recommended the following treatment: "In order to remove the cause for the pain, the valise is sent to the rear." (One has in mind the valise in which the rider's personal things are located and which is strapped behind the saddle during a campaign. Generally, then, "the burden carried by a light cavalry horse is from 112 to 115 kilograms." A cavalryman's bag and baggage that has gotten wet in the rain, naturally, adds greatly to its weight. And that is without considering the weight of victuals and plunder (trophies)). The valise, of course, as a rule was not surrendered, but even if it were, the horse remained ill for a very long time.

The most terrible horse disease which caused savage pain, which they now call *laminitis*, was classified as "inflammatory distortion of the hooves." "…It is recognized according to the difficulty with which a horse moves, it is hampered by its own members, and stands for sure on its heels, moving only when forced."

Laminitis, with nary a doubt, is what is described here in particular, and it is treated with colossal difficulty even today, for the treatment takes (if it is even possible) from several months to a year.

Cavalry practice was limited to bloodletting and an enema with a saltpeter solution. After bloodletting and a saltpeter solution in the ass, the horse was placed into the formation and marched further while slowly dying. The saltpeter did not help, so the main medicine of the military veterinarian went into operation, the cudgel and lashes.

Words fail me talking about saltpeter!

It is understood that it is preposterous. Yet very many medical and veterinarian prescriptions of the old times were absurd, but that's not the point.

We are not discussing the absurdity of old medicine. I merely have cited several examples that were the conditions for combat horses. In which connection, it was already at a relatively civilized time.

Even these two most severe diseases named off the top of my head did not presume the departure of a horse from a formation.

The horse continued to lug the cavalryman with his belongings on his back, to stand for days in the cold mud and in the rain while saddled, to attack and to maneuver both with laminitis and with painful kidneys.

And there were nearly a hundred various diseases which were typical for horses that found themselves in wartime and campaign conditions.

And in regard to practically all of them, a complete cure, which was barely possible to achieve, or the utilization of the fundamental method of military veterinary medicine (see above), was characteristic in not imparting to them any kind of significance.

The Middle Ages and antiquity were in this sense, it is understood, even worse. The conquistadors, for example, tried to treat any wounds and diseases of their horses with the fat from Indian bodies (Ann Hyland, "The Horse in the Middle Ages.")

Nonetheless, I (and de Brack) have cited sufficiently late examples when both ordinary and veterinary experience already had been built up somewhat.

In short, in this short "history of the cavalry," which I have to write now, another gloomy and savory detail comes to light. Practically all wars were carried out on ill horses, and daring attacks, bold raids, retreats and offenses were made on horses which had been struck by severe internal and external diseases.

Why am I undertaking to assert this so categorically?

For the same reason I would undertake to forecast the fate of a crystal vase dropped from any height onto a stone surface.

At times, alas, it is enough to know the properties of a subject well in order to calculate easily the degree of its deformation in different, well-known conditions.

I know very well what a horse is.

And, unfortunately, it is very well-known what war means.

The horse's physiology, psychology, metabolism, skeletal composition and myology are afflicted nearly to the point of death in the conditions which are suggested by any war, except in the movies.

The point is that the horse is strikingly fragile.

If one takes it from its domestic, natural, herd environment and plunges it into a certain stable reality, then a thousand contrivances, well-known to contemporary hippology (the science of the horse), are required for support of its elementary health.

It is quite impossible to explain throwing away money as only a vulgar desire for the indispensable fitting-out of any more or less decent stable with thermographs, ultrasound, solaria, shower stalls, automated air purification systems, service personnel who maintain those sterile surroundings, veterinarians who inoculate and make diagnoses at the proper time, special bedding of dust free saw dust or straw and special balanced fodder in which selenium or calcium are calculated to the microgram.

If the modern "great" sport kills or mutilates the horse, but nonetheless treats him (having cured him in order to finish him off), while sinking millions into him, then war, while mutilating the horse, has not treated him at all and cannot even have done so, owing to its own specific nature, so to speak.

The horse is strikingly fragile.

When he was "designed" by nature and evolution (or by god, if you want), the loads and deprivations conceived for him by man, unfortunately were not provided for and not considered.

In the "Training" chapter I talked about the special delicacy in the interrelationship with the horse's myological system during teaching the difficult Nevzorov Haute École elements.

No less delicacy and colossal knowledge are required for the problems of nutrition and care in order to preserve the horse's health.

The horse's physiology is destroyed irrevocably in captivity in several days (days!) of improper maintenance, even the most benevolent.

The entire locomotor system with its apparent power is destroyed almost as quickly as the physiological functions under the conditions of forced, wrongly organized movement beneath a rider, in harness or in reins.

War, with its absolute disregard for the observance of any standards in maintaining the horse's physiology and natural biomechanics, destroys any horse at record speed.

That is, unfortunately, axiomatic.

It is senseless to attempt to make parallels between the natural, unrestricted life of a horse and its participation in marches, bivouacs, encampments and battles.

Those same scratches, with which 100 percent of military horses of all eras suffered (except, possibly, the chariot horses in ancient Egypt and Assyria that worked in the hot sand), were never observed in horses living freely.

This is the simplest example.

It is possible to cite them by the thousands.

A horse in nature always measures his movement himself. He always selects the ground along which he will or will not go, and he always finds shelter from the elements, if necessary, or knows how to adapt to them.

Generally, the history of the cavalry is a pitiful and disgraceful history, humiliating both for the horse and for man.

And indeed there was none of the magnificence shown in the movies.

There were only hordes of lice-ridden, hungry, sick, exhausted and completely miserable horses who moved through the bloody mud of military roads with cavalrymen plopped on their backs.

And you will rightly ask, was there no compassion in the cavalryman for the horse? Were there no tears in seeing its torments?

There were both compassion and tears.

But to cry picturesquely, having placed the dying horse's head on your knees, is not a noble deed, but common sentimentality that means nothing.

The only meaningful act is rebellion against the order of things which kills the horse.

Sentimentality is very convenient: he spurred the horse, beat him, killed him, cried a little and then sat on another horse in order to spur, beat, and kill him, and then cry a little.

Aside from the sparse evidence about crying, the world history of the cavalry does not offer a single piece of documentary historical evidence about compassion for the horse.

What is striking is that the history of the cavalry could be a little more comprehensible for the normal man if the combat usage of the horse in reality had been phenomenally effective.

But it was not.

So let us not ask the military historians or the generals, they are all deceased. It is enough to turn to those who knew war well and waged it and lived with it.

Machiavelli wrote splendidly: "So that from both ancient and modern experiences, it has been seen that a small group of infantry can be very secure from, and even actually insuperable to, the cavalry" (or chariots.)

Montaigne writes: "Our ancestors, and especially at the time they had war with the English, in all their greatest engagements and pitched battles fought for the most part on foot, that they might have nothing but their own force, courage, and constancy to trust to in a quarrel of so great concern as life and honor…"

A full-fledged knight wrote this who knew his own era and his own trade well.

The most famous knight's battles of antiquity — Agincourt, Cressy, Poitiers — are all battles where the knights had dismounted.

The fates of the ancient world were decided not by riders, but by the unmounted phalanxes of Spartans and Macedonians, and later, unmounted Roman maniples. (The battles of the mounted hordes of Darius and Xerxes with the Greek infantry are very conspicuous in this regard, at Marathon, Plataea and Thermopylae.)

All of the wars that changed the map of the world at that time were infantry wars (Greco-Persian, Peloponnese and Punic). In the Battle of Marathon, the Greeks didn't have any cavalry, not a single rider, the same as in the Battle of Plataea.

The Battle on the Ice, waged by the Russian Prince Alexander Nevsky, was the absolute triumph of a united infantry over the best European knights' cavalry.

In the Battle of the Golden Spurs, the Flemish army had only 10 (!) cavalrymen and a very good infantry.

Against them were gathered nearly 15 thousand French knights. The Flemish smashed them to smithereens.

The happy burghers stripped 700 pairs of golden spurs from the dead knights and decorated the altar of a local church with them in a very picturesque manner.

A thousand Swiss near Mount Morgaten (1315), again on foot, destroyed in a flank-like formation 12,000 mounted Hapsburg knights.

The cavalry and chariots served as a kind of sauce, that was not always mandatory and that decided nothing.

Xenophon, the great horseman of antiquity, describes the senselessness and vulnerability of the combat chariots in a battle in which he participated ("Anabasis," a chariot attack at Cunaxa).

Quintus Curtius describes precisely the lameness, stupid pomposity and absolute ineffectiveness of the action of the best charioteers of that time, the Persians in the Battle of Gaugamela. "The Macedonians stabbed the stomachs of the horses headed for them from both sides, then they circled the chariots and threw their riders from them."

Even the Mongols[9] used horses only as a means to transport their huge armies.

They dismounted and fought "on foot" in all serious events or attacked the enemy (even in an open field) with their battering rams, as was the case with Kolovrat's Ryazan troops.

It is rather funny to look at the Mongols as a mounted army, considering that key Mongol victories were efficient assaults, sieges and laying hold of towns and fortresses. And here too the cavalry had nothing to do with it.

The Mongols, themselves the direct descendants of the famed Huns, also inherited Hun methods.

Assaults of towns, the brilliant possession of battering equipment, the knowledge of building round defensive walls out of carts in minutes, everything for which the warriors of Genghis Khan's heir, Batu-Khan, were famous, the Huns had invented.

It is worth recalling the history of Attilla,[10] the most celebrated leader of the mounted people, the Huns, who in the Battle of the Catalaunian Plains, was surrounded, having nearly 80,000 horsemen, instead of breaking out of the encirclement, ordered the removal of the saddles from all the horses, stacking them in a gigantic heap and setting it afire.

Attilla proposed being cast into this fire if things turned completely bad, that is, if the Romans threw back the Hun's front lines of defense.

It is a most striking illustration of how Attila himself little believed in the combat capabilities of the frightful Hun cavalry, so celebrated by artists and historians.

Such an eloquent fate awaited Theodoric, a king so loved by the Visigoths.

In a battle with the Huns, Theodoric fell from his horse and his own Visigoth cavalry trampled him into mincemeat.

And the riders saw what was happening, that they were killing their honored and beloved king, but they were unable to control their horses.

There are very many such cases in history, for example, at Sentinum the Roman cavalry, having lost control of their own frightened horses, completely trampled their own infantry.

In the Battle of Cilla as Appian of Alexandria describes it, a horse with which he could not cope dragged Scipio Africanus[11] from the battle.

Syphax, a pretender to the Numidan throne, fell from a horse that suddenly became uncontrollable in a decisive battle and was captured by his rival, Masinissa.

Claudius Asellus, a celebrated Roman rider, showing off in front of the walls of Capua which was besieged by the Romans, was not able to turn or stop his steed, and it carried him directly into the city's open gate, out of which the Capuans were attacking at that very moment.

There are tens of thousands of such examples, both in antiquity and in the Middle Ages, and even in more recent times.

The inability to control and to ride a horse properly has been the cavalry's eternal problem.

The 1830s are universally considered the years of the glorification of the "cult of cavalry" and of the European cavalry's greatest brilliance.

Which is no wonder, since a whole series of large-scale wars over three centuries had drilled and trained Europe's cavalry. Dozens of the cult's theorists toiled to publish methods and ordinances.

Having combed their whiskers and handlebar mustaches, the cavalry generals posed for hundreds of parade portraits.

The hussar, exploiting his heroic image, received instantaneous access beneath skirts, both in the provincial towns and in the capitals. England's cavalry was considered the model.

One can find a fine description of her riding talents in the work, "The Day Order of an English Cavalry Regiment," published by Lieutenant General Pavel Tsorn in 1825.

The author, not being wicked and not having any ideological purpose, describes the riding skills and level of an elite regiment of riders and noted that the famous English riders "never have any authority over their own horses, do not know how to gather (collect) a horse according to the regulations and cannot perform even a rapid turn. They believe only that the horse rush them directly forward, both straight ahead, in the attack, and in a regular gallop to attain supremacy."[12]

We can look at practically any era, at any war, and we will see the cavalry's absolute inefficiency everywhere (even to the invention of firearms) .

In principle, the last chords of the cavalry's death march were pounded out on the drum on which the Czech Hussites, fulfilling the last wish of blind Jan Žižka of Trocnov,[13] stretched his skin, which was removed from him as soon as he died.

This drum, reminding everyone, friends and enemies, of Žižka's brilliance and victories, is also evidence of the utter, hopeless shame of the knight cavalries of Germany, Italy and France which the Hussite troops and peasants took with chains, scythes and crossbows, as they wanted, killing the mounted knights by the thousands, at Shkaredny Prud, Malesov and Německý Brod, and, indeed, everywhere they were encountered.

There is supposedly only a single, indisputable example of the horse's effectiveness in war in all of mankind's history, the original story of Cortez's conquistadores.

Although, it has to be said even here that it wasn't so smooth.

To begin with, one may recall that Cortez's savage enemies, Montezuma's warriors, had never seen horses before.

It also is worth recalling that as soon as one of the horses was killed and another severely wounded, the Indians' fear of the horses was replaced by diabolical ingenuity, directed at killing as many horses as possible.

At first (after the Battle at Tobasco), Cortez very successfully tricked the savages, by appearing it seems on behalf of his horses.

They had been positioned as certain demonic creatures, thirsting for Aztec blood, fierce, uncompromising and invulnerable.

As is known, to make a great impression on the caciques who had arrived for negotiations, Cortez made arrangements to conceal a mare in one of the tents, sat the caciques with their backs exactly toward this tent, and led a stallion toward them.

The latter, sensing a near-by mare in heat, of course, demonstrated everything for which it was capable.

The historians modestly mention every pawing there of the front foot, the neighing and the rolling of eyes.

It is considered that this gimmick using the stallion even shocked Hernan Cortez's painted guests, but I suppose that the stallion allowed himself to "drop" (he had an erection).

Not knowing anything about the concealed mare, the caciques personalized everything demonstrated by the stallion.

Primarily the erection.

Finally they panicked.

They easily accepted the prospect of being killed, but they didn't really want to be raped by such a monster, too.

Everything went very smoothly for Cortez, all the way to the first battle with the Tlaxcalteca, who, it is possible, were not as afraid of sexual abuse.

All of Cortez's horses were wounded in the very first battle with them.

The Spaniards had the sense to conceal this in any way possible, but the information about the vulnerability of the horses was spread nonetheless, and Montezuma's army already had built pits with sharp stakes for luring the horses into them and destroying them.

Somewhat later (the conquistador chronicles sadly show), Juan de Escalante and his horse were killed in the region of Nautla.

The possibility of really killing a horse, which had been represented to the Aztecs as a supernatural and immortal being, transformed the consciousness of Cortez's enemies, after which all the conquered coastal regions immediately fell out of Spanish control.

In the urban conflicts that followed in Mexico and other places, the Indians first targeted and destroyed the horses.

Bernal Diaz, a chronicler of the conquistadors, carried on the legend of the horse's martyrdom perfectly.

He describes how Cortez's chestnut stallion died. The same one with whose penis Hernando Cortez had fooled the caciques in front of the tent.

He also reports how a crowd of Indians stabbed Pedro de Alvorado's light bay to death, how the black El Arriero perished, how the gray mare of Alonza died... and so on.

The conquistadors lost 45 horses in only one night while breaking out of Mexico.

Even a most superficial analysis of this war indicates that, as soon as the natives found out the degree of the horse's vulnerability, everything took its normal, military course and the conquistador's conflicts were not especially distinguished in any way from the usual conflicts of world history. The Indians had learned to kill the horses and stopped being afraid of them, and the Spaniards learned to rely only on their infantry in this savage war.

Cortez, by the way, well understood how much he owed horses, and made mention of them very emotionally, with great pain and passion, ascribing the original, initial success of his astonishing adventures, as he expressed it, "to the horse and to god."

To give him his due, he had the priorities right.

As it is remembered, Cortez sincerely did everything to maintain good relations with the conquered Aztecs: he publicly killed looters from among his own solders, judged and even somehow slightly punished rapists... overall, as it is called, he valued relations with the population. It is all the more striking that, learning about the murder by Indians of two horses, Cortez burnt eight chiefs alive who were involved indirectly in this murder. The emotions, however!

Generally, both the early and later Middle Ages know examples of weird sensibility for those times.

Rus, February, 1150. Outside Lutsk, in a battle between the Izyaslav of Kiev's people and Yuriy Dolgoruki, his combat steed was fatally wounded beneath Yuriy's son, Andrei.

Andrei Yurevich demanded Byzantine monks administer the last rites and administer the sacrament to the steed before its death. The holy men refused, saying that "cattle and horses have no place in the heavenly kingdom."

And then, despite the Christian traditions of a century and a half, Andrei Yurievich committed a sinful deed according to church measures, invoking the blessing of the old Slavic gods, he ordered the steed buried in an old heathen rite, with military honors and the erection of a burial mound over its body. "I have sinned bravely and gladly. If there is no place in the Heavenly Kingdom for this horse, then there is no place for me there."

Probably neither the brunette Spaniard in the crumpled and blood-stained cuirass nor the Russian bearded prince in his sables were cavalrymen. In the most direct meaning of this word. But both of them suspected that the horse was something more than a means of military transport. However, they were devilishly lonely in history and already, clearly, they were unable to change anything about it.

* * *

Machiavelli was right, speaking about antiquity and about his own era, and his words about the invulnerability of an organized infantry to the cavalry was confirmed repeatedly even at the latest of times.

Generally, the cavalry's tactical weakness was commonplace, everyone acquainted with military history knew it.

But surprising creatures continued to be born in the environment of the developed primates that had a special, pathological store of consciousness, in whom disregard for others' lives, human and even more so horse, was a physiological, natural manifestation.

But it could be worse! Besides disregard for others' lives, these creatures always believed that they were born into the world for a certain change in the outcome of human history.

They grew up and certainly became generals. Unfortunately, almost always in the cavalry.

And these generals a hundred, five hundred, a thousand times commanded, sending the mounted multitudes into harm's way.

In the battle of Pavia (1525), 1,500 Basques, armed with harquebuses, easily and without any losses shot down the French knights, who were thrown under the storm of bullets by Francis the First at the drop of a hat, in desperate hope of certain «moral effect» of the knights' attack.

In Sedan (1870) five French regiments (chasseurs and hussars) received an order to attack the Prussian infantry. Everything had been known in advance, but the attack took place anyhow.

In less than an hour, five regiments were destroyed by a mass barrage and practically all the people and horses perished. The Prussian infantry itself lost three men.

The year is 1941. The village of Muzino.

General Dovator's two thousand Soviet cavalrymen received an order to attack German positions of the 41st artillery brigade. Two thousand horses were killed by German machine-gun fire in less than 20 minutes. Several riders broke through to the German positions and were killed there by rifle fire.

The German unit did not lose one man.

The history of the cavalry is saturated with such attacks.

At the same time, don't forget, in addition, about the existence of the "caltrop" and all the other hazardous devices deliberately planted to injure cavalry horses. All peoples at all times made use of these devices which made any attack by cavalry both senseless and disastrous for the attackers. The fields of large clashes, where an attack of enemy cavalry was expected (in accordance with the terrain or tactical situation), were seeded with these "caltrops" as thickly as possible. A multitude of diversions and maneuvers existed, the purpose of which was to scatter as many caltrops as possible in places where enemy horses might be.

They were used everywhere.

Any museum of a historic collection, even the poorest, counts hundreds of such caltrops of very different types. With hooks on the ends of the thorns and without hooks, with faceted stingers and flat. Such a phenomenal wealth of exhibits of this type is connected with the fact that very many of them have been preserved, they are very cheap and they find very many of them in excavations and when plowing fields.

I discovered a full box (about 15 kilograms) of Swedish, Dutch, Russian and German caltrops in the Arsenal files of the Knight's Hall at the Hermitage. Even I was not able to precisely attribute all of them to their "nationality," inasmuch as the caltrop was an international, ubiquitous, conventional thing.

It is a very cunning device (see table V, **5**). When it is thrown, it always lands with the sharp end upwards and is absolutely stable any ground. And it is perfectly unnoticeable in grass, sand and even in mud.

A horse cut on a caltrop receives a terribly intense and deep puncture of the hoof. The sting of a caltrop passes through the horny sole of the hoof to the deep flexor tendon and to the navicular and coffin bones.

A horse, continuing its movement ahead through inertia, drives the caltrop ever deeper into the leg, turns it over there and converts the hoof into a bloody mass.

A wound like this was always fatal for the horse in the conditions of a lack of antiseptics and anti-tetanus vaccine.

The inability take a step on the affected leg and the terrible painful shock made the horse so lame that it was impossible to force it to move even with beatings. [b]

Caltrops were known in Assyria, Scythia, medieval Europe, in Asia, and later, everywhere and at all times.

The fates of cavalry attacks were not decided by archers and arbalesters nor bullets and grapeshot. Although they threw everything primarily at the horses, for they were larger and easier targets, their fates were decided by those small caltrops which were sown in the battlefields and engagement sites.

Everyone, in every army of the world and at all times, knew about the caltrops, about the fact that they could be everywhere, and that getting one of them into a horse's foot was the death of it. And a cavalry flying recklessly at full tilt at an enemy is a cinematic pack of lies and nothing more.

(By the way, that freedom with which the conquistadors at first made mincemeat of the Aztecs, that effectiveness of a direct equestrian attack which so astounded their enemies, was connected most of all with the fact that caltrops were completely unknown to Montezuma's warriors. They were, obviously, the only people of the world who did not know them for a long while. By as early as Pizarro's time, the caltrops would appear even here.)

Armor for horses also is a myth.

It is possible to put as much iron as one likes onto a horse, but it is impossible to protect its most fragile parts, its legs, while not paralyzing the horse's motor functions completely.

And in reality the horse's legs are strikingly fragile.

Almost any injury to the legs has major consequences for the horse. Any blow, whether with a stone, stick, axe or a shield would make the horse instantly lame and unsuitable for further combat.

In the Battle of Legnica (1241), when Batu's Mongols met face-to-face with Western European knights, the Mongols purposefully and uniformly destroyed the knights' horses in particular, hacking off and firing at their legs. It wasn't difficult for them from their short horses (nearly 120-125 centimeters high to the withers). The Mongolian bowmen at Legnica virtually didn't fire at the knights themselves or the protected chests of the horses.

Organized, precise and with fiendish accuracy, they fired at the horses legs, piercing the carpus and fetlock. (The carpus or fetlock, or the horse's hock are a rather large target for a good shot from a bow).

Grand Duke Henry II the Pious of Poland and Silesia perished in approximately the same way — the Mongols pierced all four legs of his mount, and then they beat Henry the Pious with bludgeons and hatchets.

Then the whole thing ended, by the way, with the Mongols' complete victory, as did all other clashes with heavy knight elements.

The Mongols knew better than anyone how to be merciless when it came to horses and possibly knew better than their enemies how to kill horses quickly and in huge numbers. (They had colossal experience in this matter, for the Mongols grew up only on horse meat and actually were brought up with horse blood which they drank in great quantity and with much satisfaction.)

Horse armor in no way hindered those massive horse massacres which the Mongols arranged both outside Legnica and near Sandomir, and in all the battles of the "Magyar" and "Polish" campaigns.

I had occasion to examine thoroughly the real fighting armor of European horses.

For hours, and very closely.

Only at Warwick Castle in England was I able to find on an armor crupper something looking like the marks of blows from a halberd or a large lance. But all the other horse armor does not have any combat perforations on its upper part.

The strike of a crossbow's "bolt" or a long arrow from a heavy bow leaves a very characteristic mark on any medieval armor, both a man's and a horse's.

There are hardly any of them on any piece of horse armor.

I am not talking about parade, ceremonial, gilded or inlaid chaffrons,ᶜ cruppers or peytrels.

I have in mind the relatively simple combat armor which was, by all indications, in frequent usage.

By "all indications," I mean the presence of old horse hair on the inside face, where the armor "joint" always and without fail rubbed the horse's skin.

By the way, judging by the abundance of these little hairs, which are removed easily from these joints with tweezers, there is the suspicion that often there was no horse blanket worn beneath the armor. Many horses bore this armor, since the tweezers retrieved strands of all colors from these joints and short summer strands as well as long winter hairs.

Gigantic depressions, which are created on the armor because a horse has fallen, and which was carefully straightened later, were noticed on much of the armor.

But there are hardly any signs either of arrow hits or direct blows with a sword or lance on this armor, despite the fact that they clearly were worn a lot and in very different circumstances.

It is possible to conjecture precisely from all these objects that all the blows were addressed only to the legs, stomach and underside of the neck; that is, those places where in principle no armor can go.

The bas-reliefs of Trajan's Column preserve outright fantasy depictions of Sarmatian horses dressed in a certain "tricot" of scale armor. The whole horse, including the legs, hooves and nostrils, would have been covered, as if the armor was glued to the horse, armor which, ideally, was made of boiled and straightened horses' hooves.

If this were really the case, then the thickness of the horse's legs would have been doubled, owing to the thickness of the "armor" which had a certain base and backing of horny fragments. Under those circumstances, any bending of the legs would have been absolutely impossible.

Nevertheless, the immunity of Sarmatian horses, according to the evidence both of Arrian and Pausanias, was in reality very fundamental and exceeded everything imaginable — thus giving rise to the fantasy armor "tricot" on the bas-reliefs.

The fundamental nature of the scales that covered the upper neck, chest and croup totally did not interfere with the Roman infantryman's constantly beating the Sarmatian cavalry, which they did in Moesia (winter of 69), and during the Marcomannic Wars (173) and during the Roman-Dacian wars, when the Sarmatians were loyal allies of the Dacian king Decebalus.

The transportation of horses to war is a separate history.

Let's take "civilized" times, the very beginning of the Boer Wars (1899).

Lord Blackzuoev, a lieutenant of the ninth lancers, reports in a letter to his father the details of carrying English cavalry horses via the Indian Ocean. (A short forward: they transported horses either on a ship's upper deck, partitioning off the deck into hundreds of tiny compartments with boards, or on the gun deck, the weapons deck. Aboard the "Sarah," which was carrying English cavalry horses, a procedure for the layout had been adopted on the upper deck.)

"The tossing was intolerable, and the waves huge. The wooden enclosures of the stalls did not hold out... The whole deck was covered with a mass of horses fighting for their lives mixed together with the boards from the stalls. This whole giant heap (several hundred horses) was being thrown forcefully from one side to the other. As early as the first few seconds of this horror, the majority of horses were terribly injured, their eyes put out with sharp pieces that had broken from the boards and their legs were broken. I managed to shoot my own mount with my revolver, and I am glad that not one of my horses experienced such horror as the other horses…

A huge tank with water was torn away and, while rolling about, began to crush the horses who lay on the wet deck with broken legs."

If one totals Lord Blackzuoev's letter content, the rough seas killed 83 horses in 12 hours.

To this day there are the "Horse Latitudes" on all the world's maritime maps. If a ship that was transporting horses for the conquest and settling of America was becalmed, sometimes for several weeks, and sometimes for several months, then fresh water was the first thing to run out.

Then they brought all the horses from the gun decks to the upper deck and threw them overboard while still alive.

It was all very simple, an ordinary consideration. Horses die very quickly without water. But if one waits for their death on a gun deck, then the sailors would have to drag out that 500 kilogram body by themselves.

Therefore, while the horses were still able to walk on their own, they led them to the deck and drowned them in the ocean.

Hence the name, "Horse Latitude," is in memory of the hundreds and thousands of Spanish horses who died here in the middle of the ocean.

General de Champalier, well-known for the candor of his maxims, once said: "The best military horse is a horse that can suffer for a very long time."

Probably Champalier had in mind, "to suffer while not dying."

It is possible to suspect the second meaning; however, then this general and speaker of maxims looks like a completely blunt sadist.

But he was merely a cavalry general and practitioner and, most likely, he preserved a certain solecism in his maxims.

Let's dwell nonetheless on my interpretation of the famous maxim. It becomes fully understood and sounds completely candid: "The best military horse is a horse that can suffer while not dying for a very long time." [14]

In this revelation is all the sense, all the predestination of the military horse.

It is useless to search for the secrets of relationships of horse and man in the history of the cavalry.

There is nothing in this history except the horse's pain and the horse's death.

Nothing, except the most obvious signs of man's deafness and haughtiness, his wild, stupid and primitive cruelty which characterizes his "low biological origin" better than any Darwin.

I assume I have been able to dot all the i's and demolish once and for all the myth of cavalryman.

I had to do it to teach the correctness and purity of the horse's understanding, his soul, fate and nature.

It is impossible to leave these lush mythological weeds un-pulled.

The truth is an offensive thing and it is not always absolutely necessary, but sometimes one does need to know it.

Let those who want to jump across the painted poles or ride in the troikas, or make sausage from the horse believe in the myth of the cavalry.

It is this public that, as a rule, actually cultivates this myth.

But those who desire to really understand the horse will have to say good-bye to this myth.

At the same time, we have to do the same thing with the direct descendant of the cavalry, equestrianism.

The death of another being has always been the purpose of war.

War itself was an absolute norm of the primate's life. The history of developed primates is marinated, infused, saturated with death, as the vodka of "gorilka" is infused with pepper, until obtaining today's ultimate strength. (True, today we have learned to add flavoring substances so that it isn't quite so revolting to the taste.)

But, as early as the tenth century B.C., the strength of this potion already had so alarmed mankind that they began en masse to make up a different kind of religion, the essence of which came down to the need and ability to bring the dead back to life.

There are many such religions, Christianity only stuck its own label on this most commercial and ideological success story, which had begun with Osiris. (Just about anyone was risen from the dead. Baldr, "the sanguine god of light" who was killed on the day of Ragnarök, arose from the dead, and his dad, Odin, who was crucified on the world tree named Yggdrasil and stabbed with a spear, the Sumerian Tammuz and Inanna arose, and the Finnish Lemminkäinen, the resurrected son of Zeus, Heracles, was raised into heaven, Adonis rose up, and Avalokiteshvara the embodiment of the Bodhisattvas, and even the bully King Arthur contrived to rise from the dead on the quiet.)

It is notable that the religions which assessed the world most honestly and subtly and that changed it most profoundly, such as Taoism and Zen Buddhism, didn't even hint at resurrection. They understood the extremely primitive opportunism of the subject and shunned it, leaving its manipulation to second and third class religions.

Horses somehow didn't have very much luck in this eternal mythological carnival of universal resurrections.

It is known only that the ancient Japanese Amaterasu, the sun goddess, shocked by a prank of the god Susanoò (of that same Shinto pantheon), left the world in a prolonged black shadow and flatly refused sunlight to the people and her fellow gods.

Forever.

What roused her to abandon people and the gods of the world was that Susanoò had peeled the skin off a live horse while amusing himself.

What's the big deal!

The whole history of the cavalry over thousands of years was doing just that.

Before she died, Madam Cavalry provided herself with a worthy heir in the form of equestrianism, which has continued her business, although in a somewhat more theatrical and fully senseless version.

In the times of Mama Cavalry there was at least a kind of purpose to the activity, for example, the delivery of some message, some important dispatch.

True, it was only the usual nonsense of the usual generals that was contained in the dispatch, the horses were killed off nonetheless, but at least it was not just for laughs, for entertaining the public.

Three-day eventing or the steeplechase reconstruct that very same situation. It is unclear why.

There is nothing to be achieved anymore, but they kill the horses all the same.

Probably a genetic habit, an addiction, of wanting to see pain, suffering, and the horse's death developed in mankind over thousands of years.

And this craving for torture at times is so strong and persistent, that the "junkies" contrive the 3-day event, flat races, harness racing, dressage or show jumping to satisfy it, to "get their fix."

A study of the history of the military horse and the history of the cavalry makes it possible to unmistakably determine the origin of sadism in equestrianism and the other human amusements in which the horse participates.

By the way, you remember that when beginning this chapter, I promised you to find at least one thing valuable and enlightening in the whole history of the horse at war.

Something, any small glimmer of light.

Here it is, that small glimmer.

General Custer, a regular maniacal U.S. Army cavalry general, decided to finish off the remaining Oglala-Sioux and their allies, the Cheyenne. His main enemy was a Sioux military leader of unthinkable courage by the name of Thašuŋka Witko (Crazy Horse).

A battle ensued on Saturday, June 25, 1876, near the Little Big Horn in Montana.

General Custer finally encountered Thašuŋka Witko.

When it all had ended, the carefully scalped general was cooling on the field together with his own 7th cavalry, which he, rushing to the attack, sincerely called "The Magnificent Seventh."

The "Magnificent Seventh," also completely liberated of their scalps, lay so densely, that the ground was not visible among the horse and human bodies.

Crazy Horse's warriors had killed them all and departed.

When Nowlan and Benteen's cavalry units, late for their own deaths, caught up, they didn't see one wounded man. There were neither groans nor movement. Only the dead.

The wind whistled through the multicolored feathers of the Sioux and Cheyenne arrows with which the backs, stomachs and faces of the "Magnificent Seventh" were covered.

And suddenly a steed lifted itself up from among the mass of dead and stood over the field. Wounded and bleeding, with its saddle having shifted to beneath its stomach.

Staring blankly.

Lieutenant Henry Nowlan recognized Captain Keogh's horse.

They called the horse Comanche.

He had received this lofty name at Bluff Creek in Kansas, during a war with the Comanches. He had received it for bravery and stamina, which the horse of the American cavalrymen had in common with this great tribe.

How he had survived here on the field of the Little Big Horn is completely unclear.

Without exception, all the Seventh Cavalry horses either had been killed by the Sioux or shot by the cavalrymen themselves, who then had used their bodies for cover.

As history testifies, the cavalrymen who had discovered Comanche at first wanted to kill him, to put him out of his misery.

But a certain Gustave Korn, a farrier, was found among them who decided to give Comanche a chance. Having discerned the steed's awful wounds, Korn was shattered. But then it was again decided to give him a chance, and then again Korn was so upset that he decided to shoot him anyhow. But suddenly, a threatening telegraphic order arrived from Washington where they already had heard about the horror of the Little Big Horn. "All survivors onto the steamer!"

But only Comanche had survived.

So, in fulfilling the order, they began to evacuate him with all ceremony and safeguards.

They led the horse for a long and agonizing time. Essentially, they carried him all of 15 miles, to the river head where the steamer was located and onto which the wounded were supposed to be taken away.

They made a shelter and put down bedding on the deck for him. A veterinarian fixed 12 severe wounds from arrows and bullets.

Comanche recovered from his wounds and made a complete recovery at the base of the Seventh at Fort Lincoln.

Another directive arrived from Washington on the anniversary of the Little Big Horn, the result of which was a phenomenal Seventh American Cavalry regiment order.

Here is that order (I am quoting it verbatim):

1. The horse known as "Comanche" being the only living representative of the bloody tragedy of the Little Big Horn, Montana, June 25, 1876, his kind treatment and comfort should be a matter of special pride and solicitude on the part of the 7th Cavalry, to the end that his life may be prolonged to the utmost limit.

2. The commanding officer must watch that the steed always be provided with comfortable quarters built especially for him. No one, neither a single man nor under any circumstances has the right to force it to do any work and no one can ride it…

This unique order was carried out honestly for all of Comanche's life.

He lived at Fort Riley in Kansas.

He was permitted everything.

He grazed on lawns and flower beds and he ate the first, most tender roses on the large rose bushes, but most of all he loved sunflowers bedecked with dew.

He would poke his head into windows, lay it on a window sill and was able to study human life attentively and amicably for a long time.

No one had the right to shout at or to hit him.

He wandered where he wanted with the colts who lived at the fort, and when he wanted, he dozed in his own comfortable stall or galloped about the fields.

Judging by the numerous photos preserved of Comanche in retirement, he was a bay and a very good and beautiful steed.

If Comanche decided to take a nap in the sun at a place where a regimental formation was taking place, then a certain special signal was given to the regimental bugler and the bugler, quietly, barely blew into his horn in order not to awaken the old horse.

What is most startling is, the presence of the retiree called Comanche, his happiness and tranquility, provided to the Seventh Cavalry "a kind of strange turnaround in relation to the horse."

I don't want to invent or think up anything that perhaps does not exist, I don't know of what it consisted and how this "turnaround in relation" looked, to which one of the Seventh Cavalry captains niggardly refers.

I assume, I hope, and I am certain it was a very good turnaround.

Just think, man possibly for the first time after many centuries saw what a horse's happiness looks like. And man found out that the sight of a horse's happiness is completely captivating.

And this equine happiness, under close investigation, changed people in a cardinal manner, awaking in them a sort of completely irrational desire in no way connected to the usual everyday logic of primates.

Desires, despite any expenses, to make the life of at least several more horses as happy as was Comanche's life.

For his portraits were published in all the American newspapers of that time. Everyone knew his story.

Very many maimed cavalry horses were purchased at that time and settled into a quiet happy life on small ranches a la Comanche.

American citizens who were devoted to his fate tried to buy Comanche himself, the star of the Little Big Horn, but all these attempts were decisively rejected by Washington and the "Magnificent Seventh."

Packages came for him from all over America.

"Care" packages...

Oats, sugar, choice hay, cakes covered with powdered sugar and salted toast, endless horse cloths with monograms and embroidery, with lace edgings, horseshoes cast from pure silver and the softest of brushes.

People wrote him letters!

Children wrote, and the elderly, crotchety single waitresses, sad dealers in screws, streetwalkers, sedate carpenters and hysterical men who gambled.

They consulted with him. They poured out their souls to him.

When enough letters had piled up, a pimply, melancholy corporal, having seized the opportunity when Comanche was standing relatively still, quietly read them to the steed, stopping only to sniffle and wipe his eyes clean with a dirty, purple fist.

Comanche died on November 6, 1891, at the age of 29, having lived 15 years in complete happiness.

This chapter is finished.

And the story of the cavalry has ended for mankind, thank god.

Trust me, I have spared your feelings and not described the very, very many tempers, habits and military rituals of different times and peoples known to me. Among them are those even more awful than what ended up in this, the fourth chapter of the "Horse Crucified and Risen" which is called "War."

Man has justified his stupidity and cruelty in regard to the horse with a certain need. First, the need for the military.

Now this need no longer exists.

But the craving for torture, the addiction, has remained, as I have already mentioned above.

However, this craving can be overcome. Junkies can kick the habit. As I have already said, those who are involved with equestrianism, the confirmed certified sadists, make up less than one percent. All others either do not understand what they are doing or are afraid to think about it.

Because, having thought about it, one has to change.

For the world is changing.

And a changing world gives birth to ever more and more startling people who are capable of understanding the horse and being understood by him.

---

[a]   Rustre (french) — english example "rough" or "curmudgeon".

[b]   A well-known circus figure, the "gallop on three legs" is trained for three-four months, repeated again for half a year, and only afterwards becomes the "gallop on three legs," though forced and deformed, but nonetheless a way of moving the horse around a flat arena. What-

ever Fillis lied about in this regard, it is done with typical circus cruelty: The front right or left legs are held tightly with a belt in a folded bend and picked up toward the surcingle or rib by which the horse is girdled. The horse is taught to run in a gallop in such a state with the aid of blows, of course. By the way, the circus understands how torturous this movement is for the horse, and training it takes a very long and very gradual time.

I have mentioned the "gallop on three legs" only in order to dispel any doubts about the horse's ability to move in such a way "on three legs" immediately after receiving a deep hoof wound.

ᶜ   Chaffron is a horse's combat mask (as a rule, steel or bronze).

HOME

Chapter Five

alent is a scary thing.

Gaius Suetonius Tranquillus was fiendishly talented. His book "The Twelve Caesars" has been a worldwide bestseller for 18 centuries now.

It was he who concocted the so alluring and successful genre of the dirty politician.

In particular, Suetonius made clear that spots of blood and sex form a magical pattern on the page that always will be of greater interest to the reading public than any of the letters there.

With his magic touch, people who were confused, sophisticated and intimidated by the world and who had on their imperial shoulders the whole foundation of the world, which was then ancient Rome, merrily represent rascals, monsters, perverts and schizoids.

And thus they will remain forever, for the son of a Roman legionnaire, Suetonius, besides having a colossal literary talent, also has a certain status as a primary source for historians.

A status, by the way, which is extremely doubtful, for Suetonius had never actually seen any of those about whom he wrote.

True, he had time to rummage through the old scrolls and listen to his crazy grandfather, who was the 36th extinguisher of the 84th torch at the court and was fully able to gather certain gossip and retell it to his grandson.

But no more than that.

Nonetheless, the youthful Roman emperor, Caligula, whose name literally means "Little Boots," was cut down by drunken centurions, finished off by historians and thoroughly defamed by film makers. He was the son of the emperor Germanicus, a boy who grew up behind the palisades of the legion's camps. The old praetorians would lay him down to sleep on his own cloak, sheltering him from the rains with their hacked shields. It was the same Little Boots-Caligula, who in reality was adored by thousands, and didn't even read the denunciation about an attempt on his life and wouldn't believe it, declaring that he "was not able to arouse hatred in any way in anyone." However, he was represented by the liar Suetonius as some kind of completely fanatic scum.

Caligula has remained that way in history.

No one cared about his true personality or his authentic appearance any longer; it was of no interest to anyone because the very talented Gaius Suetonius Tranquillus offered an image somewhat more tantalizing and alluring, an image of a wild libertine and a schizoid spiller of blood.

In a word, Caligula's depravity was somewhat hackneyed and commonplace, and his historic physiognomy was distorted by the grimace of lust forever.

However, if one were to rummage among those same scrolls in which the old man Suetonius rummaged at one time, it suddenly would become apparent that it was Caligula who banished from Rome the "Spintria," a sect of admirers of the vilest of sexual amusements cherished by the emperor Tiberius.

Gaius Caligula was urged not to drown the "Spintria" in the sea, which he wanted to do, obeying the natural, and judging by the scrolls, great and genuine feeling of disgust toward the libertines.

This is how talented people, historians and writers, turn white into black.

The miraculous power of art.

Tacitus and other serious historians never were so categorically negative in regard to Caligula. Nor, by the way, in regard to other heroes of their history.

But, Tacitus and others like him are "dull" and therefore read only by despondent historians who sadly burrow their own worm holes through the annals with their careful study, while picking their noses in vain and printing insipid little articles in obscure digests. Suetonius, on the other hand, was, is and will be an absolute hit.

Everyone will continue to read him as they have always read him. They will quote and make films based on his work.

Blood and sex are, after all, a way better information commodity than any kind of real history. It has been that way forever and so it will be. (By the way, even a cursory acquaintance with Josephus' "Chapter 18" easily explains both the real reasons for Caligula's murder and for his posthumous defamation.)

I read the history of the Little Boots emperor for the first time when I was about seven.

Of course, in Gaius Suetonius Tranquillus' scandalous, canonical account.

And I believed hardly a word of it.

But when I read how the centurion who struck the blow, missing Caligula's neck, cut his chin, and Caligula fell, bellowing to the conspirators: "I am still alive!" and how the ancient Roman officers finished off Little Boots before his bodyguard's very eyes, I thought about what happened with Incitatus, that very steed whom Caligula, shocking the court and the world, decided to bring into the Senate, making him a consul.

The steed's story is almost unknown.

Judging by the fact that after Caligula's assassination, a certain "centurion Julius Lupus [15] beat against a wall" even Caligula's tiny daughter, Incitatus didn't survive for long.

They probably vented their feelings on him.

The more so in that Incitatus had a "legal" home, "a palace with servants and utensils," which were presented to him by Little Boots, and secured for him in accordance with all the codes of Roman law.

Observing legal standards, it was possible to confiscate a person's home only if he was dead or had been banished.

And the house was good.

Its sweet splendor shines even through Suetonius' spiteful lines.

A black stallion in a purple horse cloth and pearls wandered in the evenings around all the rooms of his home, clip-clopping past the white rows of statues and columns in the triclinium. [a]

The servants unfastened bronze fibulae, removed the horse cloth and the stallion slowly entered a basin of warm water (steaming a bit in the cool night), in the middle of the main hall's atrium.

The praetorian guard wandered around Incitatus' house with swords drawn, insisting on quiet so that nothing bothered the stallion.

All this was thanks, of course, to the good man, Gaius Caligula, though the horse was absolutely indifferent to the level of his home's aestheticism.

The stable's beauty speaks only to the warder's nobility, but says nothing about the habits or desires of the prisoner.

This in no way detracts from Gaius' service as the founder of the ideology of correct equine management, management in which everything is supposed to serve the horse's safety and his comfort.

He wasn't right about every single thing, but he laid a fine foundation.

Moreover, I am deeply convinced that a normal stable should also be partly a religious structure, with a certain unnecessary luxury, and an excess of aestheticism.

It does not matter that the horse is indifferent to these things. Nowhere in any temple or sanctuary are the tastes and preferences of the resident deity taken into account.

Perhaps Little Boots was simply shaking up ancient Roman society, but I suppose he was frank in his desire to provide a very comfortable life for Incitatus.

He despised man's world, though he felt it and knew it well. Judging by everything, he was noble and passionate, and sought to express his sensitive nature outside the company of other people, away from the human world.

In any case, in speaking about the horse's home, that is, about a stable, I must immediately and honestly warn you that whatever we do for the delight and relief of the horse's stable life will never be appreciated by him.

In our relationship with the horse, the value of the horse's "clothing" or the presence of air conditioners or split systems or the open work structure of gratings in the stable, has no meaning or relevance.

These are all purely human amusements, and the one for whom all this splendor is created will always remain indifferent toward it, because his true home is absolute freedom.

Nonetheless, from the times of the pharaohs to the present time, people go insane erecting and decorating stables.

The stables of Prince Condé in Chantilly, not far from Paris, and now called the Living Horse Museum, have been preserved into our time as the chief example of man's romanticized notions of an equine home.

It really is a phenomenally beautiful and endlessly long building. It is highly arched and resonant, filled overhead with the squeals of bats and the coos of pigeons, and below with snoring, snorting, chewing, the delicate sounds of straw being crumpled by horses' feet, the rich sounds of dung falling from beneath their tails and the clatter of hooves on the ancient stone of the paths.

The deep, hellish bray of a gigantic Poitou donkey that also lives here destroys the nobility and harmony of this great "symphony of the stable" exactly once every other hour.

It is possible that, like all donkeys, he cannot endure the silence for too long.

The horses and ponies react philosophically to the Poitou's bray.

The infinite length of the stable building is interrupted exactly in the middle by a small manége, the circle of which is framed by carved, grey French stone that goes all the way to the incredible height of the main dome.

A youthful black woman in a red coat with a high collar eternally does a passage on the black Friesian.

Behind the manége is the lifeless museum section, where everything has been collected that has the least to do with the horse and where two endless ranks of dusty, wooden stallions demonstrate horse cloths, saddles, serreta and the stirrups of various eras and peoples.

And here are the carved gold of old round-bellied carriages and faded mummies of horses in histrionic poses.

Behind the carriage doors, inside, if one secretly opens them, are thick dust and silken seats that have been pulled apart, the wool wrenched from the cushions, as well as pigeon droppings.

On the dusty carriage floor, covered by the footprints of mice, are the crushed glass of a lorgnette and an old pistol flint.

It is quiet here. The pigeons and bats cannot be heard. But exactly once every other hour the Poitou's hellish bray reaches even here, amplified by the gigantic arches from the living stable.

There are almost no visitors here. Sometimes little old men wearing derbies wander in clacking their canes on the flagstone, cough, then disappear into the tiny, dark vaulted corridors leading to the "horseshoe" or "boots" or "anatomical" halls, where there are thousands of horseshoes, hundreds of hardened boots, rusty equipment for clipping horses and shamelessly scarlet and green plastic casts of horse intestines, hearts and legs.

The history of the stables is pompous, but nice.

Somewhere here the heart of Prince Condé rests.

His actual heart.

When Condé died and his heart had stopped, a court surgeon removed if from the prince's chest, in accordance with his dying wish.

Condé asked that his heart be buried among his horses, in the home to which he devoted his whole life and whole being.

It is easy to imagine how the wax from the candles poured in a golden rain onto the worn flagstone of the floor, how the horses snorted in the darkness behind the surgeon and the prince's valet, who, following Condé's last will and testament, rushed about the corridors of the stables with Condé's still-bleeding heart wrapped in blue velvet, seeking a place for it.

Nonetheless, the Living Horse Museum in Chantilly is not a good stable after all, despite all the romanticism, zealousness, and architectural histrionics.

Histrionics are histrionics, but some of the horses have box stalls, and the rest live in straight stalls.

The straight stalls are intolerable.

That sort of confinement implies tying the horse's head to the wall, making it impossible for him to lie down. It is an outrageous disgrace!

I fully do not intend to waste time on groaning about the freedom lost by the horse or the prison-like essence of a stable.

One may complain, of course, but that will not change the essence of it. Right now there is no other way to guarantee the horse a life, health and security except by giving him shelter.

The stables of Prince Conde at Chantilly, which are situated not far from Paris and now called "The Live Horse Museum," still remain the main example of the human romantic idea of how a horse's home should look.

Furthermore, preserving the horse's health under stable conditions is a separate, difficult job, requiring a great deal of specialized hippological knowledge and equipment, and the conscious shame of one's role as a jailer.

One could vigorously stick his thumbs into the cut of his vest, adjust his historical pince-nez and start to fulminate against the ways of life of the various stables.

It is not difficult, since mankind has exhibited and exhibits infinite ignorance, avarice and indifference to the problems of the horse's confinement.

Both in training and in confinement almost nothing but idiocy has been observed throughout history, with rare exceptions.

But everyone needs a home, a place of safety and comfort, where no one can harm him or force him to do anything against his will.

The stable has been a place of special torment for the horse for 3,000 years, with the possible exception of Incitatus' home, Comanche's last residence, and two or three other inspiring cases.

In the manége and the field, the horse, having rebelled, has at least a short bit of freedom from human stupidity and cruelty. But, in the barbarous, suffocating darkness of the stall, the horse is completely defenseless before man.

Man rules the horse completely here.

Here in the stable, man has been practicing veterinary medicine over the course of several thousand years.

The schizoid quality of these practices is incredible, but I shall not allow myself to make fun even of the most barbarous of them, since the intentions were to cure or ease suffering.

It is enough to read that Gueriniere, in the last part of his "School of Horsemanship," cites a prescription and method for treating horses.

Pumping vinegar into horse though the nostrils, the forcible feeding of fish bellies, bloodletting and repeated saltpeter enemas with eternal refrain (table 8, **9**) are still the most innocent of the veterinary "amusements" of that time.

Published in 1774, Johann Bernhard Fischer's "Medication Handbook" proposes acting in the following manner in the event of "urinary constipation." "Place a little salt into its rear, dampen the sacrum with spirits and set it alight."

And there is another prescription: "Let swarms of fleas and bedbugs into the urinary tract so that they strain the bladder with their tickling."

If setting the horse aflame and shoving fleas into his sex organs did not help, a third, radical method followed, "bury the horse up to its sacral bone in warm manure; however, so that the front part sticks out."

I am not joking about this and I do not seek out bizarre cases; I chose examples which appeared first on the page I opened at random in the "Medication Handbook."

I fully admit that a definite quantity of errors has to have been made so that veterinary medicine could become a real science and effective practice.

However, it is a disturbing fact that over thousands of years the prescriptions of old veterinary medicine have stayed roughly the same, despite their ineffectiveness or deadly effect.

Unlike veterinary medicine, human medicine has evolved; it did not deliberately seek out deadly medicines and murderous treatment methods.

Veterinary medicine, precisely reflecting public notions about the horse as a being that dies easily and is generally dispensable, has made no headway, repeating the rot about bloodletting, saltpeter and burials in dung heaps from century to century.

A comparison with human medicine is not advantageous for veterinary medicine — while human medicine has evolved, quite a lot of what veterinarians practice successfully even now is essentially the medicine of Hippocrates' time.

Nothing from the experience of 3,000 years has been included in today's veterinary practice.

Though the motives of antiquity's idiots who shoved bedbugs into the penis, were probably the best.

However, the mania with which veterinarians of the past strived to pump a saltpeter solution into every horse's butt they saw is undoubtedly amazing.

It was a very fashionable method in the 17th through the 19th centuries.

Nevertheless, let us leave the veterinary medicine of the past alone.

(But, the next time some fool begins to roll his eyes at you about the horsemen of old, their mastery or knowledge, you can put a bucket over the head of the eye-roller with a completely pure conscience and tap out something on this bucket, old-fashioned, but peppy.)

Unfortunately, the stable, the equine home, was also a place for the usage of another of man's capacity for invention, but somewhat more shameful.

Man always has aspired to improve the horse, he always has aspired to adjust its proportions and appearance for whatever fashion was in style.

The not unknown Hensler in 1851 was distressed in the following way: "The anus becomes inflamed from the immoderate insertion of pepper, ginger, tobacco and the like into it that are used, as is known, so the horse bears its tail higher, and causes pain..."

Note, "immoderate" insertion is being discussed.

Moderate insertion of "pepper and ginger"[16] was considered normal.

But in reality, almost all of the 19th century raved about uplifted horse tails, which imparted to the horses a resemblance to the then popular picturesque patterns.

They strived not simply to lift this tail artificially, which in reality is raised at moments of great excitement or joy, indicating a spirited game, but also to secure it in this position.

For beauty.

It was called "Englization".[17] "Englization" of horses wearing a lady's saddle was considered especially sine qua non.

For this, the tail was clipped with a knife or saw. Later, a tail cutter was invented, the "coupe-queue," with which the living tail is easily trimmed (table 8, 8), and in which, by the way, the spine continues, although everyone knew in what manner such amusements ended and how dangerous they were.

Let's take a look at the "Medication Handbook": "Lightening and shortening of the tail is in fact of great importance. And although the sharp knife or the axe are needed to do it however, dangerous fits are caused from it, and often indiscernible damage, reaching right to the brain itself, and it causes a deadly mouth cramp or Saint Anthony's fire[b] ensues, during which time the intestines give out from shortening the tail."

I shall add that not simply clipping the whole section of the spine, consisting of a tail dock, occurred, but it was 12–15 vertebrae and more important nerves, but methods were devised which resulted in such a twisting of the remaining fragment that it was similar to a dog's tail.

Judging by Gueriniere's description (and, one must give him his due, he is terrified by the proposed procedure), after cutting off the tail, they kept the horse motionless for a month and a half, tying the stub to a special system of blocks and fasteners on the stable ceiling (that was if the horse did not die during the week).

Docking the tail, together with an entire section of the spine, is practiced, by the way, even today.

In America, England, in France and in the Middle East.

Well alright, it's tails.

But there was no part of the horse that was not subject to degenerate and always pitiless practices in order to conform with the tastes or fashion of a particular time.

When dappled horses[18] became fashionable in the 18th century, a method was devised by which "dapples" could be applied. According to the designers, in places were dapples were desired, little circles were burnt into the horse's hide with iron heated red-hot. Then, the scabs that had formed at the sites of the burns were torn off and the exposed the wound rubbed with caustic onion juice.

The hair that grew out in half a year in these little circles was, as a rule, a white color that also created the effect of the "dapples" so beloved by the ladies and painters.

From 100 to 300 such circles were made.

White "dapples" were created by the aforementioned method.

Black or dark "dapples" on light horses were made by burning with quicklime (carbide) or lead oxide.

According to the recommendation of the specialists of that time, "take a pound of raw nitric acid, an ounce of vitriol power and an ounce of burnt silver" for obtaining chestnut color "dapples."

A description follows of nine days of torture for the horse being cauterized with nitric acid. I do not want to quote it. It is disgusting.

(The so-called "dapples" are a fully natural occurrence. Most often they appear from the uneven growth of the new coat in the spring and fall, they don't last very long and are not distinguished by brightness. Of course, natural processes were unable to satisfy the fashion tasked by the painters for a bright "dapple."

The very respectable painter, Antonio Pisanello left behind the study "Horse's Head with Slashed Nostrils" (table 8, **1**).

Pisanello did not assert the fashion in this instance, but only recorded it.

Slashing of the nostrils was done frequently, beginning in ancient times.

Up to the 18th century, when they learned to slash the vocal cords of military horses so they did not give themselves away by whinnying while laying in ambush or during an attack, the nostrils were slashed approximately the way shown by Pisanello.

This practice also deprived the horse of the ability to neigh loudly.

In which connection, one more very delicate variant of slashing nostrils was presented by Pisanello.

This manner was maintained by all peoples until the beginning of the 20th century.

Hensler records in 1851 that "the Tatars rip out their horse's snout as a precaution against snorting during secret crossings."

The race course and racing business widely practiced not just the slashing of nostrils, but carving them completely half a hand palm upwards.

It was thought that the more air the horse managed to swallow at each stride of its movement, the greater the speed it could demonstrate in a lap or race.

The nostrils, or, speaking in the language of the equestrian profiteers, the "snouts," in the opinion of the race course owners, "serve for moderating the entry of the air being breathed into the lungs during running."

So then they cut out the nostrils, too, so that they didn't hinder "the entry of air" and the setting of records.

Several decades of this absurd practice and the death of thousands of horses were needed before the organizers of the runs and races decided to abandon it.

And the practice was abandoned not out of pity for the horses, but because of the uselessness of this method for improving "rates of briskness."

The ears are a special story.

Different eras have known different fashions for the size of equine ears. Cavalrymen, as you recall, simply cut them off down to the base.

High-society riding, hunting and carriage rides, they all had forms for correcting a horse's ears.

Gueriniere describes with sadness the following method, quoting, apparently, the instructions of the Versailles court practitioners: "One must order a deft craftsman to make two hard forms from copper or iron. The form must repeat the shape of precisely the ear that you wish to obtain. Then one more such form must be built. The horse's ear is enclosed within the two forms which are fastened using a screwing device. Then, everything that lies outside of this form is cut away using a scalpel..."

If it turned out for the owner or rider that the ears were not exactly the same on the head, then five to seven centimeters of skin were cut from the horse's head, between the ears. "Then the two edges of the wound that have been created must be brought together and sutured in order to pull the ears and make them equal."

Idiocy was triumphant.

When white "stars" on horse's foreheads suddenly came into fashion, the English were first to take advantage of the opportunity.

Here is the English formula for making a white "star" on the bay or black head of a living horse: "Using a branding iron made in the form of a cobbler's awl, pierce the skin crosswise in the middle of the forehead and detach the skin from the bone using this awl. Then take four lead blades, push into the holes that have been made and place them so that they form a protuberance in the middle of the forehead..."

Further follows an extensive and openly sadistic description of how these blades "are tied together," how "they allow pus to form in the wound by not touching it..." and how, as a result of three months agony for the horse, which was supposed to be left completely immobile all this time in order not to scratch the wound, the desired white "star" is obtained.

Upon selling a horse, the following was done to conceal its age, which it was always possible to determine precisely from the teeth: "In order to sell an 8-year-old horse as a 6-year-old horse, gouge out with a chisel or remove with a cutting tool the new cups on the teeth, and for the larger part on the angled teeth, burn them out with a red-hot iron."

They were able to produce all procedures of this type, ears and teeth and "dapples," only in special frames in which it was possible to immobilize any horse by hanging it from beneath the stomach and tying each leg and the head.

One of the varieties of such a frame is depicted in figure 10 of table 8.

I can honestly say that to continue the list of tortures and humiliations which were contrived by high-society and military riding would take a very long time.

I repeat, there is not a single place on a horse's body which would not have been defaced by man either to please fashion or one's own ignorance or for financial gain.

Veterinary medicine, which could not contrive anything sensible, had contrived by that time a mass of methods, in addition to the frames, to paralyze a horse, making resistance to similar operations impossible.

This turned out well for the veterinarians.

And all this occurred in the stables, for only the four walls, the availability of the frames, the staff of smirking grooms and the ability to tie the horse tightly and immobilize him allowed the successful performance of all these operations.

All this probably was done beneath Chantilly's romanticized arches, too.

One day while disassembling one of the dusty corners of the museum, behind a stand with horseshoes, I found an old tail cutter, the oak handles of which were so stained and scoured that, obviously, they had been put to good use on more than a hundred tails.

These are all very disgusting things, but, it seems to me that a man who wishes to understand the horse must know them.

And not only because, while approaching any horse with which you intend to connect your life, it is necessary to know the whole history of the horse family, the whole chronicle of their torments and misfortunes, but in order to remember for the thousandth time that there is a way which does not lead anywhere, the way of savage, unthinking cruelty and arrogance, and that man's relationship with the horse is built most of all on the undoubted knowledge of the guilt of his type before such a great and such a defenseless type as "equus."

Denying the need for this knowledge is tantamount to denying history itself.

Manipulations with tails and ears, with "dapples" and "stars" shows unequivocally that for three millennia people have viewed the horse only as an accoutrement to bolster man's grandeur and bravado.

As a result, we had the cavalry; now we have equestrianism and the "troika," that is something that is inimitably abhorrent.

It is all so very sad.

Do not take this narrative as an attempt to in any way discredit the idea of stabling a horse.

There is no way around that.

But the stable must be a home, a true, real home where the horse knows that it is in complete safety.

Even the floating of teeth, (an indispensable procedure since the horse's teeth grow almost his whole life and are not ground down when he is stabled, but, rather grow drastically long and injure the inside of the cheeks), is better performed not in the horse's own home stall, but in a special medical cubicle where all the veterinary business takes place, and where the horse is trimmed and clipped.

If there is no such thing at the stable, then it is better to move the horse somewhere else to use a dental rasp, or to give him shots or otherwise treat him, but not his own stall.

It seems naïve, but many years of living with horses has shown me that this is the correct practice.

Generally, the ancient history of stalls is rather monotonous.

Besides the atrocities and the complete overt stupidity, nothing enlivens this doleful, bloody and crappy landscape buzzing with flies.

Unless a skinny, red-nosed veterinarian with a jar of bedbugs and a huge enema, filled with a saltpeter solution wanders by.

Or a happy mole-catcher's wheelbarrow full of different sizes of tin funnels rattles past.

Clusters of dead moles, strung on fishing line, dangle from the handles of these wheelbarrows.

There was a mole-catcher present on the staffs of the large stables and stud farms from as early as the 16th century.

Why is understood.

The moles dug deep burrows in the exercise yards that were dangerous for the horses' legs.

Mole hunting was a special art, with its own secrets and mysticism. The craft was handed down from generation to generation.

Outwardly, everything appeared commonplace at first — the mole-catcher stuck his tin funnels into various mole burrows in the field.

But then a real mole-catcher would get down onto his knees and, placing his mouth right up to the funnel's orifice, began to drone in various keys.

The droning would be replaced by a chattering of the voice and, finally, with a pronounced shriek and squeal.

Having screeched, droned and squealed a bit, the mole-catcher threw himself as fast as his legs would carry him to the one burrow known only to him (how he figured it out is incomprehensible to me) and, waiting for the appearance of the head of the mole, apparently dumb from the catcher's vocalizations adroitly hacked it with his hook on its crown, hooked it, and with exacting speed threaded it onto his fishing line which he wore as a necklace.

There were mole-catchers who pumped a special smoke into the burrows with furs and drove the moles out onto the surface, and there were those that dumped in water, but they were by no means the real masters.

The real master mole-catchers tormented the moles and drove them to the surface, with only the strength and virtuosity of their own throat, with only the knowledge of the special "mole" tones.

Notions about cleanliness, about a stable's cleanliness, were outrageous.

The stables of a Franciscan monastery in Leicester (England) were considered, if not examples, then at least extremely problem-free.

Having brought up the history of these stables, it is possible to discern a most eloquent fact which best characterizes the ideas of antiquity's horse hygiene: when they killed that poor devil King Richard III (Gloucester) at Bosworth in 1485, they quickly buried him in the Leicester Franciscan monastery.

In a "good coffin," as the chronicler notes with some reproach. (Considering this monarch's reputation, one may understand the reproach.)

In 1536, when a fine reason was found to plunder England's monasteries, which was called the Reformation, they dug up Richard III's grave, rummaged through it for any valuables which the followers of the murdered king might have buried with his body, and scattered the remains about the monastery.

And the king's coffin, that very "good coffin," was converted right there by the practical English into a "large stable feeding trough," in which capacity it remained until "its full dilapidation and chewing up."

Everything is also understood about the "chewing up." During days or months of famine, horses begin to gnaw on everything that even looks or smells a little bit like food out of melancholy and from starvation.

In all the rest, descriptions of ancient stables boil down to the most boring enumerations of saddle makers, heralds, weapons pages and so on.

True, manége water sprayers were known as early as the time of the Versailles school.

But all this is no longer very essential.

By locking a horse exasperated by boredom and despair in the dark and stinking closeness of a pen or small stall, of course it acquired a multitude of so-called "stable vices."

Tedium and complete gloom engendered "biting," "cribbing," and "weaving" (the disorder in which a horse rocks endlessly from one foreleg to the other), spasmodic digging at the floor with the feet, masturbation in stallions, kicking the hind legs against the walls, etc.

All these "vices" thrive even to this day, inasmuch as stabling has changed little.

I suppose the historian's pince-nez should be removed, since the horse in reality, having an enchanting dream in a 15th century stable stall and waking in a 21st century stable will see no difference between them.

The same flies. The same oppressive heat.

The closeness and stench.

Locks on rusty doors. A small, dingy window.

Everything just the same.

Having awoken today, the horse will hear that same anguished, "dry" cough from the neighboring stall which it heard in the 15th century; he will hear those same blows of the hind feet striking the walls, and the stupid laughter of a boozy stableman in reply. (Horses at times buck both the doors and walls from spite toward the world and frustration at incarceration, just as human prisoners throw themselves with concentrated force at prison walls and doors.)

There have been no major changes, and in speaking of stable practices, I constantly have to blend the past and the present.

The horse, in his pure essence and by his natural predisposition, is a very energetic creature who must be in constant motion.

Movement is his organic, minute-by-minute need, a need even more powerful than the need for food, sleep and sex.

At the same time, one must remember to what degree the horse loves freedom, placing it possibly ahead of everything.

Ahead of satiety, satisfaction and security.

Traditional stabling, depriving the horse of even the illusion of freedom, and at the same time depriving him of air, light and movement, really very quickly develops those "stable vices."

What the future brings is very predictable.

Not wishing to eliminate the reasons for the occurrence of these vices, and not knowing how, man wastes huge amounts of time and money to devise mechanical means of battling their manifestations and consequences.

It all resembles very much the helplessness and stupidity that man demonstrates in everything else regarding his relationship with the horse.

He grapples with the vice called "cribbing" with acrid, bitter, burning ointments based on cayenne pepper with which he coats everything in the stall that the horse can touch with his mouth.

So-called "cribbing halters" have been devised which respond in a trice by sticking steel needles onto the gums and nostrils at any attempt of the horse to grasp any prominent object with his teeth (see table 8, **6**).

Burdayevich's very well-known apparatus wounds the horse's larynx in a similar situation (**5**).

Feeding troughs and doors are either simply covered with iron or equipped with brushes having protruding nails, which do not allow horses to grasp at them with their teeth.

Iron collars have been devised, the function of which is to smother the horse in response to cribbing attempts (**3**). (These "cribbing collars," by the way, are very popular even today.)

Very recently veterinarians found out that cribbing is not only a bad habit, a "stable vice," but also a method by which a horse ill with gastritis tries at least

The Horse Crucified and Risen

a little bit, by ingesting a huge amount of air, to stifle the pain in the stomach. It is approximately the same story with masturbation.

They place a stallion, flooded with power and desires, in the same stable with mares, deprive him of any movement, bring him to madness with boredom, closeness and excessive feed and are surprised that he has begun no longer simply to frolic with slight eroticism, but seriously, to masturbate repeatedly.

This can occur five, ten times a day, to the point of reeling with complete exhaustion.

Most of the time they simply beat the stallions very harshly for masturbating.

When they get bored with the beatings, they stick a "hedgehog" onto them. A "hedgehog" is a cushion containing needles that is tied to the stomach and which prick the stallion's penis when he has an erection. (The method, while ancient, is wide-spread even today in the 21st century. So as not to wrestle with the complicated needle construction, today they sew common barbed wire onto a piece of thick felt and tie that thick felt beneath the stomach.)

In ancient times, the so-called "Benedict shield," a complex locking device, was very popular for combating stallion masturbation (table 8, 4).

If the horse, having gone crazy from the need to stay locked up for some reason in a narrow tiny room, begins to buck against walls, they beat him yet again.

Way back, somewhat greater resourcefulness appeared for this problem: in the 19th century, a cunning device was advertised: when the horse hit it, a special mechanism brought one of the wall boards into motion which beat it in response or it reacted with a sharp blow of a board from the ceiling.

And no one wants to know that the "stable vices," frequently and succulently described in literature and presented today at any stable in all its glory, in reality are a direct consequence of only boredom, despair and the horse's eternal incomprehension of his situation.

By the way, desperate opponents to common stable practices rose up at certain times.

In particular, the start of the 19th century gave birth to a short, but extremely scandalous work by an anonymous author who dared to reproach a cavalry practice, firing from pistols in the stables while the horses were being fed.

The work was called, "Gunfire in Stables Is Detrimental to Horses" (published in 1823).

Though it is written with a very thin, weak quill it is so charming that I shall quote some of it: "The habit of firing in the stable itself near horses while issuing them oats and fodder is harmful to the health of many horses."

"During shooting, which is committed in the stable, the horses usually snort terribly, tremble violently, throw themselves at all sides of the stall, kick the stall walls with their front knees and are covered with foam in several seconds, which pours from all their body, and they are terribly uneasy..."

The composition in reality evoked the fury of cavalrymen, for whom firing from pistols while the horse was eating was an indispensable practice for getting the horse accustomed to shooting.

The writer was declared to be "an ignoramus with a mind confused with pity."

A "Hussar Regiment's Captain of Cavalry and Cavalier," who appeared in some of the equestrian tracts of that time, expressed the desire personally to "flog the prankster who had lifted his hand against the indispensable traditions of many honored regiments."

Shooting in the stables, it goes without saying, continued.

As evidence of the effectiveness of their method, the officer corps demonstrated horses which reacted in no way to the firing.

Upon investigation, all the composed horses that had been demonstrated simply turned out to be deaf already from the shots that had tormented them for a long time. (One simply needs to know the structure of the horse's ear which is ten times more sensitive than the human's.)

To their misfortune, horses that live in cold countries have the habit of growing hair for the winter.

At times it is rather thick and long.

The hair is a huge inconvenience for grooms during stabling.

It takes longer and it is more difficult to clean. If the horse sweats because of the work it takes a long time for him to dry out.

The hair generally is not too decorative, presenting a shaggy appearance, a crude outline of the most perfect equine form — they say "it makes a horse artless."

These days they clip horses painlessly and quickly. At least 20 styles of cut have been conceived.

But the situation got really sad before the invention of electrical clippers.

They usually eliminated the hair that had grown out in winter by "singeing" it off.

They singed it with a special device that used acetylene or gas.

Essentially, it was a common burner, a type of blow torch, though it did not have a straight, narrow flame, but a wider mouth which applied the flame not in a stream, but as a "trowel" (table 8, 11).

Specialists could "singe off" up to ten horses an hour.

They removed the twitch (the twitch is a special cord and stick with which it is possible to firmly twist a horse's lip or ear, paralyzing the horse with pain) (table 8, 7) from a "ready," already singed, horse and, while he was still smoking and mad with pain and terror, they sprayed him with water so as to put out the smoldering hair, shoved him into the stall and led out the next one into the stable passageway.

They fastened the "twitch" on the next horse and started to burn the hair on him with the wide plume of the gas flame, in awful smoke from the hair that clouded everything.

They applied the flame to hair on the neck, on the stomach and on the head.

Baron Wrangel, a Russian enlightener and "horse lover," rather placidly speaks of this method of "removing a horse's excess hair" in his work, lamenting only that the procedure is complicated by the indispensable cleaning of the horse with a knife, which is necessary for scraping off the carbon deposit that had formed on its body.

He described even more savage and involved procedures, a type of "thinning down" of a horse, about which the baron himself also speaks with understanding and sympathy.

Fortunately, his work, the same as the work of his disciple and translator Urusov, was converted into wastepaper over a multitude of years, and it was possible to read it either only out of desperation or while tracking down absurd curiosities.

By the way, sometimes the painful, paralyzing action of the "twitch" did not help and then three to four grooms, hanging onto the horse, pressed on its head behind the halter while one or the other manipulation was performed on him.

But in the venerated former times and today, such "pressings" may lead only to injuries similar to what is depicted in figure 2 of table 8.

The "twitches," singeing, beatings, "hedgehogs," cayenne pepper, hobbling, straitjacket-like horse blankets... and so on and so forth.

Mankind's stable chronicles suggest nothing more important or instructive.

And what remains today is approximately in the same spirit.

As in the case of riding, the inability to understand the horse, to consider him, to feel and hear him is compensated for with hundreds of idiotic devices. Usually they are pitiless and cruel, sometimes they are amusing, but in any event, they are completely unnecessary. Any problems with the horse, whether in working with him or in his maintenance, are resolved very easily when there is knowledge of and respect for the horse, for his soul and freedom.

I am already tired of describing all this stable idiocy of the past and the present.

Unfortunately, because I know the world of the stable very well, I am not able to paint pleasant pictures, although, at times, I would very much like to.

Of course, the monstrous conditions of stabling, which also lead to the development of vices and to psychic disorders of horses, are not absolutely ubiquitous.

At least not 100% of stables are like that.

Only 99 percent.

There are rare, completely delightful exceptions, where the horse's home life has not turned into anguish.

Where the illusion of freedom is carefully created by man, where the opportunity for constant movement is afforded, where the horse's comfort is observed to a tee, where everything is adjusted out of respect for the horse's needs and on the basis of the modern discoveries of hippological science.

But, unfortunately, these stables are neither typical nor commonplace.

In my time in St. Petersburg, the stable of one ageless lady (whose name I do not remember since she was known more by her nickname) with a glum, orthodox expression, was, perhaps, the most characteristic.

Both behind her back and even in front of her, they called her, forgive me, the Louse.

The nickname stuck.

This name was given to her for her surprising similarity with this sweet insect as well as for her habit of getting into any male pants that came into her field of view.

The alcoholic bettors, the drunken saddle-makers, and also the farriers and jockeys, who represent the male half of the equestrian world, were not too discriminating, and after a fourth drink began to disgrace the sheep and dachshunds if such were in close proximity.

Our lady Louse was just a bit more preferable than the undesirable, in principle, dachshund and, consequently, always had great luck.

The lady made do, as is the custom, with sport dressage, rentals, as well as the buying and subsequent selling of horses.

She hung around destitute kolkhoz stables, where she bought up horses that were not yet completely broken-down, dragged them to her place, and in a few months, with beating and iron, easily made a little money, selling them for a song to the enthusiastic louts from among those who wished acquire their own horse.

She maimed horses once and for all in the process of her "retraining," making them complete invalids for life.

The louts who bought the horses did not realize this, because the lady clearly was a talented actress and very convincingly played the part of a sophisticated, all-understanding and knowledgeable horse lover.

The lady always appeared before people with a retinue of stable girls in jangling spurs, girls who were as corrupt and dirty as she herself and who showed-off in the same way.

By the way, we are speaking not about her, but about her stable.

The lady's stable was situated extremely fortuitously in an old St. Petersburg park, not far from the subway, which made it particularly desirable to private owners and renters.

The queue to the lodging, that is to the right to place one's own horse into the crib, was very long and feelings ran high.

Ladies in mink, who arrived at the stable in Jeeps, and girls with little whips, it happened, scratched each others' faces, disputing their place in line.

The stable itself was a small, plywood barracks of mysterious origin, without windows and with a very low ceiling.

Old and very frayed wires that had to be pushed to the side with the handle of a spade or mop for a horse to pass underneath hung permanently from the ceiling, sparking in the darkness.

Along both sides of a phenomenally narrow aisle, so narrow that a horse could barely squeeze through it, were located little recesses without windows, so small that a goat could hardly be kept in them.

Into these recesses the Louse's retinue in their jangling spurs crammed horses, who, as a rule, stood there, 24 hours a day.

The floors, of course, were rotten, to such a degree that they had even broken beneath the horses, and long ago had been converted into a jumble of manure, pieces of decayed boards and old toilet paper.

There was no toilet in the barracks, of course, and the renters, and even the guests, visited the horses in the recesses to urinate and defecate.

They fed the horses some kind of filth from a soft heap in the yard, the wastes of a flour mill.

But one must give her her due, for periodically they struggled with the heap's soaking, souring and formation of mold, by covering it with ragged polyethylene.

In this mysterious barracks, where it would be very difficult to place two horses, there were forty.

And the public, who wished to house its horse in a comfortable place, in an old park, where on weekends it would be so prestigious to stroll around on the horse beneath the old poplars, came and came, brandishing C-notes.

The Louse, her purplish ears eagerly perked in the direction of the rustling banknotes, affectedly distorted her face, minced about, clutched at her head, but then, after exchanging a fleeting glance with her dirty entourage, once more divided a fetid, tiny nook in half yet again with a gesture.

All the rest was a matter of technique.

A happy drunken carpenter squeezed into the little stable aisle with his boards and nails and, brushing aside the retinue's design ideas with a shake of his swollen noggin, began to make two stalls of the already tiny one — the so-called "compacting."

Then the rustling of C-notes was heard once more, and the already divided recess was divided in half yet again.

The next unfortunate horse was pressed into this very small and very fetid, new "half."

At the same time, the lady lamented continuously that only "love for the horses" motivated her. It probably could have reached 100 horses, since in their greed, both the Louse and her retinue knew no restraint.

But then the inevitable occurred — it all burnt up.

Somehow one evening the wires swung for a while and sparked, and instead of the usual small, blue sparks, they rained down huge, white flashes.

And these flashes, falling into the hay and the rotted plywood, ignited in several seconds such a bonfire that it scorched park trees far from the stable and burnt the foliage.

And forty horses were burnt in this bonfire.

Good people, who ran into the flames, still somehow managed to extricate those, who were closer to the exit, burnt, smoldering and swallowing the fire.

No one would ever have been able to save those that were further away, in the "halved" recesses.

The plywood was torn into red hot embers by the fire.

Sowing smoky debris all around, the old slate roof exploded.

And through the gaps, the raging fire wrenched itself into the sky, mixing at once with the fire from the doors and the broken walls.

The whole stable was decimated in something like 20 minutes, turned into red, glowing flakes, flying high with the souls of 30 horses over the old park's poplars.

When the barracks had been consumed, nothing was left except the distended bodies of horses which lay as close together as the live horses had stood.

The Louse, who arrived at the very end of the fire, snarling at reporters, tragically pressed the buttons of her calculator — but her view of the figures was hindered by the reflection of the fire's glow.

Within a week, the landscape in the park was cluttered with a mass of weeping little girls with whips.

The mink-clad ladies wept, not crawling out of their Jeeps.

The saddle makers, farriers, jockeys and competitors arranged an endless tearful funeral feast in a construction trailer, charging the same rate for everyone.

Various flowers were placed on the places from which the inflated bodies of the horses had been dragged away by tractors.

But some of the horses, of course, had survived.

Barely a week later, the Louse's retinue and renters, jangling their spurs, arranged jolly show jumping competitions on the site of the fire.

And the lady herself, having quickly recovered from her misfortune and some financial problems, along with the owners of the burnt horses, threw together a new stable, where her retinue, the surviving horses, the drunkard with the boards, the farriers and the competitors with the dachshund all relocated.

Things are going well for her.

She maintains that it was downright arson, and she herself claims to have seen the girls from a competing stable who, while giggling demonically had sprinkled kerosene on the walls of her barracks.

Sentimental female renters and private owners had at one time wanted to organize some kind of a granite memorial, without an eternal flame, but with verses carved into the granite to evoke a flood of tears.

They had begun to collect funds from the few crying girls, but then they shrugged off the undertaking and forgot about it.

They came down on the Louse, of course, even writing verses which were circulated in newspapers and on the internet. It was complete nonsense. These "lovers of horses" saw perfectly well where they were housing those for whom they so sweetly declare their love every minute, those for whom they are ready to write numerous posthumous verses. (Very touching and sincere, by the way.)

The Louse, showing them where their horses would live, did not fasten enchanted eyeglasses on any of their faces.

Eyeglasses that could alter reality, that could turn a terrible, fetid and horribly overcrowded barracks with sagging, frayed wires into a safe, spacious and good equine home.

To put it bluntly, the guest "consumers" happily paid for the sordid reality.

Essentially, they simply didn't give two hoots about where and how their horses lived 24 hours a day.

In this case, too, the lady Louse and her guests openly continued the same old stabling traditions, from which, despite the hearts and flowers, the expensive nutrition, the rhymes and the kisses, the same old human attitude toward the horse emerges — the attitude like the one toward cattle, which says that their proper place is in shit, darkness, and oppressive heat.

In short, we must not be distracted by the false sentimentality surrounding this documented tragedy. We must acknowledge that the horse owning public, the consumers in the "horse market," are generally quite satisfied with what "louses" have to offer.

* * *

I have reread my own text, and I have been shocked at what a record quantity of venom it is possible, as it turns out, to place on a square centimeter of paper. Zane Grey is taking a break.

But I really hate them. I hate both the lice and their breeding ground, the equestrian ladies of both sexes.

Possessed with the ability to understand and feel the horse, I am compelled to understand and share the horse's hatred for this vermin.

And solidarity with my own biological kind is not really my nature, thank goodness.

The most nightmarish reality in all this equestrian history, which spans at least 3,000 years, is indisputably the horse's biological and intellectual understanding of the savagery that is perpetrated upon him.

His awareness of the stupidity and injustice of the creature that so completely dominates this world.

Of that strange primate who pushes the horse off onto lethal friends.

On the one hand, this creature writes hundreds of poems and paints thousands of pictures dedicated to the horse, it sings the horse's praises and glorifies him, and it creates dramatic sculptures and films that bring tears to the eye.

On the other hand, this same creature locks the rusty stall bolt, leaving the praised, idolized horse immobilized in the oppressive heat and shit, without the smallest hope for bettering his life. This creature tears the horse's mouth with iron, and beats him — and the most advanced sadists in the humiliation of the horse get Olympic medals hung round their necks, medals which symbolize nothing more than an especially high level of sadism in the sadistic trade of equestrianism.

It is difficult to say what is greater here, the hypocrisy or the normal, traditional human fascism which generally is the cornerstone of any human worldview.

I am, in this case, without deprecation, for it is stupid to deprecate absolute reality.

The well-known term "fascism" seems harsh, but it explains quite a lot in this situation and will make it easier to understand its irony.

Like equestrians, guys from the Third Reich also did not wish to think about the fact that in those whom they sent to the gas chambers by the thousands were souls with destinies, intellect and the highest ability to experience love and pain.

These guys did not doubt their own right to act as they did; they seriously believed that there is a certain higher racial echelon in mankind's development and in belonging to it, they had the right to impose their will on every other living thing.

If one looks into it, German fascism was only the reduction to the logical absolute of man's position in regard to all similar living beings on the earth. For the life of me, there is no special difference between racial fascism and the evolutionary fascism which 99% of mankind professes.

German fascism was fragile. But, the universal fascism of mankind has been completely victorious for a long time and is the foundation upon which almost all of civilization has been created.

Good or bad, fascism is a philosophical question.

Being a master in the training of horses, I can only certify its complete ineffectiveness in my craft, that is, in the business of establishing a relationship with the horse and his training.

I have not been speaking about fascism by accident. Thanks to the emotional force of this offensive term it is easier to understand human motivation and psychological mechanisms with respect to traditional riding and to stabling, the subject of this chapter.

But all of this, generally, is hot air, so let us return to our stable theme, the theme of the horse's home, which can also be beautiful.

Right now I will try to briefly describe one example of how it can be.

In order to remain healthy and sound, every horse must have: a warm winter shelter (measuring not less than 20 square meters) in the event of bitter cold

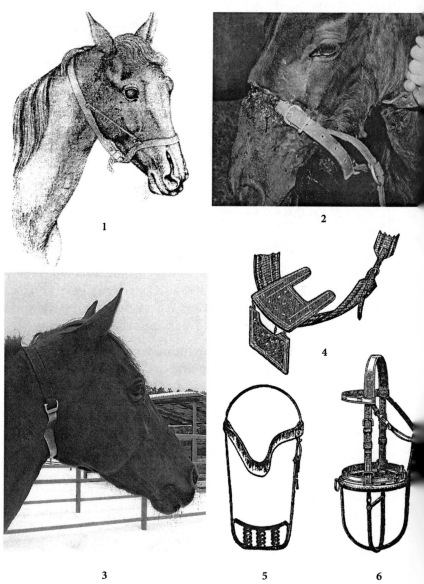

1

2

3

4

5

6

Table 8

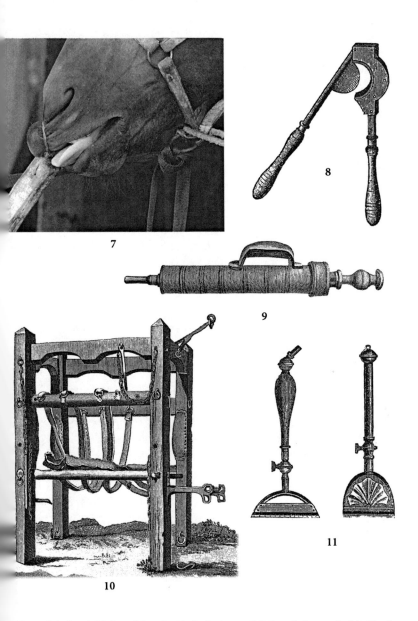

Pisanello's sketch "A horse's head with slashed nostrils"; **2** – a halter embedded in the ·rse's nose; **3** – anti-crib biting collar; **4** – Benedict's shield; **5** – Burdaevich apparatus; **6** – English halter; **7** – a twitch; **8** – a tool for tail cutting "Coupe-queue"; **9** – a clyster; **10** – a bench for the total restraint of a horse; **11** – a fur burner and storms; a summer "breathing" stall — a shelter not less than 25 square meters with its own walking yard — a paddock, and a door which should stay open in any weather.

I assume everything is clear regarding a warm shelter.

It is a fenced premise in the stable, certainly provided with a window, automatic forced air ventilation, heating that allows maintaining not less than 5 degrees Celsius at all times, rubber floors, doors, with that which in the nice language of the 19th century was called a "salt lick" and now roughly is called a "salt shaker," toys, both rolling and rocking, and a bunch of similar accessories. The horse may not spend more than the night in the stall, and by day he should be moving, spending most of his time out of doors.

Regarding the toys: these are special plastic barrels or balls that have some quantity of treats inside that the horse reaches by very accurate rolling of the barrel or ball.

Inside the toy is a kind of labyrinth.

The way to get the treat from inside to outside is devilishly complicated.

The treat comes out only if the barrel is rolled to the correct angle, stopped on time and ever-so-slightly rolled back.

I have tried it, and I wasn't able to get the damned thing.

The horses understand the meaning of the toy very quickly, and, if it is not possible to be outdoors on especially frosty or icy days, then the toy can occupy them very well for an hour or two.

Then indeed is the expertise developed.

For example, Perst contrives to empty the toy in about 10 minutes. But he worked for a long time on a very effective tactic for squeezing the toy into a corner and methodically lifting it upwards with his nose against the wall at different angles. Until it was completely empty.

Other horses, not yet being such experts, quite frankly chase the barrels and balls all over the stall.

Generally, it must first be remembered that it is necessary to occupy, divert and distract the horse from his dark prison thoughts.

Their keeper must be ashamed every minute for their captivity.

It all holds true. The toys, the special shatterproof mirrors in the stalls and the ability to communicate a lot and fully with other horses.

There also are games for the stall when the horses are training, for example, to "hand over" the rubber basins that serve as feeding troughs.

After breakfast, lunch and supper, the horse is supposed to put his empty basin into the groom's hand or throw it into the passageway.

Every two hours there is a fresh portion of hay, since food, generally, also is a miraculous distraction. Although grooming as such is completely senseless and not necessary to the horse, it has a place in certain situations because it serves to amuse the horse. Here I am describing extreme situations when the horse needs to spend a whole day in the stable, which happens very rarely.

The stall must be of such a size that the horse can both wander about a little and lie down, stretching out freely. That is, no less than 5 meter by 5 meters.

A smaller area has no right to existence.

A tank must be located alongside the stall in which it is always possible to wet the hay.

This is not necessary for all horses, but if there are even the slightest respiratory problems, the slightest cough, wetting the hay in the tank before offering it to the horse is imperative.

Soaking (not dampening it from a watering can or a wine glass) paralyzes the volatility of the spores, pollen, fine dust and microscopic fungi of which there are billions in any bale of hay, even those that look most appetizing.

Reaching the lungs, the most harmful of these fungi, and even those same fusarium alternaria, attack the alveolus and cause a cough, and eventually also emphysema.

Only an ignorant person who has not the least notion of a horse's physiology can explain away a horse's cough as a cold.

Generally, one must avoid like the plague a lengthy stay in the stall by every possible means.

No air conditioners, windows or ventilation are able to provide the horse with the amount of pure air that it needs.

Therefore, the best form of stabling for the horse is a shelter or "breathing stall."

A "breathing" stall is a covered, very roomy facility that has one solid wall and three walls that are simply fencing.

The charm of a "breathing" stall is in its provision with its own enclosure, which is paved fully or partly with rubber and enclosed, not so big that it would be possible to gallop wildly in it, but big enough so that the horse can trot and frisk about to his heart's content.

Here the horse, though limited in freedom, can nonetheless organize his own world. Here it is possible to move around, to warm himself in the sun or go into the dark shade of the shed, to visit his neighbor or roll about in the sand. The presence of a dusty place for wallowing is mandatory in the paddock.

However, for the horse, there is nothing better than freedom of life in the fields and there cannot be. A "breathing" stall is also partly an extreme measure.

The problem is that very expensive, very intelligent and eminent horses, as a rule, have been doomed to such reverent containment. The fear of the horse getting an accidental injury in freedom becomes dominate and defines the horse's life. The effort to provide him absolute security and safety results in a certain over-protection.

Almost all modern stables look like that, including even mine.

In the winter, early spring and late fall, the horses live in "breathing" stalls, in the yards and in their own exercise spaces, the paddocks, returning to the warm stable only for the night.

True, the horse spends practically all those times of the year in the "breathing stall" in a horse blanket.

On frosty days it is a very warm blanket with a hood, practically up to the ears, and when there are no frosts, the horse blanket is of warm felt or polyester padding without the hood, and on other days a very lightweight horse blanket.

Considering the circumstance that the door to the exercise yard from the "breathing" stall is always open and the horse can leave the covered area, the horse blankets should be waterproof.

Horses, as has been explained, also love a dry snowstorm very much, and a wet one, and a spitting cold rain, and a direct downpour, and even hail, and will go out from the roofed area into the yard for the express purpose of standing in a snowstorm or rain.

Even the most waterproof horse blankets get wet sooner or later; therefore, it is necessary to have, at a minimum, two interchangeable warm horse blankets for each equine soul.

Generally, the only question connected with horses where one doesn't have to listen to me is the question of blanketing horses.

Here I always go a bit too far.

I have not once resisted putting a blanket on a horse if I myself felt a bit cold.

I understand that we all have different thermal sensations. And I know that weather that seems really bitterly cold to me may just seem quite perfectly comfortable to the horse.

There must be a gate or gateway from the yards of the "breathing" stalls to those exercise spaces where the horse can have a certain illusion of freedom, that is, a place where it can graze and gallop.

The space I have is a rather large fenced garden with a pond, a peninsula, walkways and grassy plots, which on the whole are proffered for equine usage.

The soil of such spaces is a completely special story.

Considering the horse's ability to plough the ground deeply with its hooves during unrestrained gallops and pursuit of each other, complete confidence is necessary that the ground does not contain any nails, glass, iron, sharp stones, wires and similar trash, both from construction and of unexplained origin.

I have been extremely lucky in my time.

I knew a person from the tax police, whose pockets always were filled with freshly received kickbacks.

A broad and happy man, he always distributed the kickbacks collected during the day to his friends, laughing and joking. (The money, it is understood, he kept for himself. I am talking about material, objective kickbacks.)

Because he was a "big shot" unnecessary, he was given not some kind of rubbish such as candy or subscriptions to "Reader's Digest" but quality things that were very impressive.

He was extraordinarily boisterous.

"Al, get shorter, don't be a pussy, don't be shy, let all the fish come to your net" he would say to me, pulling out collections of watches and cigar cases, rings and charms.

At the same time he always uttered a mysterious, absolutely idiotic phrase, "The sun rises one time!"

The contents of his briefcase reminded one of Captain Flint's chest.

Somehow he foisted off on me a signet ring with a shamelessly enormous sapphire and a sapphire tie tack, which besides the large blue gemstone was also "finished off" with diamonds.

As I understood it, it was a modest gift from a donut maker, who was avoiding his tax assessment.

Right at that time I was making an exercise ground for the horses and already was having a thoroughly hard time with all the bits of iron and glass in it.

The workers supposedly were removing them, but very sloppily and listlessly.

They didn't dig very deeply and were not especially attentive.

The ring and pin turned out to be very welcome.

Gathering the workers, I offered them the ring, shining the blue sapphire at every one of them, and then showed them the tie tack, polished off with one more sapphire and the diamonds.

I screwed both objects into dirty, corroded foil and reported to the laborers that now I would lock them (the laborers) in the construction trailer in which there were no windows, and bury the loot in the exercise paddock.

The one who found the donut maker's sapphires would own them for the rest of his life and give them to his children.

I drove everyone into the trailer. I bolted it.

And I buried the tack and signet ring, wrapped in the corroded foil, somewhere in a half hectare space. Honestly.

The ring in one place.

The tack in another.

I dug deeply, but quickly, understanding that I had about five minutes until these folks scratched the walls of the trailer with their dark nails and got the ability to see where I was burying the valuables in particular.

I finished.

I unbolted the trailer door and barely managed to get out of the way of the small, but very excited crowd of my workers that poured out with their spades and crowbars.

Lord, how they dug!

How they raced on a motorcycle to town and returned in an hour with two metal detectors!

How they broke and took apart every earthen clod!

After two days of non-stop digging and breaking up what had been dug out, they were ready really to kill each other for the right to dig, that is, they were in good working condition.

A day later the first blood covered the spades.

The police took away one, an ambulance the other.

But the remaining wounded, having bandaged themselves up in a hurry, continued to dig and search.

Dead batteries for the metal detectors were strewn about like shells from a machine gun.

Each cubic centimeter of the paddock was ground up in black fingers.

Soon they found the signet ring.

A day later, the tack.

My loot was somewhat richer — six buckets of rusty metal and glass, which had been brought up to the surface by their bloodied spades.

I will not assert that it is without fail necessary to clean paddocks this way, but this method, you will agree, is not so very bad.

Stable life also can be happy.

And horses, despite all the limitations on freedom, while remembering the rules of the game splendidly, know somehow very cleverly and lovingly to arrange their domestic life, understanding that the world no longer belongs to them in the way it belonged to their forefathers, when the earth was free of man and traces of his life.

[a] Triclinium (Latin) — the kitchen of an ancient Roman home.

[b] Saint Anthony's Fire is gangrene.

EPILOGUE

suspected when I started to write this book that, essentially, it is for very few readers.

It is only for those who sincerely try to understand the horse's fate, his soul and his history, whose brains have not been befouled by twaddle and the fantasies of stable girls or Olympic champions.

It is for those in whom the protest against the wrongness of mankind's attitude toward and treatment of the horse always lives, even though this order of things seems unshakeable.

It is for those who know how to call things by their true names.

This book is completely useless for all others and will be incomprehensible to them.

One cannot count on certain illuminations which would have arisen under its influence.

Unfortunately, not one sportsman or jockey will be mortified and driven to hang himself.

Not those people!

I have heard many outrageous yells from titled "horsemen" about the fact that I am unfairly disregarding them.

They cite their great, or even extreme length of service as a fundamental argument in favor of their certain participation in the art of establishing a proper relationship with the horse.

It is their favorite argument.

Some of them have been tormenting horses for 20 years, others 30, and still others for 50. And the "horsemen" demand recognition and respect on the basis of this length of "service" of perpetrating narrow-minded torture, if not as masters, then at least as men who have a certain relationship with horses.

What a load of rubbish.

One can run the bow across the back side of a fiddle (where there are no strings) for 30, even for a hundred years, but there still won't be any music and the person holding the bow still won't become a musician.

The continuation of such fiddling is a sign of idiocy, not of any kind of mastery.

Though among this group of folks are a few warm-hearted, essentially good people, who have neither enough common sense nor the heart to know that they must turn over the fiddle.

It is understood that I have absolutely no interest in sportsmen.

They are creatures that are not worthy of discussion.

There is neither mastery, art, nor thought in what they do with horses.

They are legion, but not one of them is worthy of mention or discussion.

All their experience is only weakness, and equestrianism has occasioned such evil and suffering for horses that I would not want to soil the pages of this book with any of their names.

* * *

So, one may with absolute confidence assert that any search for the answer to the mystery of the equine soul in the distant and not so distant past is useless.

It is equally useless to search history for the secrets of friendship with the horse.

One now can confess, finally, that all the human experience accumulated in reference to the horse is only weakness, and, therefore, one must start from a clean slate, as if man and horse had met only today.

Everything that happened along that terrifying path to crucifixion on which the horse traveled throughout the history of the world, dragging the cross of humanity's cursed love and need for him, prostrating himself millions of times merely for man's amusement and just as many times for the sake of questionable necessity — this is one of the most disgraceful pages in mankind's history.

He who wishes to get to know the horse, become friends with the horse, establish a relationship with him that is founded on love and understanding, he who wishes to train the horse and see the staggering results of this training and this friendship, can totally scrap, can relegate to complete oblivion, the so called "experience of the ages."

The only exception is the principles of Haute École, which were formulated by Pluvinel:

1) if the horse doesn't do something, that means you did not teach him;

2) if the horse does something poorly, that means you taught him poorly (ineffectively);

3) the horse is always right.

Moreover, the "haute école founders" left very exact concepts of the technique for teaching the horse the most complex elements and figures.

The real "haute école" technique has nothing to do with iron pieces and straps, so it can be used with complete success with a perfectly "naked" horse.

The "haute école" notion about the length of an exercise with the horse, not more than 15 minutes, not counting the breathing of the opening warm-up, is very precise, and very accurate, even from the point of view of modern hippology.

It was sportsmen who brought into fashion and custom the long, hour or two-hour, training sessions, sweat dripping from the flanks, until the horse goes completely crazy.

This fashion crept into the so called "great sport" from the banal rentals, where amateurs gather. Because these "renters" often come from far away and with some difficulty, they want to justify the long and expensive trip by having a good time with the horse for at least an hour — hour and a half.

And this makes it even more convenient for the owners of the rental stables to "rip off" the renters, because an hour is after all a certain solid chunk of time for which a higher price can be demanded.

The universal stable dictatorship of the muck-stained girls who have declared themselves riding mistresses, also has led to the senseless extension of time for the exercises which are so destructive to horses.

These mucky girls, despite all their bluff and arrogance, simply cringe before the owners of the horses.

But this cringing usually consists not of kowtowing and compliance, but of a savage extension of the time of their sadistic amusements with the proprietor's horse.

A mucky girl, even knowing and understanding something, fears that they will replace her with another mucky girl if she doesn't torment the horse for a long enough time.

The 15-minute "haute école" standard is a financial death sentence for them.

In truth, the horse must be returned from the manége after the exercise, which includes such elements as the capriole and Spanish trot, almost completely dry and breathing regularly, with perhaps only a pattern of the veins on the neck and shoulders more distinct and the flanks can be a little damp but not dripping.

Anything beyond this, like the sweat, foam, heavy breathing at the end of an exercise, is a sign of absolute ignorance regarding equine physiology, myology and training on the whole.

I shall explain.

The horse understands everything in 2–5 minutes.

It is exactly the time he needs for the mastery of any new element or exercise. If after three minutes the horse has not comprehended and has not demonstrated even a trace of the movement asked of him, it means that the explanations were wrong and it is senseless to persist.

One must dismount, gather his things and go study.

But if the element has been understood and accepted for work by the horse, then 5-7 minutes a day are sufficient for perfecting it, for getting accustomed to it and developing the necessary group of muscles.

Any more is prohibited, because it is hazardous. The horse's myological system has not been designed for prolonged loads.

By the way, one may read this in any veterinary handbook or any hippologic text.

But the mucky girls think otherwise.

These girls are a special category.

A normal person, who has become the owner of a horse and who finds himself at a stable for the first time, becomes completely enslaved to the malicious, illiterate and very ambitious stable society.

At any stable, besides mold spores, flies, rats and helminth eggs, behind the heaps of old dung-filled sawdust dwell beings with strangely distorted mugs, in felt helmets that once were black, but have faded nearly yellow.

These beings, who never remove their spurs and poofy breeches, like very much to hand out aggressive advice to novices and yell at the horses.

It is impossible to establish their sex at first glance.

They themselves use the copulation method behind the dung heaps or in the tack room for determining each other's sex.

They all are finding out about a partner's sex for themselves, but, as a rule, any result suits them.

The beings know a few names of the Olympic champions, love the terms "chambon" and "ring of muscles" very much. They can, having exerted themselves until they are in pain and dirty, remember a few more terms or, moving their Adam's apple, somewhat discuss the mastery of the old cavalrymen.

These are the horsemen.

The mucky boys and the mucky girls.

The horses are absolutely subordinate to them.

And any normal person who has brought love for horses into the stable falls under their power.

They quickly hurl the wildest views at him about horse training, explaining that there are no other views, train him patiently to tolerate the beating of his horse, saying that otherwise it is impossible, and that's how their forefathers and their fathers before them did it. They easily draw him in to the slow but certain murder of his very own horse, forcing him to get involved with show jumping, dressage or 3-day eventing, depending on what these mucky overseers fancy most.

These people, the groom, the so-called riding masters and the trainers, willingly transfer to anyone who is able to pay for their services a whole list of their own mistakes and the delusions that had interfered with their own achievement at some time of something seriously significant, even in their own primitive sport.

But these unlucky sportsmen are still the best variant.

Former medal-holders, as a rule, persistently transfer those sadistic methods that once actually had allowed them to capture a few ribbons and medals.

I want to warn you honestly that, by following even one piece of their advice or taking into account only one word of theirs, you will without fail become the horse's common enemy and make the horse your enemy.

You have to run from them as you would from a fire.

Both from the medal holders and from the failures.

Plug your ears, lest you accidentally hear something that they advocate.

It must be firmly and steadfastly understood that everything coming from their mouths regarding the equestrian subject is absolute nonsense.

If, heaven forbid, you listen to them a few times and recall to your own misfortune even one thing that they said, then your vital, normal desire to understand the horse and to hear him will be killed outright.

The Olympic champions in the different equestrian disciplines can puff out their cheeks as much as they like, but, check it, their experience generally is not worth a plugged nickel and primarily merits complete oblivion.

Their jabber has no relation whatsoever to the art of relationship with the horse, to training and to true dressage.

The sporting regalia is mere certification of special cruelty toward the horse. Nothing more.

As just one example, for years on end these folks stuff the horse's mouth with iron, poke him with spurs, strike his legs with sticks, all in the name of teaching the horse the piaffe, while breaking his back and damaging his psyche at the same time. The end result is a certain repertoire of forced reflex movements which are unbearable to see.

The fact is, the piaffe can be done by any horse in a week, without any iron pieces or sticks, without beating, or forcing or even the least injury of the small of the back.

The ancient cavalry treatises, the race course tales of the "trotters" and flat racers, and the stable stories of the riding masters which the girls and boys imagine for themselves — all this is complete nonsense, a concentrate of ignorance and idiocy.

It has no relationship to perceiving the horse.

Thank god, a relatively precise science has existed in the world for many decades already that studies the horse and is called hippology. Practically all its discoveries, in any area, be they on the subject of stable management or the horse's biomechanics and physiology, are as yet in complete contradiction to the assurances of the champions and semi-champions, the renters, grooms, jockeys, horse-loving ladies and similar groups of folks.

I say "as yet" for they are heading for a showdown.

And not only in Russia.

I constantly see the fury that is aroused in horsemen when they are confronted by genuine knowledge of the horse.

Thermography (in its veterinary application), as an absolute diagnostic of equine condition, evokes horror and hatred in the mucky girls who understand that the thermographic examination of the horses with which they are involved is a condemnation of them.

They understand what thermography — which ruthlessly records in graphic detail injuries caused mainly by the rider — can reveal.

The real deadliness of show jumping for the horse (dances across the painted poles), which has been repeatedly proven scientifically and demonstrably, is still not taken into account. As always, they lead the horses to the stalls of the racecourse starting gate mainly in "hoods," so that the horses don't see where they are being taken.

In a word, a cheap, unnecessary trick.

The horse understands that they are leading him to a stall for new torture at the gallop. They usually resist it terribly. Even in the "hood."

By the way, enough already has been written about all this in the previous chapters of this book.

He who wanted to understand has understood.

And not everything is so deplorable.

Judging by the fact that this violent world after all has given birth to several people who understand that one should not go further and that 3,000 years experience of communication with the horse today can lead only to the stinking dead end of the racetrack or the sports stable, there is hope that it all will change.

The story of the new High School, the Nevzorov Haute École, is only beginning.

One of my stallions, the slender black Kaogi, about whom I wrote in such detail in the chapter about training the horse and who was in an eternally terrible conflict with the manége pigeons and sparrows, surprised me greatly the other day just as I was finishing the book.

The pigeons had appeared in the manége for some photography. We had brought them in boxes, let them out and then they got acclimated. They became comfortable in the manége and even have an important role in training.

They are so noisy and ugly, so impudent and unpredictable, turning, capering, spinning, and with the beat of their wings and headlong dives, they float in the manége air, coo so loudly and so constantly and they drop some kind of rubbish, stones and feathers right onto the heads of humans and horses, that I had decided not to evict them, but to leave them in order to train the youngest horses in the different types of surprises.

The manége's pigeon diaspora fully provides surprise and extreme behavior.

Having gotten too choosey and having a one-track mind, these white and multicolored pigeons of the "high speed" tumbler breed with beating wings and a wing-over contrive to fly within a centimeter of the horses' ears.

Or, having raised dust and debris, they can shoot themselves out of the dark carvings of the old arch precisely beneath the legs of a horse doing a passage.

Or in a swarm, hurtle from the walls like a battering ram with a crash of wings at the steed and rider.

Overall they are marvelous little birds. It was in the huge manége where, of course, all this could unfold for them.

This spring they all got it into their heads to mate.

The squawking and cooing, raging flights with straws and twigs for nests and flights without twigs already had attained a candidly maniacal nature.

Perst, who treats any unruly conduct and hooliganism with approval, has started to become friends with them and even is overindulgent, grunting in welcome and making faces at the pigeons.

The mares have started on an outright hunt, rushing at a whole swarm of pigeons during their strolls, swiping at the birds both from the rear and from the front.

But it is Kaogi who is filled with the most resentment.

The youngster, a high achiever, accustomed to absolute concentration, and one who has managed to concentrate all his boundless stallion emotions on his ideal lofty movements, has come to hate the pigeons and their interfering bustle with all his heart.

He has allowed himself to acknowledge the pigeons only a few times when being ridden, by laying back his ears and chattering his teeth in answer to their impudent flight above his head.

But this is when ridden.

Let free he has surpassed in ferocity and resourcefulness even the mares.

He has been able to gallop around the manége in pursuit of the insolent birds for hours.

He even hurt one pigeon, putting it out of action in flight with the devilish precision of a blow from his hind hooves.

Overall, the lad has declared war on the pigeons and has begun to win it.

And here, one very early morning I heard the blaring roar of Kaogi who had been strolling in the manége.

The youngster has quite a voice, but this time it was somewhat peculiar.

He was standing at the far end of the manége and bellowing continuously first at the ceiling, then at the ground of the manége, inclining his head low and touching something with a snort.

At his hoof, with an expression of extreme benevolence on its large-beaked mug, almost still completely bald, sat a young pigeon, having fluffed up its naked, rose and violet wings, and with its round stupid eyes gazed at the coal-black monster.

The pigeon bounced and retreated backwards when it was fanned with the wind from the colt's nostrils.

And Kaogi continued to bellow, and, so as not to touch the violet fool, dug carefully into the ground alongside the bird with his hoof. The pigeon's parents were occupied with more important things at the time.

Daddy Pigeon was stomping on Mommy in their slipshod constructed nest in the arch.

Kaogi waited until I, swearing, dragged over the ladder, placed the pigeon into my cap and, lifting toward the arch, shoved it into the nest, toward the stupidly cooing parents.

Having waited, he tore away in his most frisky gallop with joyful croupades and courbettes.

And since then, each time at his exercises, passing that nest, beneath that arch, either in hand or saddled, he would set his ears and give a quick snort, completely happy.

He stopped chasing the pigeons and no longer killed any of them.

I absolutely do not understand why I have told this story that makes not the slightest allegorical nor didactic sense.

The horse's intellect, lofty, pure and noble, is not even subject to doubt.

Man is not suited for the role of that pigeon, he is too strong and dangerous.

And man is not so enchantingly powerless as that lilac and large-beaked infant.

And the colt, generally, did nothing extraordinary.

Most likely this story was required at the very conclusion of the book only because it was impossible to end this narrative about the road to the cross, the crucifixion and rebirth of the horse with a conversation about mucky girls, jumps and races.

I assume that our children will read about such folks and about such amusements with the very same unbelieving grin with which we discover the "Horse Medication Handbook" of the 18th century, with its recommendation of an enema with saltpeter and bedbugs in the urinary tract.

For our children, and even more so for our grandchildren, the main words directed toward the horse, will be the words of the old grey-haired horse whisperers — the strange words of the ancient language of the prairie Sioux so strikingly understood by the horses themselves: "Shunka-wakan, nagi-ki uachi elo."

That means, as you will recall, "I need the soul of this horse."

NOTES

¹ *(Prologue, page 10)* James Fillis (died in 1914). The son of London notary officer. He was brilliant at pulling the legs of different kinds of "nonprofessionals" by publishing books along the lines of modern "How to become a millionaire" ones. Although the subject of his books was not the moneymaking kind, but about so-called "dressage." There were hundreds of pages with advice and instructions. Practically he showed utter cruelty toward horses. This cruelty, by the way, is obvious even in his fraudulent writings. The writings by themselves are the methods in which a horse plays the role of a stupid meat machine in which one should generate a servile obedience with pain induced by spurs and a curb bit. All the books contain photographs on which Fillis smugly demonstrates an incredibly ugly seat and pale walrus-like mustache. After he found himself useless in Europe, he went to earn his cash in Russia. They let him in a few barracks with his lessons, but mostly he dabbled in circuses. Impressed by his cruelty, Russian circus people (even them) provoked a loud and charming scandal. Fillis didn't speak Russian, so the carpet clown announced his appearance with such words: "An English breaker, a true horse sy-Fillis! A plague for all the horses"! The so-called "methods" of Fillis are still studied thoroughly by Russian sportsmen. They sincerely try to discover the secrets of dressage in this rubbish.

² *(Prologue, page 12)* Zhuangzi. Ingenious Ancient Chinese philosopher, one of the founders of Taoism, the religious-philosophical system which proposes not to hope for something supernatural, but to seek for freedom, happiness, truth and scorn for death inside oneself. His treatises were reprinted thousands of times. Little is known about Zhuangzi himself, but world philosophy is charmed by him for the last two and a half thousands of years.

³ *(Chapter 1, page 29)* "Historical small potatoes." I'm a bit shy of my own term "small potatoes," but in comparison with such giants as Pluvinel, de Nestier and Guérinière this description of all the "lesser" masters of Haute École, to my regret, is the most suitable one. Though there were brilliant, legendary riders among these "small potatoes," such as de Solverg, de Neuilly, Marquis de la Bigne and Viscount d'Abzac, Montfaucon de Rogles, de Loubersac, Dougast, De Villemot and Dupaty de Clam, the author of a few clever (for their time) books. For exam-

ple this particular one published in 1771 "The Science and Art of Riding, Demonstrated in Accordance with Nature." Gaspard de Saunier finds himself among those "small potatoes," according to my logic, although, he was very talented rider and writer. All who were mentioned above, despite their obvious talent, were either born too late, after all the main discoveries of the School were made and all the laurels were shared, or they were just adherers of one or another Haute École branches. For example, de Solverg and de Neuilly all their lives imitated the super-star of Haute École, de Nestier, with whom they were friends. Although they were always cognizant of his superiority, they were great at imitation. They even copied de Nestier's reticence, his mode of dressing and saddling a horse, and his habits and views. De Solverg and de Neuilly served in the Versalles School under de Nestier's lead. They were well-known and respected, but in the history of Haute École they are mere shadows of de Nestier. This is a telling example. Among the listed seemingly brilliant persons there are only pale duplicates of Pluvinel, de Nestier, Guérinière and Pignatelli and other founding fathers of the School. Marquis de la Bigne and Viscount d'Abzac, Gaspard de Saunier and Montfaucon de Rogles, Coulon, de Cirineille, de Rochefort, de Bournoville and De Plessis were examples. We can give a salute to the rough limestone of their graves with our great respect, but we should remember that they hadn't discovered anything and that they were not the teachers, but mere students. Of course, I beg their ghosts pardon for this bad name "small potatoes" which I used regarding them as well. A fortiori, William Cavendish, the Duke of Newcastle should be considered a "small potato." For all his life he struggled to be a true master, but all these struggles were vain. Although he had called himself one of the pillars of Haute École whenever it was possible, we still remember the spur wheels which he attached to the tail of the chambrière, his constant use of serreta, the habit to "bend the head to the boot" and other manifestations of Newcastle's cruelty, which always stood in contrast with the true spirit of the School. The anxious fanfaronade of Newcastle to become the great master of the School came at a high cost to the horses whom he trained. His constant desire to show off with an incredibly high capriole, duration of terre à terre, his urge to grade up to Pluvinel or Salomon de la Broue made Newcastle's riding "affected," rude, nervous, conceited and, in its essence, not truly "Haute École." If I could, I'd rather cross out Newcastle from the annals of Haute École, but, of course, I'm not the one to make such decisions. I also open-heartedly consider all the nobles "small potatoes." Those like "the grand equerry" le Grand and boastful Baron d'Eisenberg, another "grand equerry," but this time it happened at the court of the Naples vice-king. The "small potatoes" are all those people, who entered the history of the School via cumshaw. For example, le Grand (the Duke of Bellegarde) bitterly envied Pluvinel all his life and played mean tricks on him at the court whenever he could. By the way, it was le Grand who with the help of his sidekick Thalman de Roe nicknamed the great Pluvinel Rustre. It was le Grand who mimicked the harsh old man (Pluvinel) wincing and rolling his eyes for the pleasure of ladies and idlers. If the king would not have favored Pluvinel, this "grand equerry" would have ruined the great master at the drop of the hat. Le Grand had clout at the court and a lot of power in everything concerning horses. During his lifetime he tried to harm the School, but always was somewhere near it, and the weak-eyed history, as it happens quite often, numbered le Grand among the brilliant galaxy of Haute École founding fathers. Pluvinel was aware of le Grand's power and was a little afraid of him. The master had to shuffle for le Grand all the time, but in his main treatise "Exercise de Monter à Cheval" he made le Grand one of the characters and very respectfully put into his mouth the dumbest words. A charming revenge. Marquis of Marialva belonged to this rank of the ones who "got into" and the ones who were "gotten into" by history.

[4] (Chapter 1, page 61) The amazing thing is that while studying any Antique war theorist or practicianer who wrote his treatises on tactics and strategy — Apollodorus, Eneus the Tactician, Athineus, Sekstus Julius Frontinus, Flavius Vegetius Renatus, Marcus Vitruvius Pollio — you will find out that there is not a single word written on cavalry and its use. Serious Antique authors wrote on the army setup as if there was no chivalry at all or as if it played only the moral, theatric role and had no use in any real stratagems and battle instructions. And despite this fact, all the treatises mentioned above contain all the kinds of information — from the methods of well digging to the technique of cleansing the armor. Only Flavius Vegetius Renatus in chapter 23 of the third book mentions briefly that the cataphracts (heavy horsemen) are highly vulnerable, and in chapter 24 there is a brief mention of chariots. I mention chariots here for it shows distinctively how antiques thought of this stupid device which was later anthemed by artists and cinematographers: "The kings Antioch and Mithridates used scythed chariots with four horses in their military campaigns. At first those chariots evoked great fear, but later they became the figures of ridicule. It is hard to find an even field for such a chariot with scythes, the smallest obstacle will hold it, and if one horse of the four gets injured or killed the chariot comes out of action. But those chariots lost sense mainly because of this Roman trick: when the battle started, Romans quickly threw tribules on the field. When horses stumbled on tribules, they died. Tribula is a defensive piece made of four sharpened stakes. Whenever you throw it, it will stand firmly on three of its stakes and is harmful by the fourth one pointing upwards. Besides large wooden tribules which were used against chariots the small iron or copper tribules were scattered around. They smashed the attack of any cavalry without the slightest effort from the offended side. The only leader who had managed to neutralize tribules (or, as I call them in Spanish "espinas") was Frederick of Prussia. This beast, after finding out that the field on which he was supposed to move his chivalry was sown by espinas, placed there by the ill and injured and riderless horses from the trains and infirmaries. The horses were raced across the field ahead of the attacking regiments. These ill and injured horses, which Frederick didn't need any more, gathered espinas with their

hooves. They stayed on those fields forever. In all the armies of the world horses were the main aim for archers, slingers, arbalesters, musketeers and artillerists. This is an ancient practice. The Ancient Indian sources like Mahabharata describe it this way: "And then Virata pierced Susharman with ten arrows and also pierced his four horses with five arrows each."

5 *(Chapter 3, page 149)* Ulrich von Jungingen (killed in 1410), was the Grand master of Teutonic order. He was a valiant but very feisty knight who had started the war of the Order with Poland in 1410 and lost it in the battle of Grunwald (Tannenberg). Von Jungingen got off cheap as he was killed during the battle. And Teutonic order after Grunwald was "brought down" for a long time and in different ways. It was deprived of its lands, castles, coats of arms until it was "brought down" completely and eliminated.

6 *(Chapter 3, page 203)* There is a common canonic cliché which claims that the sign of the good seat of a rider are dropped heels. This is nonsense. A rider who rides bareback, i.e. one who had harmonically adjusted himself to the horse's movements, a relaxed rider always and surely will have not his heels, but his toes dropped. It is obvious that the most natural position of a rider's feet would be the one with its toes dropped a little. But the rules of the stiff, made-up seat which is common in modern dressage demand to drop heels. As this position is unnatural and tense, it deprives the seat of lightness, harmony and the ability not to mess up a horse's movement. There are dozens of tools which make an illusion of dropped heel. Those tools are rubber liners on the stirrups which are sloped one side or another, or special "under heels" which are put in riding boots. "Under heels" is some kind of an inner heelpiece pointing upwards which is hidden inside riding boots, it makes a visual illusion of a dropped heel. But it is only an illusion. Poor goofs, who have watched a lot of dressage videotapes without knowing this small secret, pull their heels down till their eyes pop out. They stiffen their legs and entire body and gain this way that decoratively-stiff seat that is loved so much by ignoramuses. In fact, this seat is the sign of a complete dilettantism and dangerous stupidity, because a tensely sitting rider will certainly fall down from his horse. After all, there are as many seats as there are allures. There are as many seats as figures. The only goal of a rider is to make his presence on the horse's back as imperceptible and light as possible. So, the main goal of a good rider is something that founding fathers of Haute École called "depriving oneself of his own weight". And it is one's task to decide how to reach it. Some slouch a little like Luraschi and Oliveira, some move legs ahead and some sag a bit. All in all, everybody solves this problem according to the horse's movements and their own physique.

7 *(Chapter 4, page 228)* After burying their chief and building a mound above his body and the bodies of his horses, wives and servants, Eastern Scythians didn't settle down. Depending on the size of a mound, they killed twenty to thirty

horses and riders. Dead horses with dead men on their backs were put around the mound like guards. It was made in an easy way; three stakes were pegged into the ground and on those stakes dead men and horses were strung. There was a crossbar on the two stakes on which a horse was put to support its belly so the horse wouldn't fall.

[8] *(Chapter 4, page 229)* King David, one of the main characters of the Scripture, is honored by the Christian church as a saint, godfather and prophet. From the look of it, he was a complete paranoid. Horse tortures were not the only deeds of this saint prophet. In addition he intricately and often indulged in debauchery which was a cumshaw. Also he wrote poems known now as "Psalms of David" and invented new ways of murder, indiviual ones as well as mass ones. In particular, after he had won one of the Ammonite cities, David, as the Scripture tenderly puts it, "took the people of this city and put them under saws, iron hammers, iron axes and threw them into the burners" (poem 31, chapter 12, The Second Book of Kings). David was noted for his hysterical piety and whim.

[9] *(Chapter 4, page 251)* Mongols. After studying all the main sources of that time, which are scarce — "The History of Mongols" by Plano Caprini, "Chronicles" by Thomas of Split, annals of Rashid-Ad-Din, "Man-da bay-lu" (the complete description of Mongol-Tatar) by Chou Hun, which is the deepest Chinese source; "Hay-da Shi-lyue" (the brief information on black Tatars) by Pan-Day and Suy-Zin, "The Great Chronicle" by Matthew of Paris and a few Russian annals — it becomes obvious that almost all of the Mongol-Tatar victories had no connection to mounted fight and horses. Mongols were the best archers and had a great skill in using stone mortars, glaive throwers, double-bow and triple-bow ballistas and fire-throwers of Chinese type. The main force of their armies, at least since 1223, was Chinese engineers who invented different catapults, and created and maintained them. The second Mongol's grand trump card was "Hasharas", siege crowds of local people. These people dragged catapults, gathered and tooled missiles for them (they were pulling up the stones and beveling them). Those same "Hasharas" pelted moats with hurdles, earth and wood. And they were the ones to get molten lead, tar, pitch, stones and logs from the top of the fortifications on their heads. Rashid-ad-Din points that during the siege of Khujand, for example, "There were fifty thousand "Hasharas" and twenty thousand Mongols." In the book "Man-da" the full description of this event is given: "Every time they advanced toward a big city, they first conquered some small towns and took people for prisoners. They chased them with the horde and used them as sieges. When there were enough people, they were ordered to gather a lot of stones and to carry a lot of wood and earth. When captives arrived at the big city, they began to pelt the moats at the fortifications with what they had brought with them until the moats were even with the ground. "Hasharas" were used to maintain chariots with ballistas and stone mortars, assault domes, catapults and battering rams." "Hasharas" were used in field

battles and sieges as well. But there were few real field battles and information on them is contradictory and not accurate. The main list of the Mongol-Tatar victories contains sieges and assaults of fortresses and cities, i.e. the operations where the cavalry had no part at all. Those sieges and assaults "made" the war as it was during the Russian and the European campaigns of Jahangir Batu Khan. The cities of Vladimir-Suzdalskiy, Ryazan, Vladimir-on-Klyazma, Torzhok, Kozelsk, Kiev, Krakow, Wroclaw, Buda, Pest, Bratislava, Pucanec, Krupina, Esterholm, Swach, Drivasto, Catarro, Dubrovnik, Zagreb, Uglich, Yaroslavl, Kostroma, Galich, Rostov, Tver, Pereyaslavl-Zalesskiy, Yuryev-Polskiy, Suzdal, Moscow and others were besieged and assaulted. Almost the same things happened during the Asian campaign of the Jahangir's predecessor. The same sieges and assaults — Bukhara, Samarkand, Choresm... I can list them for eternity; there are a lot of fortresses and cities in Middle Asia and China. And they all have been conquered by Mongols. Every assault, every capture of the city is, first of all, a melée combat on foot with the use of "high-tech" of that time. And this is what makes war history of Mongols, even if it sounds paradoxical.

[10] *(Chapter 4, page 251)* Attila (395–453). The ultimate ruler of the Huns (Hunnu), who had somehow managed to fuse one of the greatest armies in the world history of enormous quantity of wild nomadic tribes who held no sympathy for each other, and to belabor with it the space from China to France. Considering the public dramatics he displayed in the Battle of Cataluanian Fields where he had ordered the gathering of the saddles from all the army, to make a mound of them and to set it on fire so he could thrust himself into the fire if he had lost the battle, Attila was a very artistic psychopath. It is not exactly clear to me, why he wanted to burn the saddles which had massive wooden arches in them and were skillfully crafted and richly ornate. If Attila's desire to fry himself in the face of his whole army was so irresistible, he could use the pieces of ten carts of the 20 thousands carts and wagons the Huns had with them and by which they surrounded themselves while waiting for the Romans and their allies (for that moment) the Vestgotes to attack. Though, the battle at the Cataluanian Fields had no winners or losers. Vestgotes had arranged the funeral feast for their king Theodorich whom they had trampled themselves; the Romans didn't take the chance to attack on their own, and Attila fell back snarling only to safely and with comfort die a bit later a wonderful death of sexual overstrain.

[11] *(Chapter 4, page 252)* Publius Cornelius Emilianus Scipio (The African) (235–183 B.C.). The highest standard of Roman military aristocrat and warlord. Cruelty, mercy, valiance and caution were never the motives of his deeds but they were mere tools for his work as a warlord. With the admirable nonchalance of a great surgeon, Publius Cornelius Emilianus Scipio used those tools to operate on the Ancient world of his time and to remove the enormous Carthage ulcer which threatened Rome and therefore the civilization. He had overrun Hannibal

and later destroyed Carthage. Some historians explain the embarrassing episode when Scipio was carried away from the battlefield by his horse with the scratches the horse got and which frightened him. I, on the contrary, think that the cause of this episode was a complete absence of real riding skills which could not be present at that time. The wounded horses, as all the history of war shows, prefer to stay in ranks following their herd instinct and the will to be near their kin. Only the rudeness and the stupidity of the rider can provoke the real disobedience and the so-called "bolting" to which Scipio fell victim. He himself provoked his horse to do it, for sure. As Roman sources put it, Scipio engaged into the combat on his own and started to bandy some darts with Hannibal or the Carthaginian he took for Hannibal; then Scipio freaked out, pulled the horse's mouth too much with the dreadful Roman iron of his and the horse, crazed by pain, bolted away from the battle. Scipio should have thanked his clever horse for dragging him on the Roman side and not into the Carthage camp.

[12] *(Chapter 4, page 253)* Russian cavalry wasn't better. The fame of the Cossacks is phony. The main "style" of the Cossacks was barbaric, cruel riding without collection, with the horse's back sagged and head tilted upwards, "like an axe" as the Cossacks called it themselves. The cruel and primitive Cossack riding can be compared only to the riding of Nigerian or Afghan tribes. For example, Tirion reports that the French Marshall Murat during the war of 1812 never used his saber in the encounters with Cossacks. He used only his whip in such fights. Only those Cossack squads who fought on the German side during the World War II as a part of "SS Cossack cavalry corps" got some rudiments of horseback riding knowledge.

[13] *(Chapter 4, page 253)* Jan Zhizhka (1360–1424). Genius of a warlord, the instigator of the Hussite Wars who had kept all the knightly Europe on its toes as long as his health let him. In his youth he took part in the battle of Grunwald (1410) where, possibly, he had begun to enjoy his part in the public events of this sort. In 1419 Zhizhka, who was apparently bored and litigated with his neighbors, heard that the clerics had burned Jan Hus with whom Zhizhka had been friends. I don't think that Zhizhka had seriously entered the Hussite casuistry and understood the dogmatic essence of the conflict between Hus and Roman Catholicism. I suppose that Zhizhka took it as a personal insult that his friend was burnt and that he felt the mood of the streets and understood that he stood a wonderful chance to enter the war with almost all the civilized world. I should say that for Zhizhka this was far more interesting than lawsuits and almost bloodless boring fights with his neighbors. As he was an extremely talented warlord (as the results of his actions show) and a powerful leader, Zhizhka easily joined everyone in Czech lands who were annoyed by anything. The next Crusade came along. It came to Czech lands and its goal was the smashing of the Hussite heresy (the followers of Jan Hus) which Papists found very harmful and utterly intolerable. Zhizhka easily thwacked the first Crusade, then the second one, and then the blood purge of

the European knighthood became his habit. He was bored to death if the warriors of the Holy See didn't appear for long. As soon as he saw them, he was childishly amused. And at once battered and smashed them. He never took captives or ransom. He just killed, but did it merrily, with zest and inventively. The knighthood was upset with his bad manners and absolutely refused to bring Crusades to the Czech lands. Zhizhka was terribly bored and to get himself something to do he started to kill those same Hussites on behalf of whom he fought with Crusades. After there was no one left to kill, Zhizhka got bored again. This time he was bored virtually to death. Zhizhka was a big joker and a visionary man. It concerned his battle tactics as well as such a small things as a death-wish. After his death, the followers of Zhizhka skinned him, according to his will and used part of his skin to make a drum, the sound of which should have inspired the followers of Zhizhka to kill everyone they saw. The other part of Zhizhka's skin was used for more mundane needs. At least, my Czech friend Frantishek who sells antiques and besides knight spurs and iron gathers everything medieval, a few times offered me, with his eyes artistically popped out, for sale a powder bag sewn of Zhizhka's skin, a handwritten Bible of XVI century cased in Zhizhka's skin, a "misericord" in the sheath lined with Zhizhka's skin, etc. After thoroughly examining a few of the coeval portraits of Zhizhka I hadn't found his close resemblance with Shar-Pei dog, so I don't understand where all those objects made of Zhizhka's skin which are passed between antiquarians are from.

[14] (*Chapter 4, page 264*) Something Marshal de Saks had claimed. He was not as aphoristically precise, but still he formulated quite well the principles of training the war horse. Marshal wrote honestly, that the love of a horse ruins cavalry. He claimed that it was "necessary to cause pain to horses and to make them stronger with races and severe training."

[15] (*Chapter 5, page 276*) Julius Lupus. One of the participants of the plot against Caligula. He made it into history not only as a big fan of smashing babies against the walls, but as an exceptional coward. The plot-makers, including their leader Cassius Heraeus were put to death under sentence of Senate for the murder of the emperor Gaius Caligula which was committed on January 24 of the year 41. Among the sentenced to death was Julius Lupus. When he was brought to the scaffold, he started to cry, whine and beg, that is he behaved absolutely gracelessly.

[16] (*Chapter 5, page 283*) Fashion of 18th and 19th centuries. G. Tennecker, the author of the popular book of that time "Stable Order" published in 1820 describes this fashion thoroughly: "As we like a horse only when it holds its tail high, which demonstrates its power and nature; it is not sufficient only to watch that a tail is always in good position. The Englization (cutting a tail) — as good as it is — is not always sufficient for this purpose. So we have to use different means to achieve our aim. One of these means is the administration of pepper, after which a horse

not only lifts its tail better, but becomes more tempered, livelier and moves more freely. For this purpose the whole peppercorns are put in the horse's rectum, or balls made of ground pepper, flour and water, which are also put in the rectum a few at a time. This artificial irritation of the rectum makes the horse not only carry its tail better, but it seems more tempered and even fatter and wider while the irritation continues. It is because the horse tenses its belly and tries to push away the irritating object. Also it lifts its loins and back. The movement of its hind legs becomes easier and the horse looks powerful, speedy and beautiful". Today this tradition is kept only in circuses and corridas.

[17] *(Chapter 5, page 283)* Englization. I shall quote sources of that time once more. The way they are formulated will show better than any proof that this idiotic tradition was common almost everywhere. The same Tennecker in his "Stable order" writes this: "The one who wants to sell horses without improvements, without englization or tying up tails, if he doesn't want to sell only peasant horses, has no idea what real horse business is and will never profit from it... A horse which is lazy, inattentive, stiff in its legs, exhausted by work and with its legs damaged, after englization, twisting and tying its tail becomes lively, quick and even more free in its movements as long as the pain in its wounds and tension continue."

[18] *(Chapter 5, page 284)* Although, fashion changed from time to time at the end of 18th century, instead of "dapples" the "tiger stripes" became fashionable. G. Stuthaim describes how after prolonged procedures with different recipes the coats of gray horses became striped like tiger's fur. "To turn a light-gray horse to a mottled one or a tiger and to make other marks on it the hell stone is used. It leaves reddish-brown spots on the coat. I've often seen how a tiger was made of a gray horse, and everyone took it for a real one. À propos, I remember the light-gray horse of Mister Sh., with whom we did our military service in Saxon hussar regiment. His horse was painted so skillfully, that regiment's officers at first thought there were natural markings on its coat. Also a famous circus rider Ciarini had a painted tiger among his horses, and spectators took it for a real one."

BIBLIOGRAPHY

Albrecht, K. *Principles of Dressage*. London, 1981.

Ammianus Marcellinus. *Roman History*. Moscow, 1994.

Appian of Alexandria. *Roman History*. Moscow.

Appian of Alexandria. *Roman Wars*. Moscow, 1950.

Archaeological digest. Vol. 1–34.

Archeology of USSR: Ancient Realms of Caucasus and Middle Asia. Moscow, 1985.

Archeology of USSR: Ancient Russia. Moscow, 1985.

Archeology of USSR: Antique Realms of the Northern Black Sea Region. Moscow, 1984.

Archeology of USSR: Corpus of the Archeological Sources. All issues.

Archeology of USSR: Finno-Ugres and Balts in the Middle Ages. Moscow, 1987.

Archeology of USSR: Plains of Eurasia in the Middle Ages. Moscow, 1981.

Arrian. *The Campaigns of Alexander*. Moscow, 1993.

Back, W., Clayton, H. *Equine Locomotion*. Saunders, 2001.

Baker, G. J., Easley, J. *Equine Dentistry*. Saunders, 1999.

Balme, M. de la. *Essais sur L'Équitation:* ou, *Principes Raisonnés sur L'Art de Monter et de Dress-er Les Chevaux*. Paris, 1773.

Barroil. *L'Art Équestre*. S. I, 1887.

Baucher, F. *Dictionnaire Raisonné d'Équitation*. S. I, 1833.

Baucher, F. *Dressage Méthodique du Cheval de Selle*. S. I, 1891.

Baucher, F. *Methode D'équitation Basée Sur de Nouveaux Principes*. S. I, 1859.

Baucher, F. *Passe-temps Équestre*. S. I, 1840.

Bichko, S. V. (Iyvachchin). *Russian-Lakota Phrase Book*. Saint Petersburg, 2005.

Bourgelat, C. *Le Nouveau Newcastle, ou Traité de Cavalerie*. S. I, 1771.

Brack, F. de. *Light Cavalry Out-Posts.* 1906.

Bregrieres, C de. *Manuel des Écuyers.* S. I, 1725.

Brereton, J. M. *Horse in War.* David & Charles, 1976.

Bricks, G. *Annotation.* In: Denison, G. History of Cavalry. Moscow, 2001.

Broue, Salomon de la. *Le Cavalerice François.* S. I, 1602

Budenny, S. *The Book on Horses.* Moscow, 1959.

Capitaine Picard. *École de Cavalerie.* Paris, 1880.

Carnat, G. *Le Fer à Cheval à Travers L'Histoire et L'Archéologie.* S. I, 1951.

Cavendish, W. *Methode et Invention Nouvelle de Dresser les Chevaux.* S. I, 1658.

Clam, Dupaty de. *La Science Et L'Art De L'Equitation.* S. I, 1776.

Comte D'aure. *Cours Déquitation.* Paris, 1888.

Cornelius Tacitus. *The Annals.* Moscow, 1969.

Curnieu Baron de. *Leçons de Science Hippique Générale Partie 2.* S. I, 1857.

Dalmatov, V. *Cavalryman Handbook.* Moscow, 1921.

Darwin, Ch. *Collected Edition.* Saint Petersburg, 1908.

Denison, G. *History of Cavalry.* Moscow, 2001.

Directions and Orders for the Cavalry of the King of Prussia Frederick the Great. Saint Petersburg, 1903.

Domnin, A. *Cutting and Applied Swordcraft in Cavalry.* Moscow, 1927.

Edwards, E. H. *Bits and Bitting.* David & Charles, 2000.

Fiaschi, C. *Trattato dell' Imbrigliare, Maneggiare e Ferrare Cavalli.* S. I, 1556.

Flavius Josephus. *The Antiquities of the Jews.* Rostov-on-Don, 2003.

Flavius Josephus. *The Jewish War.* Minsk, 2004

Fillis, J. *Journal de Dressage.* S. I, 1903.

Fillis, J. *Principes de Dressage.* S. I, 1891.

Franconi, V. *Cours d'Equitation Pratique.* S. I, 1855.

Frouville de. *Manière de Dresser les Chevaux.* S. I, 1784.

Fisher, I. B. *Cattle Doctor Book.* Moscow, 1774.

Gail. *Oeuvres de Xenophon*. S. I, 1795.

Gaius Sallustius Crispus. *Jugurthine War*. Moscow, 1891.

Gaius Suetonius Tranquillus. *The Lives of the Twelve Caesars*. Moscow, 1966.

Gensler, I. *Equestrian Handbook*. Saint Petersburg, 1851.

Gerlach. *Cours d'Equitation Militaire*. S. I, 1830.

Geschvend. *The Guide to Understanding a Horse*. Saint Petersburg, 1868.

Grisone, F. *L'Écuirie du Sr. Federic Grison, Gentilhomme Napolitain*. S. I, 1559.

Gueriniere, F. R. de la. *École de Cavalerie*. S. I, 1733.

Gueriniere, F. R. de la. *Écuyer du Roi et d'Aujourd'hui*. Belin, S. I, 2000.

Gumilev, L. *History of the Hunnu People*. Moscow, 2004.

Hammond, I. *The Conquistadors*. Moscow, 2002.

Herodotus. *The Histories*. Moscow, 1885.

Hippica, or the horse science. Moscow, 1685.

Hippocrates. *Selection*. Rudnev, V., trans. Moscow, 1994.

Hodgson, D., Rose, R. *The Athletic Horse*. Saunders, 1994.

Horse-breeding and Hunting Magazine. Saint Petersburg, 1850–1854.

Hunersdorf, L. *Equitation Allemande*. S. I, 1843.

Hyland, A. *The Horse in the Ancient World*. Sutton & Sutton, 2003.

Hyland, A. *The Horse in the Middle Ages*. Sutton & Sutton, 1999.

Hyland, A. *The Medieval Warhorse*. Sutton & Sutton, 1994.

Hyland, A. *The Warhorse*. Sutton & Sutton, 1998.

Instruction on How to Break Horses by Antonio Pluvinel, French Royal Grand Equerry. Moscow, 1670.

Knottenbelt, D., Pascoe, R. *Diseases and Disorders of the Horse*. Mosby, 1999.

Knottenbelt D., Pascoe, R. *Manual of Equine Dermatology*. Saunders, 1999.

Kraft zu Hohenlohe-Ingelfingen. *Conversations on Cavalry*. Warsaw, 1889.

Le Cheval et la Guerre. Paris: Association pour l'Académie d'art équestre de Versailles, 2002.

Loch, S. *Dressage*. London, 2001.

Machiavelli, Niccolo. *The Art of War*. 1939.

Malm, G. A. *Bits and Bridles: An Encyclopedia*. Grasshopper Publishers Kansas, 1996.

Markovin, V. *Zandack Burial Mound of the Early Iron Age on the River Yarik-Su*. Moscow, 2002.

Matthew, P. *The Great Chronicle*. Moscow, 1979.

Mauleon de. *Méthode de Dressage*. S. I, 1895.

Mauricius. *Tactics and Strategy*. Moscow, 1903.

Mazhitov, V. *Kurgans of the Southern Ural*. Moscow, 1981.

Memoires de Mr D'Artagnan, Capitaine-Lieutenant de la Premiere Compagnie des Mousquetaires du Roi. A Cologne: Chez Pierre Marteau, 1701.

Men-da. *Bay-lu*. Moscow, 1957.

Menou, R. de. *Exercice de Monter à Cheval*. S. I, 1651.

Miura, I., Sasaki, R. F. *Zen Koans*. Saint Petersburg, 2004.

Mogilnikov, V. *Nomads of the Northwest Altai Foothills in 9–11 Centuries*. Moscow, 2002.

Mommzen, T. *History of Rome*. Moscow, 2004.

Montaigne, M. *Essais*. Moscow, 1979.

Munenori, Y. *Haiho Kaden Se*. transl. by Hiroyaki Sato. Saint Petersburg, 1998.

Musany. *Dressage des Chevaux Difficiles*. S. I, 1880.

Musany. *Dressage Méthodique*. S. I, 1879.

Nitobe, I. *Bushido*. Sofia, 2004.

On the Horse-Breeding Arrangement. 1687.

Osipov. *The Newest and Perfect Russian Horse Expert, Rider, Breeder and Horse-Doctor*. Saint Petersburg, 1791.

Pausanias. *Description of Greece*. Moscow, 1996.

Plano Carpini, J. *History of Mongals*. Moscow, 1957.

Pliny the Younger. *Letters*. Moscow, 1984.

Plutarch. *Vitae Parallelae*. Moscow, 1961.

Pluvinel, A. de. *L'Instruction du Roy en L'Exercice de Monter à Cheval*. S. I, 1666.

Polybius. *The Histories*. Moscow, 1899.

Prince Scherbatov and Count Stroganov. *Book on Arabian Horse.* Saint Petersburg, 1990.

Procopius Cesarean. *The Vandal War.* Saint Petersburg, 1993.

Rashid-ad-Din. *Annals Collection.* Moscow, 1946, 1952, 1960.

Richardson, C. *The Horse Breakers.* J. A. Allen, 1998.

Rosche, A. *The Pocketbook on Light Cavalry Military Service.* Saint Petersburg, 1834.

Saint-Phalle. *Dressage.* S. I, 1904.

Saunier, G. de. *La Parfaite Connaissance des Chevaux.* S. I, 1734.

Saunier, G. de. *Principes de la Cavalerie.* S. I, 1749.

Sokho, T. *Letters from the Zen Master to the Fencing Master.* Saint Petersburg, 2003.

Solleysel de. *Le Véritable Parfait Maréchal.* S. I, 1672.

Susane. *Cavalerie Française.* S. I, 1874.

Swift, J. *Essays.* Moscow, 1947.

Tao-te Ching translated by Jan Hin-Shun. Kharkov, 2002.

Tao-te Ching translated by V. Malyavin. Moscow, 2003.

Tao-te Ching translated by V. Pereleshin. Moscow, 2000.

Taratorin, V. *Cavalry at War.* Minsk, 1999.

Titus Livius. *The History of Rome from its Foundation.* Moscow, 1989.

Toudouze, G. *Le Roy Soleil.* Paris, 1908.

The Bones and the Flesh of Zen: Hundred and One Stories of Zen. Saint Petersburg, 2004.

The Description of the Outlandish Horses. 1686.

The Holy Bible. Moscow, 1999.

Thukydides. *History.* Moscow, 1981.

Urusov. *The Book on Horses.* Saint Petersburg, 1911.

Vallet. *Le Chic à Cheval.* S. I, 1902.

Vitt, V. *Horses of Pazyrik Kurgans.* Moscow, 1952.

Waring, G. *Horse Behavior.* S. I, 2003.

Wrangel, P. *The Book on Horses.* Saint Petersburg, 1903.

Xenofon. *Anabasis.* Moscow, 1951.

Zhang Zhen-Zi. *Practice of Zen.* Saint Petersburg, 2004.

Zhuangzi translated by V. Malyavin. Moscow, 2004.

Zorn, P. *Notes for Hunters of Horses.* Moscow, 1822–1827.

APPENDICES

APPENDIX 1

STATEMENTS

ПРАВИТЕЛЬСТВО САНКТ-ПЕТЕРБУРГА
КОМИТЕТ ПО ЗДРАВООХРАНЕНИЮ
**САНКТ-ПЕТЕРБУРГСКОЕ
ГОСУДАРСТВЕННОЕ УЧРЕЖДЕНИЕ
ЗДРАВООХРАНЕНИЯ
«БЮРО СУДЕБНО-МЕДИЦИНСКОЙ
ЭКСПЕРТИЗЫ»**
195067, Санкт-Петербург,
Екатерининский пр., 10
тел. (7-812) 544-1717;факс (7-812) 545-0340
ОКПО 01932390 ОКОГУ 07185
E-mail: sudmed@zdrav.spb.ru

14.12.2006 г. № _356_ /01-4

А К Т

испытаний по установлению силы
рывкового и штатного воздействий средств управления,
используемых в конном спорте (мундштук, трензель),
на рот лошади

Цель испытаний: установление максимальной силы рывкового и штатного воздействий средств управления, используемых в конном спорте (мундштук, трензель), на рот лошади.

Задачи испытаний:
– установление силы рывкового усилия средств управления, используемых в конном спорте (мундштук, трензель), на рот лошади при воздействии людей, обладающих разной физической силой;
– установление силы штатного усилия (относительно медленного натяжения) средств управления, используемых в конном спорте (мундштук, трензель), на рот лошади при воздействии людей, обладающих разной физической силой.

Условия постановки экспериментов:
Экспертные исследования проводились на манекенах (синтетических моделях), геометрические и механические показатели которых полностью соответствовали голове лошади (с полуоткрытым ртом) в момент воздействия на нее средств управления.
Перед экспериментами манекены (синтетические модели) головы лошади прочно закрепляли в положении, обеспечивающем обычное соотношение рук «наездника», повода и головы лошади в момент воздействия на нее средств управления.
В качестве средств управления ходе экспертизы были применены стандартные средства управления в виде мундштука и трензеля, выполненные из желтого металла.
Для укрепления на голове средств управления (мундштука и трензеля) были использованы штатная система ремней в виде «уздечки» или «оголовья».
В экспериментах рычаг, придающий воздействию силу и эффективность, т.н. «повод» был идентичен применяемому в конном спорте.
Воздействие осуществлялось через прочный повод (с длиной стороны 1 м).

Для установления площади механического контактного воздействия на рот лошади использовали специальное приспособление, используемое в медико-криминалистических экспериментах.

Общая сила воздействия замерялась специальным динамометром с фиксируемой на максимуме стрелкой и шкалой до 350 кг с ценой деления 5 кг.

При проведении испытаний исполнителями физических воздействий (рывкового и штатного натяжения), влекущих болевое воздействие на рот лошади были выбраны:
– мальчик 13 лет;
– девушка 23 лет;
– мужчина 43 лет.

Результаты испытаний:

В результате проведенных экспериментов установлено, что:

1. Общая максимальная сила воздействия повода на модель головы лошади была зафиксирована:
– при натяжении от 50-100 кг;
– при рывковых воздействиях 220-300 кг.

2. Сила исследованных специальных металлических инструментов, именуемых «трензель» и «мундштук» составила на 1 кв. см поверхности рта:
– при обычном натяжении: от 50 до 100 кг;
– при рывке средней силы: от 180 до 220 кг;
– при сильном рывке: свыше 300 кг.

3. Зарегистрированные в экспериментах механические воздействия указанной интенсивности могут приводить к различным повреждениям тканей ротовой полости лошади: от ссадин, кровоизлияний и разрывов слизистой оболочки, до возникновения ушибленных ран и даже переломов костей.

Кроме того, выявленные уровни максимальных нагрузок на модель головы лошади, особенно сильные рывки, могут быть опасными с точки зрения возникновения повреждений связочно-суставного аппарата шейного отдела позвоночника лошади.

Судебно-медицинские эксперты:

Заместитель начальника Бюро
по экспертной работе
доктор медицинских наук, профессор
Заслуженный изобретатель РФ   Исаков В.Д.

Заведующий отделом экспертизы трупов Бюро
кандидат медицинских наук,
врач высшей квалификационной категории   Сысоев В.Е.

NEVZOROV Haute école
RESEARCH CENTRE

GOVERNMENT OF SAINT-PETERSBURG
HEALTH PROTECTION COMMITTEE
STATE INSTITUTE
OF HEALTH PROTECTION
OF SAINT-PETERSBURG
"COURT-MEDICAL EXPERTIZING BUREAU"
195067, Saint-Petersburg,
Ekaterininskiy pr. 10
tel. (7-812) 544-1717, fax. (7-812) 545 0340
OKPO 01932390 OKOGU 07185
E-mail: sudmed@zdray.spb.ru
14.12.2006 No 356 /01-4

STATEMENT

of examinations to define the force
of common and jerk torque impact of control means
used in equestrian sports (snaffle, curb)
upon a horse's mouth

Purpose of examinations: definition of the maximum force of jerk torque and common impact of control means used in equestrian sports (snaffle, curb) upon a horse's mouth.

Examinational tasks:

–   definition of the maximum force of jerk torque impact of control means used in equestrian sports (snaffle, curb) upon a horse's mouth by people possessing different physical strength.
–   definition of the maximum force of common impact of control means used in equestrian sports (snaffle, curb) upon a horse's mouth by people possessing different physical strength.

Experimental conditions:

Experiments were carried out on mannequins (synthetic models), with geometric and mechanical properties that are completely corresponding to head of a horse (with mouth half-opened) at the moment of impact of equipment for control.

Before the beginning of every experiment mannequins (synthetic models) of a horse head were firmly fixed in a position, providing a common physical correlation between rider's hands, reins and a head of a horse ridden in the moment of impact of control means.

As control means standard control means in the forms of a snaffle and a curb, made of metal of yellow color were used.

For proper fixation of control means (snaffle and curb) on the mannequin head a common strap system (in the form of a "bridle" and a "head-band") was used.

In the experiments performed, the lever, providing correspondent force and efficiency (so called "reins"), was identical to the one used in equestrian sports.

Impact was exercised through durable reins (with a long side of 1m in length).

For determination of the square of mechanical contact impact upon a horse's mouth a special device was used, commonly utilized in medico-criminalist expertise.

The total impact force was measured by a special dynamometer with a pointer fixated at maximum value and a scale up to 350 kg with scaling factor equal to 5 kg.

During the experiments the following people were selected to be producers of physical effects (jerk and common drawing), entailing painful impact on the horse's mouth:

- a boy of 13 years old
- young woman of 23 years old
- a man of 43 years old

Examinational results:

In the course of experiments carried out it had been defined, that:

1. The total maximum impact force of reins upon the horse head mannequin was fixated at the respective levels:

- for drawing: from 50 to 100 kg;
- for jerking: from 220 to 300 kg.

2. The impact force of the subject metal instruments (control means) named "a snaffle" and "a curb" aggregates (per 1 sq. cm. of mouth surface):

- for drawing: from 50 to 100 kg;
- for an average force jerk: from 180 to 220 kg;
- for a strong jerk: over 300 kg.

3. Mechanical impacts of mentioned intensity, registered during experiments, may lead to various damage of oral cavity tissues: from abrasions, hemorrhages, mucous tunic ruptures up to compound wounds and even to bones being broken.

Besides that, detected levels of maximum impact force upon the horse head mannequin, especially for strong jerks, may be dangerous in the way of causing damage to ligament-articularis apparatus of the cervical part of a vertebral column of a horse.

Medico-legal experts:

Deputy Chief of Bureau for Expertise
Doctor of Medical Science, Professor
Honored Inventor of Russian Federation
Isakov V. D.

Head of Corpse Expertise Department
Candidate of Medical Science
Doctor of Higher Qualification Category
Sysoev V. E.

Head of Nevzorov Haute École Research Centre
Nevzorov A. G.

ПРАВИТЕЛЬСТВО САНКТ-ПЕТЕРБУРГА
КОМИТЕТ ПО ЗДРАВООХРАНЕНИЮ
**САНКТ-ПЕТЕРБУРГСКОЕ
ГОСУДАРСТВЕННОЕ УЧРЕЖДЕНИЕ
ЗДРАВООХРАНЕНИЯ
«БЮРО СУДЕБНО-МЕДИЦИНСКОЙ
ЭКСПЕРТИЗЫ»**
195067, Санкт-Петербург,
Екатерининский пр., 10
тел. (7-812) 544-1717;факс (7-812) 545-0340
ОКПО 01932390 ОКОГУ 07185
E-mail: sudmed@zdrav.spb.ru

14.12.2006 г. №   366 /01-4

А К Т

испытаний по установлению силы возможных ударов
стандартным хлыстом, принятым в качестве штатного
средства воздействия в конном спорте,
и особенностей повреждений кожи и мягких тканей лошади,
возникающих в результате таких ударов

1. Цель испытаний: установление максимальной силы возможных ударов стандартным хлыстом, принятым в качестве штатного средства воздействия в конном спорте, а также особенностей повреждений кожи и мягких тканей лошади, возникающих в результате таких ударов.

2. Задачи испытаний:
– установление максимальной силы динамического воздействия стандартным хлыстом при ударах разными способами, с разной скоростью (от воздействия людей, обладающих разной физической силой), в разных направлениях по биологическим и небиологическим имитаторам, а также на специальном стенде;
– определение возможности образования повреждений кожи и мягких тканей лошади, возникающих в результате ударов разными частями стандартного хлыста с разной силой и скоростью.

3. Методика исследований и условия постановки экспериментов:

Экспертные исследования проводились согласно общей методике, применяемой в судебной медицине для медико-криминалистического изучения поражающего воздействия тупых предметов, а также механизмов огнестрельной и взрывной травмы (в том числе, так называемой «забронивой травмы» тела человека, одетого в средства индивидуальной бронезащиты, например – бронежилет).

3.1. На первом этапе проводилось <u>изучение и обобщение данных</u>:

а) специальной литературы по конному спорту, фото- и видеоматериалов различных соревнований, где всадниками использовался спортивный хлыст. Исследовались принятые в конном спорте виды замаха и амплитуда ударов хлыстом, а также возможная сила наносимых ударов;

б) специальной судебно-медицинской литературы о видах и свойствах повреждений, возникающих:

— от воздействия тупых твердых предметов с ограниченной травмирующей поверхностью с разной энергией (силой и скоростью) на различные биологические объекты;

— при тупой заброневой травме тела человека, одетого в средства индивидуальной бронезащиты (бронежилет, бронекостюм, каску и др.).

в) архивных материалов судебно-медицинских экспертиз повреждений у пострадавших, получивших травму от ударов тупыми предметами с ограниченной травмирующей поверхностью небольших размеров, то есть в условиях, характерных при нанесении ударов хлыстом в конном спорте;

г) архивных и видео материалов ветеринарного исследования трупов погибших лошадей со следами от ударов спортивным хлыстом.

В результате исследований баз данных были составлены дифференциально-диагностические таблицы (Приложение 1).

3.2. В качестве <u>средства воздействия</u> применялся стандартный спортивный хлыст (бывший в употреблении) фабричного производства с кожаной ударяющей частью, прошитой вдоль четырьмя рядами машинного шва толстой нитью.

3.3. <u>Для нанесения ударов</u> использовались статисты, обладающие разными физическими характеристиками и силой.

3.4. <u>При нанесении ударов</u> их сила, виды замаха и амплитуда движения руки с хлыстом соответствовали вариантам штатного удара, принятого в конном спорте.

3.5. <u>Для объективной проверки силы наносимых ударов хлыстом</u> выполнялись опыты по аппаратному замеру данного параметра на специальной экспериментальной установке для изучения баллистики запреградной тупой травмы.

3.6. <u>Опыты выполнялись на</u> биологических и небиологических имитаторах, аналогичных по плотности мягким тканям живой лошади (блоки баллистического пластилина).

Для точно установления границ повреждений, а также имитации зон осаднений на коже использовался следующий приём: поверх поражаемых объектов последовательно помещались чистые листы писчей бумаги и копировальной бумаги (пигментным слоем вниз).

4. Результаты экспериментов детально изучались (с использованием стандартных приемов морфоскопии и морфометрии), а также фиксировались путём фотосъёмки на цифровую камеру (Приложение 2).

В результате исследований физических параметров ударного воздействия концевой части спортивного хлыста с помощью специальных экспериментальных установок было зафиксировано, что общая сила воздействия хлыстом была не менее 19 кг/см^2, а удельная энергия удара составляла около 20-25 Дж/см^2.

В ходе дальнейших экспериментальных исследований установлено, что в результате ударов спортивным хлыстом стандартного образца (и при штатной амплитуде ударов такого типа) на имитаторах мягких тканей лошади формировались следующие повреждения:

– на листах бумаги: стойкая деформация и сквозные разрывы неправильной овальной формы размерами до 6х1 см с неровными, рваными краями, окруженные зоной отложения черного пигмента шириной до 0,5-1,0 см (имитирующего зону осаднения вокруг основного повреждения);

– на блоках баллистического пластилина формировались вдавления, по форме и размерам соответствующие характеристикам ударяющей поверхности спортивного хлыста фабричного производства:

а) от ударов плоскостью – общими размерами 9-10 х 2-3 см;

б) от ударов ребром – общими размерами 10-11 х 1,0-1,5 см.

Такие повреждения на имитаторах мягких биологических тканей обычно соответствуют следующим видам реальных повреждений:

• очаговые ссадины;

• очаговые кровоподтеки, подкожные кровоизлияния и гематомы;

• размозжения подкожно-жировой клетчатки;

• отслойка кожи в месте травмирующего контакта;

• разрывы кровеносных сосудов;

• пластинчатые кровоизлияния под мышечную фасцию;

• очаговые и инфильтрирующие кровоизлияния в подлежащие мышцы;

• частичные разрывы и размозжения мышц.

5. Результаты изучения архивных материалов судебно-медицинских экспертиз повреждений у пострадавших, получивших травму от ударов тупыми предметами с ограниченной травмирующей поверхностью небольших размеров, в условиях, аналогичных вышеописанным экспериментам (характерных при нанесении ударов хлыстом в конном спорте), а также на биологических имитаторах, показали, что в таких случаях как правило, формировались следующие виды повреждений:

• ссадины;

• кровоподтеки и гематомы;

• размозжения подкожной основы;

• отслойка кожи;

• разрывы кровеносных сосудов;

• кровоизлияния под фасцию мышечной ткани;

• разрывы и размозжение отдельных мышечных волокон.

6. Результаты изучения архивных и видео материалов ветеринарного исследования трупов погибших лошадей, имеющих следы от ударов спортивным хлыстом, свидетельствуют, что в местах действия хлыста выявлялись аналогичные повреждения:

* осаднения, кровоподтеки и внутрикожные кровоизлияния;
* размозжения подкожной жировой ткани и разрывы кровеносных сосудов;
* кровоизлияния под фасцию мышц;
* частичные разрывы и размозжения мышц.

7. Сопоставление полученных данных.

7.1. Все вышеописанные данные, полученные в результате разных видов исследований, экспериментов и опытов были сведены в табл. 1 и сопоставлялись между собой.

Таблица 1

Результаты сопоставления данных по видам повреждений

Основные виды повреждений	Наличие повреждений по результатам:				
	обобщения спец. литературы	архивных материалов		экспериментов на имитаторах	
		экспертных	ветеринарных	биологич.	небиологич.
Осаднения	+	+	+/–	+	+
Кровоизлияния:	+	+	+	+	+
- кожные, внутрикожные	+	+	+/–	+	+
- в подкожную жировую ткань (клетчатку)	+	+	+	+	+
- в подлежащие мышцы	+	+	+	+	+
Размозжение:	+	+	+	+	+
- подкожной клетчатки (с отслойкой кожи)	+	+	+	+	+
- мышечных волокон	+	+	+	+	+
- подлежащих органов	+	+/–	+/–	+/–	–
Разрывы кровеносных сосудов	+	+	+/–	+	+/–

В результате сравнения данных табл. 1 было установлено, что они практически полностью совпадают, что свидетельствует об устойчивости и закономерности полученного комплекса морфологических признаков, характеризующих травму спортивным хлыстом (фабричного производства бывшим в употреблении).

7.2. В условиях многократного нанесения ударов по одному и тому же месту объём вышеописанных повреждений пропорционально возрастает.

7.3. Помимо регистрируемых местных признаков ударного воздействия по телу животного необходимо отметить, что частые многократные кровоизлияния, а также размозжения тканей могут приводить и к общему страданию организма в целом. Механизм данного влияния связан с процессом рассасывания постоянно образующихся множественных кровоизлияний (гематом) и других пораженных тканей.

В ходе рассасывания из травматических очагов выделяются составные части и элементы клеток, в том числе кровяных телец (эритроцитов) в виде свободного белка – гемоглобина и миоглобина. Эти белки и их крупные осколки, имея высокий молекулярный вес, обладают способностью накапливаться в мелких сосудах (капиллярах), в том числе в почках, и забивать их. Формируются так называемые гемоглобиновые (и миоглобиновые) цилиндры, что может приводить к нефрозу (воспалительному заболеванию почек).

Всё это ухудшает процессы фильтрации и выделения из организма вредных продуктов обмена веществ (частичная или хроническая почечная недостаточность), что не может не влиять отрицательно на здоровье и общее состояние животного.

В Ы В О Д Ы

В результате проведенных исследований и экспериментов установлено, что:

1. Общая сила ударного воздействия концевой части спортивного хлыста составляет не менее 19 кг/см2, а удельная энергия удара – около 20-25 Дж/см2.

2. Зарегистрированные в экспериментах механические ударные воздействия указанной интенсивности могут приводить к различным повреждениям биологических тканей тела животного: от ссадин, кровоизлияний, до локальных размозжений подкожной жировой клетчатки, разрывов кровеносных сосудов и частичных разрывов подлежащих мышц.

3. Частые, многократные местные признаки тупой травмы мягких тканей от ударного воздействия хлыста по телу животного в виде кровоизлияний и размозжений подлежащих тканей могут приводить и к общему страданию организма в целом, в том числе почек.

Судебно-медицинские эксперты:

Заместитель начальника Бюро
по экспертной работе
доктор медицинских наук, профессор
Заслуженный изобретатель РФ   Исаков В.Д.

Заведующий отделом экспертизы трупов Бюро
кандидат медицинских наук,
врач высшей квалификационной категории   ...соев В.Е.

NEVZOROV Haute école
RESEARCH CENTRE
THE GOVERNMENT OF SAINT-PETERSBURG
HEALTH PROTECTION COMMITTEE
**THE STATE INSTITUTE
OF HEALTH PROTECTION
OF SAINT-PETERSBURG
"BUREAU OF FORENSIC SCIENCE"**
195067, Saint-Petersburg,
Ekaterininskiy pr. 10
tel. (7-812) 544-1717, fax. (7-812) 545 0340
OKPO 01932390 OKOGU 07185
E-mail: sudmed@zdray.spb.ru
14.12.2006 No 366 /01-4

STATEMENT

of experiments to define the force of possible strike by a standard whip,
which is used as a standard means of influence in equestrian sports,
and to determine the extent of damage to skin and soft tissues of a horse
that appear as a result of such strikes

1. **Purpose of examinations:** determination of maximum force of possible strikes by a standard whip that is used as a standard means of influence in equestrian sports and to determine the extent of damage to skin and soft tissues of a horse that appear as a result of such strikes.

2. **Experiments:**

– definition of the maximum force of dynamic impact of a standard whip under strikes in different manners, with different speeds (by people possessing different physical strength), from different directions on biological and non biological models, and also on a special stand.

– Determination of maximum force of dynamic influence by a standard whip while striking with it in different ways, with different speeds (from the influence of people possessing different physical abilities), in different directions at biological and non biological models, as well as on a special stand.

3. **Methods of analysis and conditions of setting of the experiments:**

Analysis was carried out with coherence to general methods used in forensic science for crime-detection studies to identify the effects of a striking effect by blunt objects and also of mechanisms of bullet and explosive trauma (including "through the armor trauma" to the human body when wearing types of individual body-armor, i.e. a bulletproof vest).

3.1 The first stage included **studying and generalization of the data:**

a) Equine sport literature, photo and video materials from various competitions, where riders were using an equine sports whip. Types of strikes and amplitudes of whip strikes accepted in equestrian sports, as well as possible force of given strikes were investigated.

b) Expert crime detection literature about the types and qualities of damages that appear:

- From the strike by hard blunt objects with limited traumatic surface applied with different amounts of energy (speed and force) on different biological objects;
- During blunt "through the armor trauma" to the human body, dressed in means of individual armor protection (protective vest, helmet and etc);

c) Materials from the archives of crime-detection records of damage done to victims who received trauma from a strike by a blunt object with a traumatic surface of small size, i.e. in conditions typical to those of strikes by a whip in equestrian sport;

d) Archival and video materials of veterinary studies of corpses of horses with welt marks from a whip used in equine sports;

As a result of the studies databases were gathered with differential-diagnostic tables (See appendix 1).

3.2. As a means of influence, a standard mass-produced whip used in equestrian sports was used (one that had been used previously) with popper/flapper made of leather sewn lengthwise with thick thread in four rows of machine-sewn stitches.

3.3. For the application of strikes, people that that had different physical characteristics and different abilities to apply force were used.

3.4. The application of strikes, their force, types of strikes and amplitude of movement of hand with the whip were in coherence with variants of regular strikes, accepted within equestrian sport.

3.5. For objective verification of the force of given strikes by the whip measurement of this parameter on special measuring system for studying ballistics of trauma by blunt object to a subject behind a barrier were used.

3.6. Experiments were done on biological and non biological models, analogical in its density to soft tissues of a living horse (blocks of ballistic plastic).

In order to define the exact boundaries of damage, as well as imitation of the zones of graze wounds on the skin the following method was used: in consecutive order blank sheets of writing paper and carbon paper (pigment side down) were placed on top of the objects to be struck.

4. Results of experiments were studied with detailed care (using standard methods of morphoscopy and morphometry), and were also recorded by photography using digital camera (see appendix 2)

As a result of studying the physical parameters of the striking effect of the popper/flapper of a whip used in equestrian sport with help of special experimental settings it was found that the general force of the whip was no less than 19 kg/cm^2 and the maximum energy of the strike was about 20–25 joule/cm^2.

During the following experimental studies it was found that as a result of strikes by a standard type of whip used in equestrian sport (with standard amplitude of strikes of this type) on a model of soft tissue of a horse, the following injuries were observed:

-   On sheets of paper: deformation and trough ruptures of long oval form in size up to 6x1 cm with uneven, ruptured borders, surrounded with a zone of deposit of black pigment in width up to 0.5–1.0 cm (which follows the zone of a graze wound around the primary injury);
-   On blocks of ballistic plastic impressions were formed, identical in form and size to the features of the striking surface of a mass-produced whip used in equestrian sport:

a) From strikes by flat surface – with total size of 9–10×2–3 cm;

b) From strikes by raised surface – 10–11×1.0–1.5 cm.

Damage on models of soft biological tissues like this usually coheres with the following types of injuries:

•   Multifocal injuries;
•   Multifocal bruises, subcutaneous hemorrhage and hematomas;
•   Crushing of subcutaneous tissue;
•   Detachment of skin in place of traumatic contact;
•   Ruptures of blood vessels;
•   Lamellar hemorrhage under the muscle fascia;
•   Multifocal and infiltrative hemorrhages into underlying muscles;
•   Partial ruptures and crushing of muscles.

5. Results of the study of the materials from the forensic science archives of injuries of victims who were traumatized by being struck with a blunt object with a limited traumatic surface of small size, in conditions analogical to those experiments described above (those which are typical while giving strikes with the whip in equine sport) and also on biological models have shown that in cases like this, as a rule, following types of injuries were formed:

•   Graze wounds;
•   Hemorrhages and hematomas;
•   Crushing of subcutaneous skin base;
•   Skin detachment;
•   Ruptures of blood-vessels;
•   Hemorrhages into the fascia of muscle tissue;
•   Ruptures and crushing of separate muscle fibers.

6. Results of the study of archival and video materials of veterinary necropsies of horses that had welt marks from the sport whip testify that in places of impact by the whip the following damages were discovered:

Graze wounds, hemorrhages and intradermal hemorrhages;

Crushing of subcutaneous tissue;

Hemorrhages under fascia of muscles;

Partial rupture and crushing of muscle tissue.

7. Comparison of obtained data.

7.1. All the data that has been described above, which was received as result of different studies and experiments was put together into table 1 and was compared in-between.

Table 1.

Results of comparison of data by types of injuries

Main types of injuries	Presence of injuries by results:				
	Generaliza-tion of special literature	Archive materials		Experiments on models	
		Expertise	Veteri-nary	Biological	Non-bio-logical
Graze wounds	+	+	+/−	+	+
Hemorrhages in:	+	+	+	+	+
– skin, intradermal	+	+	+/−	+	+
– the mass of subcutaneous tissue	+	+	+	+	+
– underlying muscles	+	+	+	+	+
Crushings of:	+	+	+	+	+
– the mass of subcutaneous tissue	+	+	+	+	+
– muscle fibers	+	+	+	+	+
– underlying organs	+	+/−	+/−	+/−	−
Ruptures of blood vessels	+	+	+/−	+	+/−

As a result of comparison of data in table 1, it was determined that they are almost completely identical, this signifies the reliability of the data received regarding morphological signs that characterize the trauma caused by a previously used, mass-produced whip used in sport.

7.2. In the event of repeated strikes on the same area of the body, the size of injuries that were described above grows proportionately.

7.3. Aside from the local signs of the striking effect on the animal's body it is significant to note that frequent repeated hemorrhages and also crushing of tissue can cause general suffering of the organism.

These traumas are connected with a process of reabsorption of repeatedly induced hemorrhages (hematomas) and other tissue injuries.

During the process of reabsorption, cells are detached including hemocytes (erythrocytes) from the center of traumatized areas in the form of free protein – hemoglobin and myoglobin. These proteins and their debris, having a high molecular weight, have the ability to accumulate in small vessels (capillaries) as well as in the kidneys, obstructing them. Hemoglobin and myoglobin cylinders are formed, which can lead to nephrosis (an inflammatory disease of the kidneys).

All of this compromises the processes of filtration and discharge of waste products of metabolism, which cannot not affect in a negative way the health and general state of an animal.

SUMMARY

As a result of studies and experiments undertaken, it was identified that:

1. The general force of the striking effect of the popper/flapper of the whip used in sport is not less than 19 kg/cm^2 and the maximum energy of the strike is around 20–25 joule/cm^2.

2. Striking influences of given intensity may cause different injuries to biological tissues of an animal's body: from wounds, hemorrhages and to local crushing of subcutaneous tissue, rupture of blood-vessels and partial ruptures of underlying muscles.

3. Frequent multiple local signs of trauma by blunt object of soft tissue from striking effect of the whip on animals' body leading to hemorrhaging and crushing of underlying tissues can cause general suffering of the organism in general, including damage to the kidneys.

Medico-legal experts:

Deputy Chief of Bureau for Expertise
Doctor of Medical Science, Professor
Honored Inventor of Russian Federation
Isakov V. D.

Head of Corpse Expertise Department
Candidate of Medical Science
Doctor of Higher Qualification Category
Sysoev V. E.

Head of Nevzorov Haute École Research Centre
Nevzorov A. G.

APPENDIX 2

CATALOG
OF ANTIQUE HORSE BITS,
STIRRUPS AND SPURS

Table I

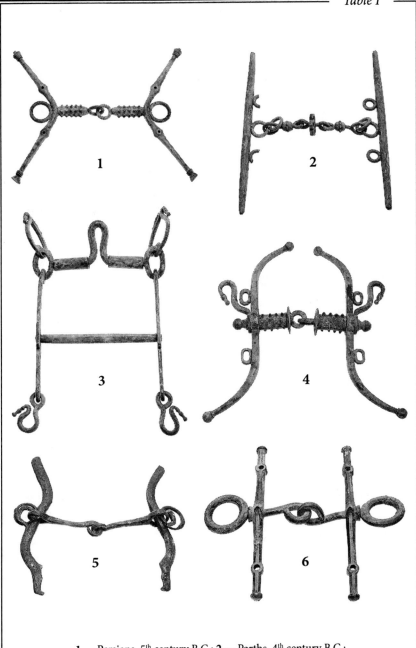

1 — Persians, 5th century B.C.; 2 — Parths, 4th century B.C.;
3 — Rome, 1st–3rd centuries; 4 — Greeks, 5th century B.C.;
5 — Sarmats, 2nd–4th centuries; 6 — Transcaucasia, 8th century B.C.

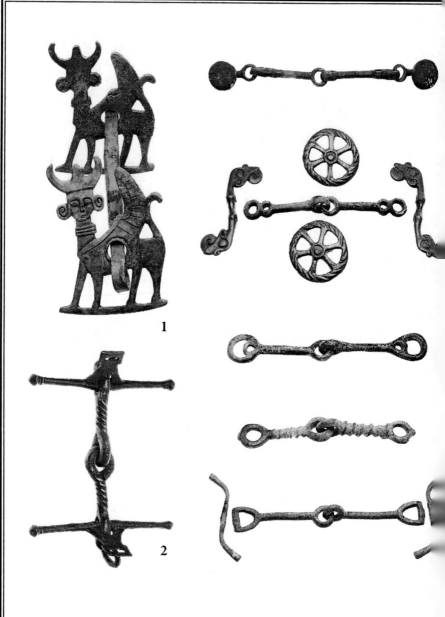

1 — Lurians, 10th–8th centuries B.C.; 2 — Sarmats, 2nd–4th centuries;
3 — Cimmerians, 7th century B.C.; 4 — Scythians, 6th century B.C.;
5 — pre-Scythian time (8th–7th centuries B.C.);

Table II

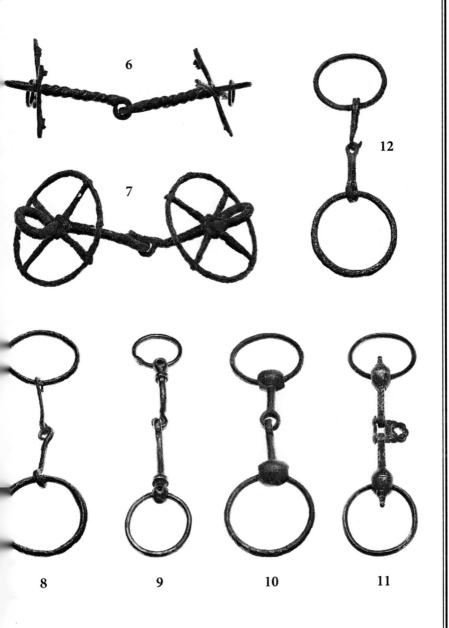

6 — Scytho-Meotian period (4ᵗʰ century B.C.) («barbed psalia»);
7 — Sarmats, 1ˢᵗ century B.C.; 8 — Russia, 10ᵗʰ century; 9 — Alans, 10ᵗʰ century;
10 — Antes, 1ˢᵗ century; 11 — Khazar, 10ᵗʰ century; 12 — Mongols, 13ᵗʰ century

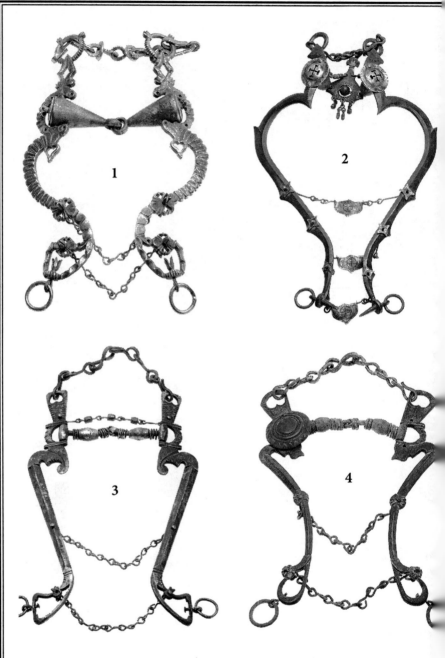

1 — Europe, 17th century; 2 — England, 15th century;
3 — France, 16th century; 4 — Europe, 17th century

Table III

5 — Europe, 17th century; 6 — France, 17th century;
7 — Europe, 17th century; 8 — Europe, 17th century

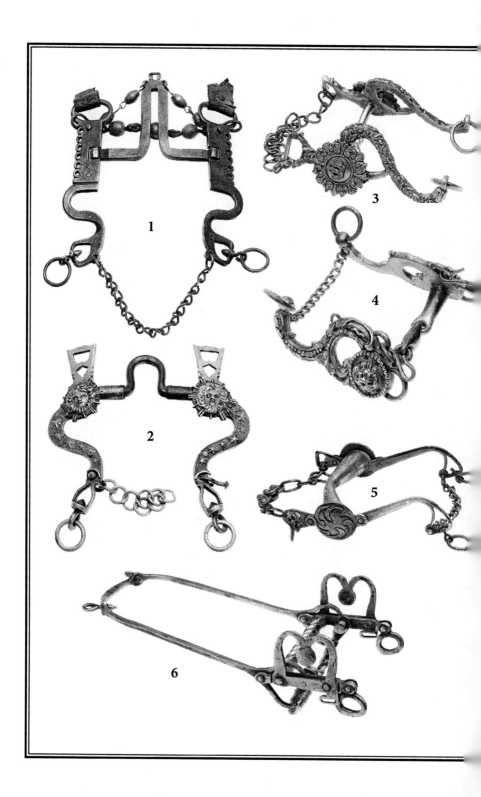

Table IV

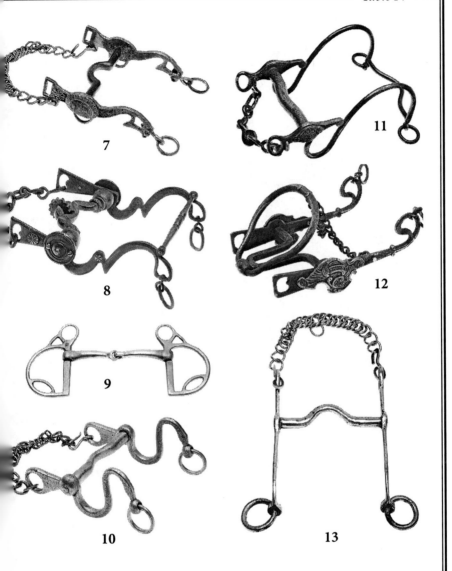

1 — Conquistadors (unidentified age); 2 — France, late 18th century; 3 — France, early 19th century (mouthpiece is substituted with a mouthpiece from a modern "mild" snaffe); 4 — Poland, 18th century (mouthpiece was subsituted with a jointed piece in 20th century); 5 — England, 18th century; 6 — Europe, 12th–13th centuries; 7 — France, early 19th century; 8 — Europe, middle 18th century; 9 — Mario Luraschi's curb bit, 20th century; 10 — Germany, curb bit of WWI; 11 — France, middle 19th century; 12 — Italy, early 18th century (ganette); 13 — modern curb bit

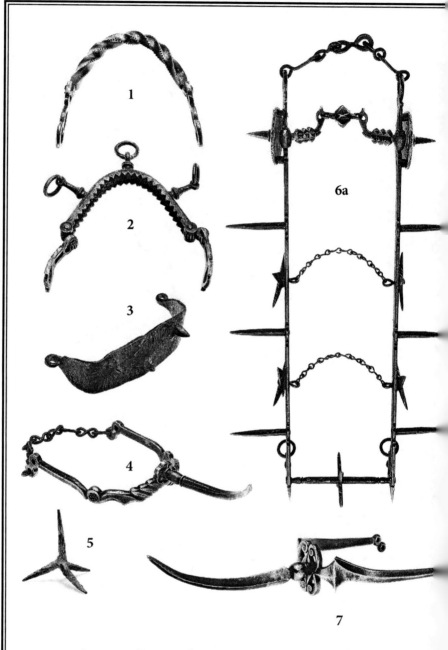

1 — seretta (Europe, 16th century); 2 — seretta (Austria, 18th century); 3 — Hun spur, 3rd–5th century; 4 — Arabian East, 11th–15th century; 5 — espina (tribula) (unidentified age); 6a — war curb bit with spikes (England, 14th–15th century)

Table V

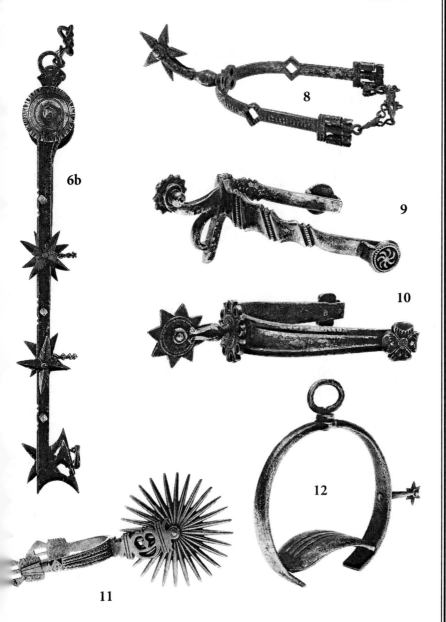

6b — war curb bit with spikes (England, 14th–15th century); 7 — Gothic knight spur, 13th–14th century; 8 — Europe, 15th century; 9 — Austria, 18th century; 10 — France, 17th century (Haute École); 11 — Mexico, 19th century ; 12 — England, 18th century

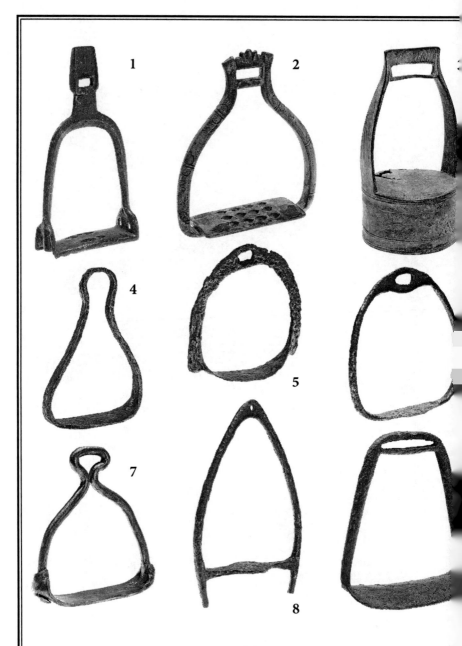

Stirrups

1 — 8th century; 2 — Xianbei, 5th century; 3 — Alans, 5th-6th century; 4 — Huns, 4th century; 5 — Slavs, 8th century; 6 — Pechenegs, 8th century; 7 — Franks, 7th century; 8 — Normans, 10th century; 9 — Mongols, 11th-13th centuries

Table VI

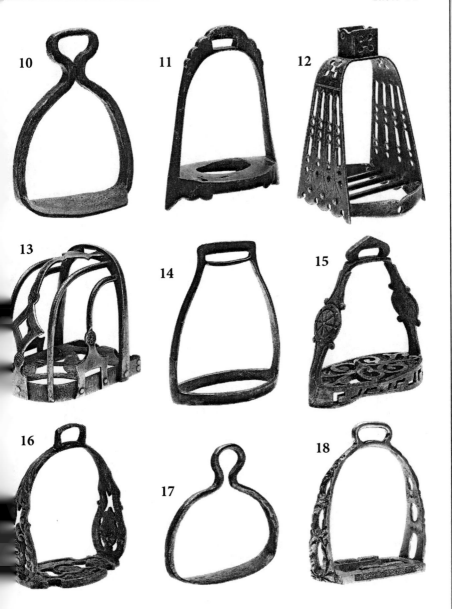

10 — Saxons, 10th century; 11 — China, 15th century; 12 — Italy, 14th century;
13 — England, 14th century; 14 — Russia, 16th century; 15 — Europe, 19th century;
16 — Italy, 18th century; 17 — Cumans, 10th century; 18 — France, 18th century

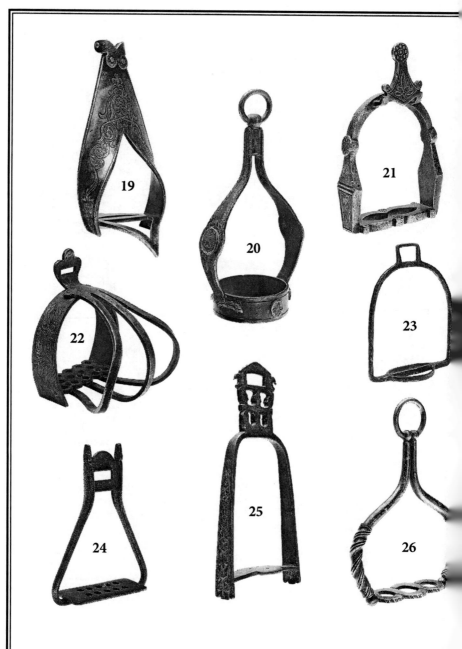

19 — Italy, 15th century; 20 — France, 17th century; 21 — Russia (?), 19th century; 22 — England, 15th century; 23 — Flanders, 18th century; 24 — Lithuania, 17th century; 25 — Afghanistan, 18th century; 26 — Austria, 18th century

Table VI

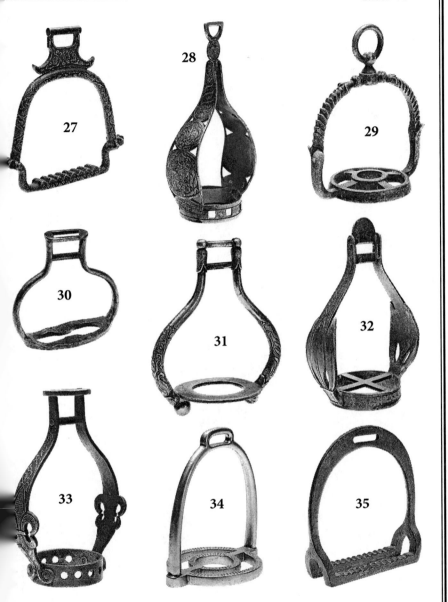

27 — China, unidentified age; 28 — France, 17th century; 29 — Saxony, 18th century; 30 — Poland, 18th century; 31 — France, 18th century; 32 — France, 17th century; 33 — France, 18th century; 34 — France, 19th century; 35 — Germany, early 20th century

Table VI (end)

36 — Italy, 14th century; **37** — Russia, 19th century; **38** — South America, 19th century; **39** — South America, 18th–19th centuries; **40** — Portugal, 17th–20th centuries (is used till modern times)

CPSIA information can be obtained at www.ICGtesting.com
Printed in the USA
LVOW120841140113

315554LV00011BA/454/P